W9-BWY-809

Trust Women

A PROGRESSIVE CHRISTIAN ARGUMENT FOR REPRODUCTIVE JUSTICE

Rebecca Todd Peters

Beacon Press, Boston

BEACON PRESS
Boston, Massachusetts
www.beacon.org

Beacon Press books
are published under the auspices of
the Unitarian Universalist Association of Congregations.

Printed in the United States of America

21 20 19 18 8 7 6 5 4 3 2 1

This book is printed on acid-free paper that meets the uncoated paper ANSI/NISO specifications for permanence as revised in 1992.

Text design and composition by Kim Arney

Portions of ch. 3 were originally published as "Considering Social Policy on Abortion: Respecting Women as Moral Agents," *Journal of Feminist Studies in Religion* 30, no. 1 (Spring 2014).

Library of Congress Cataloging-in-Publication Data

Names: Peters, Rebecca Todd, author.
Title: Trust women : a progressive Christian argument for reproductive justice / Rebecca Todd Peters.
Description: Boston : Beacon Press, 2018. | Includes bibliographical references and index.
Identifiers: LCCN 2017042045 (print) | LCCN 2017061131 (ebook) | ISBN 9780807069998 (ebook) | ISBN 9780807069981 (hardback : alk. paper)
Subjects: LCSH: Abortion—Religious aspects—Christianity. | Abortion—United States. | Motherhood—United States. | BISAC: SOCIAL SCIENCE / Abortion & Birth Control. | SOCIAL SCIENCE / Women's Studies. | RELIGION / Christian Life / Women's Issues.
Classification: LCC HQ767.25 (ebook) | LCC HQ767.25 .P48 2018 (print) | DDC 362.1988/80973—dc23
LC record available at https://lccn.loc.gov/2017042045

To my mother, Becky,
whose moral wisdom continues to guide me

To my husband, Jeff,
whose love and friendship sustains and holds me

To our daughters, Sophie and Eve,
who inspire me to continue to fight for social justice

and

In memory of Beverly Wildung Harrison,
who taught me how to be a social ethicist

CONTENTS

INTRODUCTION

On a hot and humid August evening, I trail down the aisle at the local drugstore looking for pregnancy tests. I'm twenty-six and married, but I'm still embarrassed and I glance around to see if anyone is looking, like a teenage girl buying condoms and trying to pretend she isn't. I do not want to be pregnant; I do not want anyone to see me with a pregnancy test. There are several tests to choose from, and I have no idea how they differ from one another. Out in the parking lot, I climb into the car, where my husband is waiting, and we head home. The tension in the car is palpable. After we get home, he tries to persuade me to eat dinner before I take the test, but I need to know now. I go into the bathroom, read the directions, and pee on the little white stick. Urine splashes everywhere. I lay the stick on the sink while I clean up the toilet and wash my hands. I watch as the plus sign emerges and darkens with each passing second. I stare at it intently, willing it to turn back. Maybe the horizontal line that transforms the test into a plus sign is supposed to surge like this right before it disappears. It doesn't. I am devastated. Utterly and completely. I do not want to be pregnant. I do not want a baby. Though I have only been married for nine months, I can feel my marriage falling apart around me. I love my husband, but I do not know what is happening between us. Every day, I wonder if we are going to weather this storm. All I know is that there is barely room for the two of us in this relationship, never mind three. We've only lived here a month. I don't even have a doctor. The next day, my husband finds an ob-gyn who does abortions in her office and I make an appointment. After the procedure, I lay in our bed and cry. I cry because I am scared that my marriage is ending. I cry because I had wanted to have children with this man, just not right now. I cry because sometimes you just need to cry. One week after the abortion, my husband and I separate. This is my first abortion experience. I have never regretted it.

I AM A CRADLE CHRISTIAN and an ordained Presbyterian minister. I did not choose to end my pregnancies despite my Christian identity and faith but rather because of it. My faith is not a tangential part of my life; it is a defining feature of my identity and my work as a feminist social ethicist. Like many women, I make reproductive decisions that align with my values. Decisions that reflect and respect the commitments I have made to my marriage, to being a good parent, and to my moral obligation to "love myself."[1]

Every year in the United States, 6.4 million women get pregnant, and *half* of these pregnancies are unplanned. With my first pregnancy, I joined their ranks. Like me, 50 to 60 percent of the women who have abortions were using birth control during the month that they got pregnant.[2] And here's yet another relevant statistic: Forty percent of unplanned pregnancies end in abortion, meaning that roughly one-third of US women will have an abortion by age forty-five.[3] Whether planned, unplanned, chosen, avoided, or unattainable, pregnancies are part of the stories of women's lives. Yet, considering that one in three women have abortions, we can see that abortion is also a *normal* part of women's reproductive lives.

Despite the normalcy of abortion, we live in a culture that largely assumes abortion is wrong. Certainly, not everyone believes it is wrong, but the assumption that abortion is wrong frames both the contemporary abortion debate and how our culture responds to and discusses the issue. This moral judgment is evident in recent legislation that interferes with women's access to abortion or seeks to persuade women to continue their pregnancies. It is evident in the increased policing and incarceration of women who seek to end their pregnancies. It is evident in the culture of shame that deters the majority of women from telling others they are having or have had an abortion. It is evident in every statehouse and public hearing across the country where the moral character of every woman who has had an abortion is put on trial. These women are denounced for being selfish, careless, or irresponsible; for killing their children; and for other moral infractions against idealized versions of femininity and motherhood.

Even people who are pro-choice often go out of their way to clarify that they are not *pro-abortion* (heaven forbid!) but that abortion should be legal as a matter of public health. Since Bill Clinton first introduced the idea that abortion should be "safe, legal, and rare," the idea has become a favorite pro-choice rallying cry of politicians. By focusing on making abortion "rare," they seek to appease a public uncomfortable with any attitude that challenges the consensus that abortion is morally wrong.[4] This stance is not surprising given that the theoretical framework that shapes how we think and talk about abortion requires women to justify why they are having an abortion.

"I do not want to have a baby" is the logical reason most women seek an abortion, yet it is not considered adequate. Women are required to have "good" reasons, "acceptable" reasons, reasons that outweigh or override the prevailing moral injunction against abortion. Requiring women to justify why they seek to end a pregnancy assumes that abortion is wrong unless one is able to make a convincing argument otherwise. But what are the origins of this supposed moral injunction? Why do so many people *assume* that abortion is morally wrong? Society hasn't always assumed that abortion was wrong. As we will see, abortion was actually a common form of birth control through much of the nineteenth century. Even today, there are many people who do *not* consider abortion immoral. So, in a country where abortion is legal and women do not have to explain to their healthcare providers why they wish to end a pregnancy, why does our cultural debate continue to judge and shame women for having abortions?

JUSTIFICATION FRAMEWORK

There is an unexamined pronatalist bias in this country. An attitude that reflects deep, often unspoken patriarchal assumptions about women and women's sexual activity. Consider these examples:

> Responsible women don't have unplanned or unwanted pregnancies.
> Women who have abortions are sexually promiscuous.
> Women who get pregnant have to live with the consequences of their behavior.
> If you don't want to have a baby, you shouldn't have sex.

These assumptions are at the heart of what I call the *justification paradigm* that frames the contemporary conversation about abortion in the United States. In this framework, when women get pregnant, we expect them to have babies. Abortion disrupts this narrative. Consequently, women are required to offer socially acceptable reasons for ending their pregnancies. In short, they must justify their moral decision. The necessity of justification permeates the very language of the debate itself—pro-choice arguments seek to justify women's right to abortion, while pro-life arguments seek to limit and even eliminate acceptable justifications.

In fact, the public has developed rather rigid perceptions about when abortion is morally acceptable and when it is not. *P*renatal health, *r*ape, *i*ncest, and life of the *m*other (PRIM) are accepted as "justifiable" reasons for abortion. Since 1972, some 87 percent of the US public has consistently approved of abortion when a woman's health is endangered, 78 percent approved of it in circumstances of rape, and 77 percent in cases of serious prenatal health issues.[5] However, only 1 percent of abortions are a result of rape and less than 0.5 percent the result of incest. About 12 percent of abortions are sought to protect a woman's health, and 13 percent for prenatal health issues. Thus, almost three-quarters of the women seeking abortions in the United States do so for other than the PRIM reasons.[6] These women are routinely caricatured as selfish, irresponsible, immature, or sexually immoral—accusations that show up not just in public debates and discussions of abortion, but also in church discussions about abortion. In fact, such characterizations dominate debates about abortion in many Christian denominations that support the continued legalization of abortion while explicitly rejecting abortion for "convenience," birth control, or sex selection.

The language of justification reveals a moral debate rooted in the largely unacknowledged premise that continuing a pregnancy is a prima facie moral good. This premise, however, reflects deeper cultural expectations about women's sexuality, including their obligation to bear children as part of women's essential or ontological purpose and cultural assumptions about the moral status of what I call the *prenate*. These cultural assumptions often reflect particular theological claims that pregnancy is a blessing, children are gifts from God, and prenatal life is sacred. Claims that require deeper interrogation.

Because the current available language is inadequate, morally loaded, or both, I have coined the term *prenate* to refer to the developing entity as long as it resides inside the pregnant woman. From clinical and emotionally detached scientific terms (*fertilized ovum*, *blastocyst*, *zygote*, *embryo*, *fetus*) to emotional and morally laden terms (*baby*, *unborn child*, *mother*, and even *pregnant woman*), our words are charged. More importantly, they constrain our moral imagination and fail to adequately describe the moral, physical, developmental, and social uniqueness of what happens over the nine months of a pregnancy. I have based the term on the word *prenatal*, which refers to the state of the pregnant woman, and on *neonate*, which refers to the infant after birth. In this book, I argue that only through the physical experience of birth does the prenate cross the threshold into life, securing its status as a member of the human community.

Modern medicine's capability to allow increased control over human fertility through contraception and abortion is a morally relevant factor that has changed women's historic relationship with pregnancy and childbirth. The idea that women must passively accept pregnancy and motherhood as the consequence of sexual activity is simply not true. Ninety-nine percent of sexually active women use contraceptives, and abortion is not only statistically safer than childbirth, but one of the most commonly performed medical procedures in the country.[7] The ability to share sexual intimacy in ways that no longer make pregnancy and motherhood a consequence of sexual activity has changed people's experience of their sexuality. These changes also push us to think more critically about our moral understanding of sexuality, parenting, and family.

My point here is not to imply that in our contemporary circumstances pregnancy or abortion is morally inconsequential. Rather, quite the opposite. Because childbearing is a deeply moral act, we ought to take the decision to continue a pregnancy far more seriously than we do. When women can safely and effectively prevent or end pregnancies, the decision to have a child is no longer simply a biological reality; it becomes a moral act. Rejecting the premise that pregnancy is a prima facie moral good not only recognizes that the moral landscape of sex and reproduction has shifted over the past 150 years, but also acknowledges the moral seriousness of pregnancy and childbearing in a world of limited resources.

By beginning with the premise that women should continue their pregnancies, the justification framework misidentifies the act of terminating a pregnancy as the starting point for our ethical conversation. It reduces the conversation to an abstract question of whether abortion is right or wrong, creating a binary framework woefully inadequate for the complexity of the moral questions surrounding abortion. Abortion, however, is never an abstract ethical question. It is, rather, a particular answer to a prior ethical question: "What should I do when faced with an unplanned, unwanted, or medically compromised pregnancy?" This question can only be addressed within the life of a particular woman at a given moment in time. When a woman is faced with this ethical question, her answer will vary depending on the individual and the many factors—social, economic, personal, religious—that define her life at any given point.

Once we have identified the right ethical question, we can begin to recognize that abortion is not the problem. Claiming abortion as the problem not only is misleading but also identifies the wrong starting point for the conversation. Starting in the wrong place interferes with our ability to understand, discuss, or address a social problem in a meaningful way—a way that could impact the root causes. By focusing public attention on the morality of abortion, the justification paradigm has eclipsed the much more morally significant reality of women's sexual and reproductive health. When we recognize that the moral question begins when a woman is faced with a problem pregnancy, we see that the starting point of our ethical conversation should be women's lives.

The problem that we face in this country is our failure to trust women to act as rational, capable, responsible moral agents. At its root, this inability to trust women stems from the ongoing legacy of misogyny and patriarchy that continues to shape a cultural desire to control the lives and bodies of women. This failure to trust women is at the heart of the justification paradigm, which is rooted in essentialized ideas about women's nature and their moral obligations. The justification framework is morally inadequate in ways that distort and damage our ability to have productive conversations. Far more importantly, however, the moral failure of the justification framework is the way it actively harms the health and well-being of millions of women as well as their existing children and the future of their families.

Women's reproductive lives are about more than their bodies and their sexuality, although these aspects are central. Their reproductive lives encompass the health and well-being of their children, their grandchildren, and their communities. Although it only takes nine months to gestate a baby and bring it into the world, it takes at least another eighteen years to raise that child into a healthy, loving, and well-adjusted member of society. The degree to which a parent can accomplish these tasks successfully and without excessive stress depends on whether they have access to safe and affordable housing, an education system that teaches kids what they need to know to succeed in life, a job that pays a living wage, and a community where their race or ethnic background does not put them at risk. In short, the ethics of reproduction are much more comprehensive than the current justification framework allows.

This book aims to shift how we think about, talk about, and legislate women's reproductive health and well-being from a framework of justification to one of reproductive justice (RJ). RJ has three primary principles: the right *not* to have a child, the right to *have* a child, and the right to *parent* in safe and healthy environments.[8] It is an intersectional approach grounded in the multiple challenges and social realities that women face during their entire reproductive lives. This intersectional approach also recognizes the moral complexity of individual women's life situations, rejects the position of moral absolutism, and holds that moral meaning and value can only be measured within the context of an existing moral life.

The RJ movement grew out of the lives and experiences of women of color who found the reproductive rights movement too narrowly focused on abortion rights and not adequately attentive to the reproductive healthcare concerns that enable all women to live healthy and full lives. Comprehensive reproductive health care, which is often taken for granted by middle-class white women, is often more difficult for women of color to obtain. In a context where women of color have been targeted for sterilization, where the maternal mortality rate is not only four times greater for black women than white but rising, where access to contraception is increasingly threatened, it is not insignificant that the actual bodies that are being policed by the state under the mountain of new "regulations" of abortion and abortion providers since 2011 are primarily the bodies of poor women, of young women, of black and Latina women.[9]

I was introduced to the RJ perspective many years ago through my work with and support of the Religious Coalition for Reproductive Choice and the writings and activism of women of color. As a white, middle-class, intersectional feminist whose work on questions of poverty and oppression has always embraced a hermeneutic of justice I was excited by how the RJ frame created a space for activists of color to change the language of the reproductive rights debate and to push forward concerns of social justice—concerns that moved beyond a liberal, feminist focus on rights. As I began to research and write on reproductive issues, I was invited to participate in professional conversations with RJ activists and scholars, a group that includes women of color and white women. The support I have received from women of color in the RJ movement for my work has been inspiring and challenging, and it continues to push me to think beyond my own social location and circumstances and to consider more broadly what justice looks like in the reproductive lives of women who are most marginalized by current public policy. Pioneering RJ activist Loretta Ross described RJ at one meeting as "open-source code" that creates a framework that all people committed to overcome reproductive oppression can share. She cautioned that while people using RJ can't change the basic code, new people will build "new ideas and platforms on it."[10] I hope my work in these pages to challenge the justification framework and reframe how we think about abortion builds faithfully and respectfully on the RJ source code.

In this book, I will show that the justification framework not only harms women but also has disrupted our ability to have authentic public discussions about the health and well-being of women and their families. The argument proceeds in three steps. First, we must reclaim and reframe conversations about abortion within the context of women's lives, where abortion decisions are made on a daily basis. Part 1, "One in Three," examines the material reality of women's sexuality and abortion in the lives of real women and the consequences of social policies based on social control. Allowing women to decide when and if they will bear children is the only way to ensure that women will not be coerced into pregnancy and childbearing. Second, to understand why our public policy is rooted in an ideology of the social control of women's sexuality, pregnancy, abortion, and mothering, part 2, "Why Misogyny and Patriarchy Matter," traces how philosophical, legal, and religious attitudes about women allow us to accept the social control of women as the dominant legal and political approach to women's reproduction. This section challenges the social control of women by deconstructing the justification framework. Finally, in part 3, "Moving from Justification to Justice," we move beyond justification and toward a model of justice. Here I reimagine pregnancy and prenatal life in ways that offer a new theological foundation for reproductive justice.

Polls suggest that it is largely Christians who find abortion morally unacceptable, with three-quarters of Jews and those who claim no religious affiliation finding abortion morally acceptable. Meanwhile, only one-third of Catholics (38 percent) and Protestants (33 percent) and 18 percent of Mormons find it morally acceptable.[11] While the most public opponents of abortion come from evangelical and Roman Catholic backgrounds, the relevance of Christianity to the conversation is more complicated than the contemporary positions of some Christian politicians and faith leaders on questions of sexual morality and the moral status of the prenate. For centuries, Christianity has been used and abused to shape how people think about women, sexuality, and families. Uncovering Christianity's deep and abiding role in how we think and talk about abortion is essential, whether we are Christian or not.

Perhaps in response to the outspoken public Christian voices that denounce the morality of abortion, increasing numbers of people—perhaps as much as one-third of the US public—are indicating that they do not think that abortion is a moral issue at all.[12] While I can understand the logic behind this move—if abortion is not a moral issue, then perhaps we will stop arguing about it—the problem is not in recognizing that abortion is a moral issue. The problem is that we do not trust women to make moral decisions about their bodies, their lives, and their families. To say that abortion is not a moral issue is to tacitly agree that women are not capable of making moral decisions.

Shifting the moral conversation from abortion to reproductive justice acknowledges the moral weight of the decision either to end a pregnancy or to continue one. It requires that a new public conversation about pregnancy, abortion, and women's reproductive healthcare be rooted in trusting women as capable moral agents. It creates a space for meaningful ethical discernment and, in doing so, opens up the possibility of recognizing that abortion can be a moral good.

The principles of RJ form the theoretical foundations of my analysis and my commitment to building a world of justice and peace where women are trusted to make the moral decisions that shape their lives. In such a world, women have access to the resources and support that enable them to make truly uncoerced reproductive decisions. I want nothing less for my own daughters. How can I want anything else for all women?

One in Three

CHAPTER 1

You Shouldn't Have a Baby Just Because You're Pregnant

IN MY EARLY TWENTIES, I volunteered as a clinic escort at the local Planned Parenthood in my town. That was my first real introduction to the hatred, ugliness, and emotional manipulation aimed at women who have abortions. While I had grown up the daughter of a Presbyterian minister, I got an intimate look at a very different form of Christianity when I was serving as a clinic escort. I was shocked by the cognitive dissonance of people who professed to be Christians while using their theological beliefs to verbally attack others: they spewed some of the most venomous, hateful, and demeaning words I had ever heard at the women they encountered at the clinic. These protestors, who claimed to be Christian, clearly did not understand what it meant to live faithfully in the same way that I did. It was my faith that had brought me to that clinic to stand in solidarity with my sisters who needed the simple moral support of someone walking compassionately by their side in a moment of great need.

As escorts, that's what we did. Wearing bright orange vests that identified us as clinic supporters, two of us met each woman at the door of her car and offered to escort her to the clinic entrance if she wanted it. They all did. Placing ourselves on each side of her, we would lock our elbows through hers and keep up a constant chatter about the weather, the hostility of the protestors, and any other small talk that we could think of. The women we supported reacted in different ways to the protestors. Some women ignored them and chatted with us; others were angry and resentful of the intrusion into their private lives. For others, who were already sad, the goading of the crowds brought on more tears. But none ever turned away. As studies across the country have shown, the women who showed up for their abortion procedures had already made their decision. They knew what they were doing.[1] For these women, the presence of the protestors was harassment, pure and simple, and the crowd represented just one more barrier to be overcome on the women's path back to normal life.

At the time I was volunteering as an escort, I was working at the national headquarters of the Presbyterian Church (USA) in its women's advocacy office. One of my responsibilities was to observe a task force on problem pregnancies that was looking at the issue on behalf of the denomination.[2] At one of the public hearings, I even testified that if my birth control were to fail, it was very likely that I would have an abortion. I was young and single and trying to figure my life out. I wasn't ready to be a mother. A couple years later, I went to seminary and got both a master of divinity degree and a PhD in Christian social ethics. During these years, in addition to being an activist, I became a scholar. My work addresses social problems based on the commitment to justice that I find within the Christian tradition. My commitment to the well-being of women, children, families, and all marginalized communities also undergirds my attention to questions of sexuality and sexual ethics.

Approaching sexuality and reproduction as a question of justice can shift our ethical orientation in ways that allow us to see the problems and the issues in new and different ways. In turn, how we identify and frame a social problem is the most relevant factor in our ability to devise effective social policies that address the problems of injustice that have the most direct impact on society. We must also identify the right moral question to provide meaningful moral guidance for Christians and other people of goodwill who seek to navigate the rocky terrain of moral discernment for themselves and as the basis for social policy. To identify the right moral questions to ask as we think about abortion, we must begin with the most basic questions of sexual ethics—when and why do we have sex, and what do babies have to do with sex?

While examing questions of sexual ethics, we must be careful not to fall into the trap of reducing abortion to questions of individual sexual morality. Abortion, which is defined as the termination of a pregnancy, is also about babies, families, motherhood, and community. This is not to equate prenates with babies but to say pregnancies lead to the birth of babies and, thus, abortion is always about whether to accept the potential inherent in any given pregnancy. "What shall I do when faced with an unplanned or medically complicated pregnancy?" is always a moral question, just as "Do I want to be a mother?" is a moral question.

Moral questions are common in all cultures. Sometimes, the answers to these questions are not obvious. Moral questions ask how we are to live in ways that honor and uphold our personal and collective values as a human community. They require moral discernment as we seek answers. For Christians, moral discernment is a process of deciding how to respond to a particular moral question that involves seeking wisdom and guidance from our faith tradition and community as well as from our family and friends. The capacity to discern right from wrong is what makes us moral beings; as a fundamental task of human existence, moral discernment forms the basis of culture and society.

I was five when *Roe v. Wade* became the law of the land. I have only ever known a world in which US women have a legal right to end their pregnancies. Born in the late 1960s, I grew up in a generation that reaped the benefits of second-wave feminism, the civil rights movement, and the sexual revolution. In this chapter, I use my own sexual and reproductive history to set the cultural stage for an examination of the ethics of abortion by illustrating the shifting attitudes about sexuality and sexual ethics that have marked the last fifty years. The decision to tell my story in these pages is a methodological one. Stories matter, and abortion cannot be understood—culturally, theologically, socially, or politically—outside the lives of the women who have abortions.

My abortions are not a secret in my life. Although I have never felt compelled to hide them, I have never felt the need to broadcast them either. Even so, I debated for years about whether to write about them publicly. After all, to be public about having had abortions is to open yourself up to an uncomfortable degree of moral scrutiny. Given the culture of shame, few women are willing to publicly share their stories and experiences. I tell my own story, not because it is compelling or unique. My story is, in fact, unremarkable in that it is like many situations that women face daily across the country. I tell my story because as a married, white, professional woman, I can and there are so many other women who cannot. In this chapter, my story serves as a vehicle to raise questions and offer insights about sexual ethics and how our ethical thinking is shaped by the assumptions we make, the questions we ask, and the context in which we examine those questions. It also illustrates how the creation of knowledge (or what we know and how we know it) is at least partly informed by our lived experience. Since my story is illustrative and not universal, in later chapters, I also share the very different stories, experiences, and social situations of women whose lives are different from my own.

THINKING ABOUT SEX

I came of age during a time when premarital sex was losing some of its stigma and young people were having sex at earlier and earlier ages. More than half of Generation Xers (people born in the late 1960s through the early 1980s) had had sex by the time they were eighteen.[3] Critics often marshal this observation to denounce the "loose morals" of younger generations. But contrary to popular belief, the *incidence* of premarital sex has not changed that much from one generation to the next. By age forty, 85 percent of my parents' generation (1939–1948) report having had sex before they married; the number rises to 93 percent for those born 1949–1968 and stays steady for succeeding generations (1969–1988).[4] What has shifted over time is the age at which young people become sexually active, falling from a median age of 20.4 for the Silent Generation to 18 for Gen Xers and to 17 for the millennials.[5]

These changes in sexual behavior reflect shifts in cultural norms related to sexuality that have been changing for some time. From the destigmatization of premarital sex to the rising numbers of babies born to single women to the increasing acceptance of same-gender relationships, many of our ideas and practices about sexual behavior have evolved dramatically over the past hundred years. While some religious conservatives want to use these cultural shifts to attack the morality of younger generations or to try to shore up flagging notions of appropriate Christian virtues and ideals, the reality is that Christian attitudes toward sex and marriage have also altered over time. Even a cursory read of the Bible demonstrates that sex was never exclusively reserved for heterosexual, married couples. Sexual activity was certainly controlled during biblical times as well, with dire consequences for those who transgressed the established sexual norms; it's just that the norms were different.[6]

Marriage in the Bible was much more about property rights, the paternity of offspring, succession, political alliances, and tribal stability than it was about companionship, mutual support, and affection—the way we tend to think about marriage today. The patriarchs of the Jewish and Christian tradition often had sex with multiple women, sometimes, but not always, for the purpose of procreation. Many of the women in the Bible who were slaves, servants, or handmaids were reportedly "given" by the legal or primary wife to her husband for the purposes of securing children. The origins of the twelve tribes of Israel are traced back to the biblical patriarch Jacob, who, after marrying two sisters, Leah and Rachel (offered to him by his uncle Laban), then also took one maidservant from each of his wives as a concubine. The notion of consent, particularly for women, in matters of sexual intercourse is not a relevant moral norm in most of scripture.

During the earliest years of Christianity, belief in Christ's imminent return shaped how people thought about marriage and sexual activity. Given Paul's expectation that Christ would return any moment and that the community should be spiritually prepared, Paul advocated celibacy, which he describes as self-control. Paul's concern for sexual immorality, which in his definition includes prostitution, adultery, fornication, and sodomy, is legendary. In offering celibacy as a model for other Christian disciples, he elevates his own choice as spiritually superior to those who experience sexual desire, which he describes as being "aflame with passion." In light of his denunciation of sexual immorality, Paul concedes that marriage is the appropriate setting for sexual relations, but he clearly views this choice as less honorable than celibacy.

Clearly, there are limitations in seeking direct ethical guidance for contemporary sexual behavior from a book that reflects sexual and cultural attitudes two thousand years old. Recognizing that attitudes toward sexual morality in the Christian tradition have changed over time does not mean that Christian values should simply capitulate to culture or that sex outside marriage is OK simply because that is the prevailing cultural practice. Christians are right to care about sex and to approach it as a moral issue. Sex is a sacred and wonderful activity that can be shared between two people in ways that deepen and reinforce mutual bonds of caring and commitment. And it's fun!

When I was in high school and trying to figure out how I felt about sex, I sure could have used some moral guidance to help me navigate the waters of teenage hormones, young love, and discernment about sexual readiness. As a Christian, I believed that sex was a sacred gift to be shared with someone special. I did not see casual sex as a good moral choice, but waiting until marriage didn't make sense to me either. At sixteen or seventeen, I didn't want to get married for a long time—if ever. All my friends were having sex, and my boyfriend (who was three years older than me) was not a virgin. I knew these were not good reasons to have sex, but when I sought moral guidance from mentors (inside the church and out), the response was a simplistic "wait until marriage." I knew where my parents stood on the issue, as one of the most memorable scenes of my childhood was the day my father found my older sister's birth-control pills. It didn't matter that she was in a long-term relationship with a man that she eventually married or that she was actually being sexually responsible by using birth control; my father made it clear that all that mattered was that she was having sex before marriage and that she shouldn't. I got the message, but it didn't make any more sense to me than it had to my sister.

While my high school boyfriend never pressured me to have sex, clearly he wanted to. And so did I. Absent a meaningful sexual ethic to help me think through vulnerability and what it means to share one's body with another sexually, or what questions to ask about the quality of one's relationship, or even how to assess one's maturity and readiness for sexual intercourse, I was left to figure it out on my own. I knew in my soul that "sex only in marriage" didn't cut it, but I didn't have the tools that I needed to make some of the most important moral decisions I would make in my life about how and when to share sexual intimacy with another person.

Absent any guidance from my church or from Christian leaders and elders, at the end of an inadequate moral discernment process, I became sexually active at the age of seventeen. It's not that this was a bad moral decision and I certainly don't think it was sinful or immoral. I was in a long-term relationship with someone I loved; we cared deeply for one another and were each committed to our relationship. I don't think premarital sex is always wrong, but I do think the quality of the relationship and the commitment of sexual partners to the integrity and health of the relationship are important, as is maturity. That, perhaps, is what I was most lacking.

Today, there are better resources out there to help Christians think and talk about sexuality, sexual intimacy, justice, and right relationship. Increasingly, Christian moral norms about sex are shifting from "sex belongs within marriage" to a more rigorous moral norm of "sex as right relationship." The idea that sexual activity is only morally acceptable within the bounds of marriage is a weak moral norm on two levels. First, the traditional argument that sex belongs in marriage is based on the belief that a two-parent family is the best place to raise children. This reasoning assumes that the purpose of sexual activity is to have children and, therefore, sex belongs in marriage. Yet, in our world today, most heterosexual sexual activity does not produce children; nor does it have to. Second, the argument that sex belongs in marriage also ignores factors of consent and the quality of the relationship between a husband and a wife. The recognition of marital rape is just one example of how our attitudes about the quality of sexual activity, even within marriage, have improved over time. The idea that a woman can be raped by her husband recognizes the agency of women and affirms the belief that sex should be consensual, even within a marriage.

An ethic that makes the morality of sex contingent on whether or not the sex occurs within a legal marriage is a two-dimensional ethic that is only concerned with the right container for controlling sexuality and sexual activity. Two-dimensional ethics offer simplistic answers to complex questions; they ignore depth, complication, and moral agency. They also attempt to provide definitive answers for people rather than teaching them how to engage in complex and nuanced moral discernment.

Christian ethicists who are engaging in new models of sexual ethics are shaping robust three-dimensional models of sexual ethics. Three-dimensional ethical thinking looks beyond the surface configuration of a relationship (i.e., marriage) and asks challenging moral questions about the quality of the relationship, the behavior and attitude of the partners toward one another, and why they wish to share physical intimacy. Questions like these offer a more rigorous ethical standard for sexual intercourse than a marriage certificate offers: an ethical standard rooted in the values of mutuality, justice-love, and right relation.[7] Because Christian values, like all moral teaching, exist within particular cultural contexts, they must respond to those realities in ways that help interpret the core spiritual and moral values of the tradition in each age and place. New ways of thinking about sexual morality—like justice-love and right relation—reflect the important ways in which Christian theologians and Christian communities have sought to engage in difficult conversations about sexual identity, sexual activity, and the different ways in which people can engage in sexual activity rooted in intimate relationships that reflect equality and justice between partners. I am teaching my two daughters to respect their bodies and respect themselves as the foundation for recognizing the importance of consensual sexual activity between partners in a committed relationship—a lesson that I didn't learn until my twenties. Although attitudes in many Christian communities about same-sex relationships, same-sex marriage, and justice-oriented sexual activity have clearly shifted in my lifetime, cultural and religious attitudes about abortion have been relatively stagnant for the past forty years. This intransigence is deeply problematic; our collective thinking and moral reasoning about abortion must also move into the twenty-first century. The development of my own moral understanding of pregnancy and abortion was deeply influenced by my Christian faith and my mother's practical moral wisdom.

THINKING ABOUT ABORTION

In high school, one of my friends got pregnant. She asked me to go with her to the "clinic" for a pregnancy test, as teens had no easy access to reliable home pregnancy tests in the early 1980s. Growing up in a country where abortion was legal, I was vaguely pro-choice but hadn't particularly thought much one way or the other about my own attitudes about abortion before she got pregnant. We accidentally ended up at a pro-life "clinic" that required my friend to watch a film before the staff would give her the test results. She told me that the film was gruesome, full of images of bloody fetuses and designed to horrify.

It turned out she was pregnant. She was shaken up when we left, not so much by the confirmation of her pregnancy, since she had been pretty sure about that already, but by the film. Everything that happened from the moment we walked in the door of that clinic, from the posters on the wall of smiling babies with their mothers, to the constant reproachful banter of the women who offered "counseling," to the film itself—everything was designed to shame and guilt my friend into continuing her pregnancy. Of course, the visit to the pro-life facility didn't change her mind. She was dating someone off and on who was out of high school but not in college and didn't have a steady job. She liked him, but she knew she didn't want to have a baby with him. She didn't want a baby at all right then. She wanted to graduate from high school and go to college.

She was my first friend who had an abortion, but certainly not the last. I don't remember any of my friends getting pregnant in college, but that doesn't mean it didn't happen. What I remember most about the issue of abortion in college was a casual conversation I had with my parents over a break. I don't remember what prompted it, but I told my parents that I was pro-choice, although I would never *personally* have an abortion. My mother looked at me and said, "Why not?" She said that if I got pregnant while I was in college, she wouldn't expect me to have a baby unless she knew that was what I wanted.

Now, let's get one thing straight. My mom does *not* believe in premarital sex or sex outside marriage, period. Remember the debacle with my older sister's birth control? It wasn't that she thought I was having sex or that it was OK if I was, but she recognized that the question of an unintended pregnancy in my late teens was a larger and more complex moral question than whether I should have been having sex. My mom was able to frame the question of an unwanted pregnancy in the context of motherhood and the larger life that lay ahead of me. She said to me, "You shouldn't have a baby just because you are pregnant. You should have a baby because you want to be a mother, because you want to have a child, because you are ready to raise a family."

My mother's practical moral wisdom is also deeply theological. She was expressing a profound theological affirmation of the sacredness of the covenant bond of parenting and family. As a Presbyterian, I am part of the Reformed tradition where the term *covenant* often describes sacred relationships. Covenants are sacred relationships like those between God and God's people, between married partners, and between parents and children—relationships with particular obligations and commitments. Said to me in the context of our own covenantal bond of mother and daughter, these words reflected her sincere hope and desire for my well-being as her child. They also expressed her responsibility to teach me to respect and love myself as a child of God. I also learned in that conversation that my father had been part of a clergy consultation network in New Orleans before *Roe* and that he had helped connect women with safe places to have abortions. Although my father was a minister and a member of the Silent Generation, which held strong beliefs that sex belonged inside marriage, his beliefs did not prevent him from ministering with compassion to the women who came to him seeking help with their unwanted pregnancies.

However, compassion is often not the response to women who have had abortions. Despite forty-five years of overwhelming support for legal access to abortion, acceptance of the legality of abortion does not mean that the general public feels positively or even neutrally about abortion. Nearly half of the public have indicated to pollsters that they think abortion is morally wrong.[8]

The comment I made to my parents—that I was pro-choice but would never have an abortion—is something I have heard repeatedly throughout my life. The statement seems to epitomize the "yes, but" feeling that so many people have about abortion. It's a statement full of ambiguity. Implicit in this seemingly supportive statement affirming the need to keep abortion legal is a subtle judgment of the women who have abortions. To say that you support abortion as a legal option but that you personally would never have one is also to imply that there is something morally wrong with having an abortion and thus with the women who have them.[9]

I pressed a friend of mine who said this to me recently about what she meant by the statement. Her response was, "Well, I just can't imagine being in a situation where I wouldn't be able to welcome a child into my life." Even though this woman is a dear friend and a politically active, pro-choice clergywoman, there was a need to clarify, to distance herself from the circumstances of abortion. The not-so-subtle subtext of this sentiment is that abortion is OK for *those* people, but not for me. There is a clear posturing in this statement, a distancing between those of us who have children and those women who have abortions. This posturing is possible because so many women keep silent about their abortions and because most people don't know that 60 percent of women who have abortions *already have children*.[10] As my friend and I talked, we acknowledged the ambivalence associated with abortion, particularly for many Christians who struggle with questions about the moral status of the prenate.

Each of us has our own unique set of life experiences associated with pregnancy, childbirth, and babies. Experiences of our own families of origin and our relationships (or lack of them) with our mother or father, or both, also shape us in often unknowable ways. For some of us, these are positive experiences; for some, they are strained or even deeply painful; and for others, the experiences are mixed. Each of us brings this body-knowledge with us to the table as we seek to make sense of how we feel about abortion. How we understand and know the sacred always influences our thinking about the world around us. When it comes to these most personal and emotional topics of sexuality, pregnancy, prenates, children, and parenting, our moral intuition is deeply shaped by our experience.

I think the security of her own experience is probably why my friend said she supported abortion but would never have one. Given her health, and her supportive husband, family, and congregation, she could not imagine any circumstances in which she would not be able to welcome a child into her life.

Neither did I. Until it happened.

ABORTION AS NORMAL *OR* BEING PART OF THE ONE IN THREE

The first time I got pregnant, I was twenty-six. We had been married for eight months. I was commuting to graduate school and my husband was a first-year family practice intern at a local hospital. Some weeks, he worked more than a hundred hours a week. I used a diaphragm and kept a very careful record of my cycles. One evening, as were picking up some Chinese food, I mentioned to my husband that my period was late. So we swung by the drugstore for a pregnancy test and headed home. He wanted to wait until after dinner for me to take the test, but I couldn't wait. I peed on the stick, and a plus sign showed up immediately. I went into the kitchen and laid it on the table saying, "The instructions say to wait five minutes before reading it." In my panic, I actually thought the test might turn back. In case you are wondering, that's not how they work. My husband, a doctor, did know how they worked.

Before we got married, we talked about what our future family might look like. We both wanted to have children, but we were also young, relatively poor students with a lot of educational debt. We felt that it was important to build up our relationship and to spend some time with each other before we had kids. We talked about waiting four or five years before we started a family, and we consequently used birth control to prevent my getting pregnant. Eight months later, I found myself pregnant as a newlywed. For some newlyweds, this might have been a welcome delight. For others, while it might have been unplanned, it could have become a wanted pregnancy. After all, we were young and healthy, and although we were struggling economically, we had enough to get by. From the outside, it probably looked as if we ought to be able to handle an "accident" like this. After all, 60 percent of unplanned pregnancies become wanted pregnancies.

But we were miserable. We fought a lot and sat in quiet tension much of the rest of the time. We were both stressed with the pressures of our work, with living in a community where we knew no one (literally, I knew not one person in the town where we lived), and with the fear that our marriage was falling apart. We were in counseling, but it wasn't really helping. We recognized pretty quickly that while both of us wanted children, we were not ready to be parents. I had confirmed my pregnancy so early that the doctor didn't want to schedule a procedure for two more weeks. Those two weeks were torture. I felt as if my body were occupied by an alien, hostile force. I couldn't eat, I couldn't sleep. I certainly couldn't focus on my coursework. There was nowhere I could go to get away from it. My husband and I drew further and further away from one another. One week after my abortion, we separated.

As I was considering ending my pregnancy, I certainly recognized the gravity of being pregnant. I knew that whatever decision I made in that circumstance would be a moral decision. I was unexpectedly pregnant, and the question was, What should I do? I knew I didn't want to have a baby at that point in my life. I loved my husband, but things were bad between us. I was in seminary, and having a baby right then would seriously interrupt my studies and my future career. I believed that my work on issues of social justice was important; it was my calling in my life. In my prayer and my discernment, I knew that this was not the right time for me to become a mother.

Having an abortion at such an early stage of pregnancy was, for me, different from using contraception to prevent a pregnancy. The potential for life represented by the dividing cells in my body required that I consider what it would mean to embrace that pregnancy and make a covenant commitment to bear a child. The truth was, I didn't want it—the pregnancy or a child. I had regularly used contraception to prevent it, I didn't bond with it, and I never entered into relationship with it. For me, it was an *it*. Those dividing cells were never a child for me.

Having had three subsequent planned and wanted pregnancies, I know the difference between embracing and rejecting a pregnancy. A miscarriage at the same point in a wanted pregnancy would have been a much more tragic loss for me. It was a pregnancy, but it was never a "baby." While I recognized the moral weight of the situation, I have never believed that a prenate holds the same moral position as a baby. I had been pro-choice as long as I could remember. I had testified before Presbyterian committees and general assemblies that if my birth control failed, I would likely have an abortion if I wasn't ready to be a mother. Although I weighed my options and considered what it would mean if I kept the pregnancy, the decision to have an abortion was neither traumatic nor tragic. I did not experience it as a theological crisis or as an act that separated me from God. It was a loss, but it was the loss of a road not taken, the loss of a potential child with a partner with whom I had very much wanted to have children. A loss, but neither a tragic nor a life-defining loss.

My abortion was the right decision, a sentiment shared by 95 percent of women terminating pregnancies.[11] I have never regretted my decision or felt any lingering guilt or sadness after my immediate experience of the pregnancy and abortion. My first abortion was not a tragic decision. The tragedy was my failing marriage. Ending that pregnancy opened up the space for us to separate. Separation gave us each the opportunity to be apart and to figure out what we wanted, from ourselves and from each other. It allowed us the chance to come back together and find a better marriage counselor.

The most important lesson I learned in my first five years of marriage is that marriage is hard work. I have learned this lesson over and over again throughout our twenty-five years of marriage, though nothing will ever compare to those first five years. In those years, we learned how to communicate, we rebuilt our broken trust, and we practiced listening and caring and kindness. We learned how to fight in ways that shared our pain and vulnerability rather than attacking one another, and we learned how to care for one another even in the midst of arguments. Only after we did the hard work on our marriage could we imagine welcoming a child into our family.

Four years later, when we were ready to be parents, I got pregnant right away. This time we had a solid marriage and we had found a caring church that embraced us with open arms, brought us food for weeks after the baby was born, and otherwise supported us. We were still students, we still didn't have much money, and the three of us lived in a tiny rental house. But we were emotionally and psychologically ready.

My husband and I finished our training and finally both landed professional jobs that we loved. Pretty soon, we were ready for another child. I was teaching full time and had a three-year-old, so I don't remember much about my early pregnancy except the constant nausea. At thirty-five, I was labeled *advanced maternal age* and given the standard warnings about the increased risks in my pregnancy. But my husband and I decided not to have an amniocentesis, given the potential risk of miscarriage and our assumption that I would have a healthy pregnancy and a healthy prenate. I had my routine prenatal tests as scheduled, not thinking much about them, until there was a message on my answering machine from one of the doctors in my practice to call her.

It was Christmas Eve. As any pregnant woman knows, she was not calling to tell me my tests were normal. My doctor's office wouldn't even be open for another three or four days, and I was sixteen weeks pregnant. After a few insistent conversations with answering services and on-call midwives, we finally got a call from the doctor who told us that my alpha-fetoprotein test had shown an increased risk for Down syndrome. She arranged for an amniocentesis and an ultrasound for the day after Christmas. I remember bundling our three-year-old off to church for the Christmas Eve pageant, where she played a sheep, and I sat with her in the hay at the front of the sanctuary while my husband sat alone in the pew, silently crying as we both wondered what we would do if something was wrong.

The next two weeks were a blur. They involved ultrasounds and perinatal cardiologists, two painful amniocenteses, and finally by my eighteenth week, a diagnosis of multiple severe heart defects that would require open-heart surgery in the first year of life and Down syndrome. While we never thought we would have another abortion, we were suddenly faced with another unexpected life situation that required serious moral reflection. Fifty years ago, we would not have known the diagnosis ahead of time. There is an increased possibility that I would have miscarried or had a stillbirth. If the prenate had made it to full term, I would have given birth and our child would have died within the first year of life. Medical technology has advanced in truly remarkable ways. In our situation, it offered both the advanced knowledge of our prenate's diagnosis and the possibility of open-heart surgery. It was now our responsibility to figure out what to do with this information.

We had to discern whether we were prepared and willing to parent this medically and socially fragile potential child that I carried. The fact that this was a deeply wanted pregnancy meant that this situation was nothing like my first abortion. Although my marriage was now solid, I was still concerned for the health of my marriage and I had to think about the obligations that we had to our three-year-old, my calling and vocation as a Christian ethicist and college professor, and my awareness of my own gifts and limitations as a parent. Even though I had welcomed this pregnancy and deeply wanted another child, my moral obligation to the prenate in this case was not simply to ensure that it be born, but to make the best decision that I could make in the situation.

My husband and I knew that ending the pregnancy was the right decision for us. But in contrast to our first experience of abortion, this experience was wrenching. We grieved deeply over our loss, but the loss was the loss of our imagined child, the social being we had created in our minds as all would-be parents do. The death of the imagined child we were expecting happened when we received the prenatal diagnosis, not with the abortion. Abortions of wanted pregnancies are widely regarded as comparable to the miscarriage, stillbirth, or newborn death of a wanted child.[12] If we had decided to continue the pregnancy, no doubt we would have built a new social relationship with that prenate and we certainly would have loved any child that we would have had. But whether we terminated or continued the pregnancy, we would have needed to grieve the loss of the child we had imagined. For very personal reasons, we decided to end the pregnancy. Two years later, I got pregnant again and gave birth to our second daughter. Again, we welcomed a child into our family.

Both of my abortions were legal. Both of my abortions were decisions that my husband and I made together after considering our situation and our existing resources and obligations, including our emotional energy and capacity to parent. When I had my second abortion, one of my best friends said to me, "But what will you tell your children?" Despite her long-standing pro-choice political position and her support of me through the crisis of my pregnancy, her question indicated that she thought there was something wrong with my decision. From my perspective, I planned to tell my children the truth because it was the right decision for me and my husband and our family. Clearly, my friend did not feel the same way. For her, there was something shameful in my decision and she couldn't quite imagine how I could explain that to my children.

The decisions to end two of my pregnancies were important moral decisions in my life, but they were no more important than many other moral decisions I have faced. In fact, the decision to have two children has been a far more profound and life-changing decision than either of my abortions. My abortions do not define my life; they are episodes in a larger life story. Like one in three women in this country, I have a reproductive life story that includes abortion. And those abortions are the backstory that has shaped the family that I have now. I would, most likely, still have two children, but the complete randomness and serendipity of sperm and egg joining means that I would not have had these particular children. The children that I have are not unwanted children or socially imagined children or potential children. They are real children, my children. And I have no regrets.

My abortions don't make sense outside of the larger story of my life, my whole life. And this is why I've written about them. My decisions to terminate my pregnancies were made within a particular context; they were not abstract decisions. Rather, my abortions were part of exercising my responsibility as a fertile woman who believes that parenthood is a sacred calling; they were rooted in my theological understanding of pregnancy, life, children, and parenting. My abortion experiences also represent the two primary categories of abortion in the United States—abortion of an unwanted pregnancy and abortion of a wanted pregnancy. The circumstances of each situation are both morally significant and morally distinct. For this reason, in the next chapter we will look more broadly at the real-life circumstances and demographic realities of women who fall into each of these two categories.

CHAPTER 2

Abortion in Real Life

RECENT ATTACKS ON PLANNED PARENTHOOD, combined with the regressive laws being passed across the country that seek to limit women's access to abortion, have prompted increasing numbers of women to share their personal stories of abortion. This trend includes a Twitter campaign to "shout your abortion," which went viral in September 2015. The campaign began with Amelia Bonow posting this Facebook status update:

> Hi guys! Like a year ago I had an abortion at the Planned Parenthood on Madison Ave, and I remember this experience with a nearly inexpressible level of gratitude. . . . I am telling you this today because the narrative of those working to defund Planned Parenthood relies on the assumption that abortion is still something to be whispered about. Plenty of people still believe that on some level—if you are a good woman—abortion is a choice which should [be] accompanied by some level of sadness, shame, or regret. But you know what? I have a good heart and having an abortion made me happy in a totally unqualified way. Why shouldn't I be happy that I was not forced to become a mother?[1]

Bonow ended her post with the hashtag #shoutyourabortion. The post was picked up by Lindy West, a writer, activist, and friend of Bonow's who tweeted it to her sixty thousand Twitter followers. Within ten days, the

Twitter hashtag had more than 150,000 posts. The *New York Times* did a piece about the success of the campaign and the backlash it engendered—a backlash so threatening and extreme that Bonow temporarily moved out of her apartment building.[2] The #shoutyourabortion campaign was conducted at the same time as Congress's investigation of Planned Parenthood, a farce that included a grueling four-hour interrogation of Cecile Richards, the president of Planned Parenthood. Most importantly, however, the investigation provided an opportunity for Republicans to grandstand on the issue of abortion.

The women across the country who broke their silence and shared their abortion stories rejected the assumption that abortion is shameful. But all too often, shaming and blaming women for ending unwanted pregnancies drives women to hide their stories. Because the tactics of shaming force women out of the public square, the very real circumstances that gave rise to their abortion decisions are erased, to be replaced by caricatures and stereotypes—the selfish coed, the career-driven wife, the crack whore, the promiscuous teenager. While some prominent women have "come out" about having abortions, many women have not felt comfortable telling their stories—particularly women who do not have what I referred to in the introduction as PRIM stories. PRIM abortions, as I've noted, represent only one-quarter of abortions nationwide. The stories of the other 75 percent of women are too little heard.[3] But these stories help us better understand the most common reasons that women in this country end their pregnancies.

In this chapter, we will look more carefully at who has abortions in this country and why. In a debate often driven by emotion and speculation, more comprehensive data can present a more accurate picture of the landscape of fertility, reproduction, and parenting that shape women's decisions about continuing or ending a particular pregnancy.

ENDING UNWANTED PREGNANCIES

Just over six million women in the US every year get pregnant, and almost half of those pregnancies are unintended.[4] In fact, the average US woman spends 2.7 years pregnant, postpartum, or trying to become pregnant, and 31 years trying to avoid becoming pregnant.[5] It's the avoidance of pregnancy that's difficult. Every year in the US, 2.8 million women who want to have sex but don't want a baby get pregnant anyway.[6] Studies demonstrate that between 50 and 60 percent of women who have abortions were using some form of contraceptive the month they got pregnant.[7] This statistic is not surprising, given contraceptive failure rates. These graphs show the percentage of women who are likely to get pregnant using various forms of contraceptives over a ten-year period.

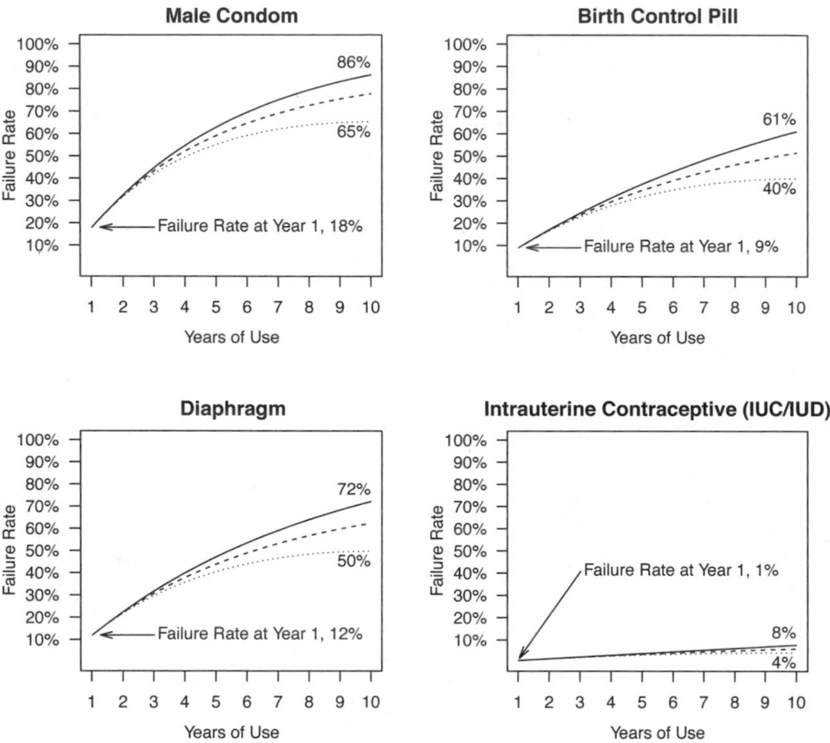

Most people are familiar with one-year failure rates for contraceptives, but failure rates increase over time. These images offer projections for three sets of assumptions of how failure rates may change over time. Solid line: constant failure rate; dashed line: failure rate dropping by 50 percent over ten years; dotted line: failure rate dropping to 0 percent over ten years.[8]

One of the many assumptions about women who have abortions is that they are irresponsible. While the label of *irresponsibility* is often code for judgmental attitudes about the behavior of young women who are sexually active, part of the accusation of irresponsibility is the charge that they "should have known better" or that they should have used birth control. This accusation entirely ignores the fact that roughly one-quarter of the women who get pregnant every year in the US are using birth control.[9] Given the stunningly high failure rates of the most commonly used forms of birth control in this country, it's no wonder that 50 percent of pregnancies in the US are unplanned. What's surprising is that the rate isn't higher.

Although these graphs represent projections, they illustrate an important, unacknowledged aspect of contraception: failure rates increase over time. Contraceptive failure rates are higher than most people realize, because we are used to seeing failure rates based on one year of usage. That's how they are most often presented. But women have sex over their lifetime, not at one-year intervals. Probability rates increase over time because the risk is compounded. So, whereas your risk of pregnancy might seem reasonably low when measured over a year, the risk of unintended pregnancy increases over time.

When I was fitted for my diaphragm at a Planned Parenthood clinic during college, I remember that the staff talked to me about the failure rate, which is estimated at about 6 percent with perfect use (also referred to as "efficacy," which assumes ideal conditions). They emphasized the importance of using it correctly, and they meticulously went over the details with me. I can't remember if they told me that the failure rate with typical use (also referred to as "effectiveness," which assumes actual or typical use, which reflects imperfect and inconsistent use) is 12 percent. Even if they had, the 12 percent rate probably still seemed like pretty good chances. It was at least in the same ballpark as condoms and birth-control pills, and I liked that a diaphragm is noninvasive and that I had control over it. I also didn't have to remember to take a pill every day. What I didn't know was that the failure rate for perfect use over a ten-year period could approach 46 percent and that, with typical use, there might be as much as a 72 percent chance I would get pregnant within ten years. In retrospect, I was playing Russian roulette and I didn't even know it. It was only a matter of time. Not until I got pregnant did I find out that the failure rate with diaphragms is even higher for women with a tilted uterus—which I have.[10]

The various available forms of contraception have a wide range of effectiveness. Although female sterilization is highly effective and is used by

25 percent of women using contraception, it is not easily reversible and therefore not practical for women who might not be finished with (or ready to start) their childbearing.[11] Another 25 percent of women use the pill (with a ten-year typical-use failure rate potentially as high as 61 percent), and 15 percent rely on male condoms (with a ten-year typical-use failure rate approaching 86 percent). All told, contraceptive failure translates into roughly 1.6 million unplanned pregnancies per year.[12]

Those numbers still only account for just under half of the 3.4 million unplanned pregnancies that occur every year.[13] The other half of the unplanned pregnancies happen to women who are sexually active but not regularly using contraception, even though they don't want to get pregnant.[14] This group, while statistically small (only about 10 to 16.5 percent of women), is the one that garners the most public hostility.[15]

Rather than blaming and shaming these women, it seems more productive to try to understand them. Since almost all women use some form of birth control at some point in their lives, why a persistent group of sexually active adults do not use birth control is a striking public-health question. William Mosher and colleagues' recent study of women who gave birth after an unintended pregnancy found several characteristics that stood out among groups with higher rates of nonuse of contraceptives.[16] The data shows no identifiable groups of women who reject contraception outright. There are, however, some groups with an increased risk of unprotected sex. For instance, women who have recently become sexually active are more likely not to use contraception than are women who have been sexually active for more than one year. Both teenagers and women over thirty-five also have higher rates of unprotected sex. Women who are cohabiting are almost twice as likely as married women not to use birth control. Black women have higher rates of lack of contraception (25 percent) than white women (14 percent), and foreign-born black women have the highest rate of all (30 percent). Education also plays a factor: 24 percent of women with an education up to a high school diploma don't use birth control, compared with 12 percent of women with a bachelor's degree. But the percentage increases to 18 percent for women with a master's degree or higher. Clearly, women not using contraception represent a wide-ranging and diverse group.

Not surprisingly, some of the same groups that have higher rates of nonuse of contraceptives also have higher abortion rates—black women, poor women, young women. However, the cultural narratives about *why* these women do not use contraception are more problematic. The dominant charge is that women are careless, lazy, or simply happy to use abortion as their primary means of birth control. Not only do these attitudes reflect a lack of knowledge or understanding about the social realities of these women's lives, but they are part of a prevailing cultural attitude that singles these women out for public shaming. Rather than making assumptions about these women's motives, let's examine the evidence.

First, even though many women who don't use contraception may not be trying to get pregnant, 20 percent of women with unplanned pregnancies who give birth indicate that they "didn't really mind getting pregnant."[17] After all, only 40 percent of women with unintended pregnancies will decide to have an abortion. Women who have "mis-timed" pregnancies, meaning they want children but the pregnancy happened earlier than desired, are much more likely to continue the pregnancy than are women with unwanted pregnancies.[18]

The Mosher study indicated that one-quarter of the women were not using birth control because they didn't expect to have sex, another 12 percent indicated that their male partner either didn't want to use birth control or didn't want them to use birth control, and 10 percent were "worried about the side effects of birth control."[19]

While there are numerous forms of contraception, from hormonal to barrier methods, many women experience negative side effects from some methods and find it difficult to find forms of contraception to use. Perhaps the most surprising explanation that women give for not using birth control is that more than 40 percent of them didn't think they could get pregnant.[20] This perception is a pervasive finding in numerous quantitative studies.[21] Some women think they won't get pregnant because they have had unprotected sex in the past and had not gotten pregnant. Others have had medical conditions or procedures that they believe have compromised their fertility, or they have a history of infertility personally or in their family. Some women have partners who have led them to believe that they (the men) are sterile, and still other women are simply misinformed about the risk of pregnancy and the efficacy rates of various forms of contraception. Misinformation about pregnancy risk is a serious problem, but also a manageable one. Indeed, one study demonstrated that women who received contraceptive counseling in the past year significantly increased their use of birth control.[22]

Women also face a host of barriers when trying to obtain birth control: cost and lack of insurance; challenges in scheduling appointments and getting to a clinic or doctor's office; no regular doctor; language barriers; and difficulty accessing a pharmacy.[23] One study found that almost one-third of the women interviewed had encountered problems getting prescription contraception at some point in their reproductive lives.[24] These barriers were much more prevalent for women living below 200 percent of the poverty line. For many women, such obstacles can make them vulnerable to unintended pregnancies. When the flaws lie in the healthcare system, it is unhelpful to single out the behavior of individual women. It is unreasonable to expect women to stop being sexually active when the healthcare system fails them.

We've now examined the data that shows why roughly three million women in the US have unintended pregnancies every year. The moral question these women face is what to do about it. Although 60 percent of those women will decide to continue their pregnancies, 40 percent decide to terminate.[25] To correct the prevailing characterization that these women are selfish, callous, and irresponsible, let's look at the social-scientific research to get a better picture of who these women are and why they make the decisions that they do.

For many women, specific disruptive events like a divorce or separation, moving two or more times in a twelve-month period, losing a job, or experiencing domestic violence played a large role in their decisions to end a pregnancy.[26] Sociologist Rachel K. Jones and her research team found that 57 percent of women who have abortions experienced a potentially disruptive event in the previous twelve months.[27] While this observation is not surprising, the compounding role that poverty plays in the lives of women with unintended pregnancies is noteworthy.

Forty-nine percent of women who had abortions in 2014 were living below the federal poverty line, a measure that is widely regarded as ineffective in measuring real economic deprivation and stress. In 2014, the federal poverty line was $11,670 for a single adult and $15,730 for a two-person household. Most economists recognize that to get a more accurate picture of poverty in this country, we need to look at people whose income falls below double the federal poverty line (also referred to as 200 percent of the federal poverty line). When we do that, we add another 26 percent of the women who had abortions in 2014.[28] In total, that means that fully 75 percent of women who had abortions in 2014 were poor or low-income, living in or near the bottom quintile (household income up to $21,432), which represents the poorest 20 percent of people in the country. Sixty percent of these women already have at least one child, and their daily lives are often a struggle.[29]

Jones found that more poor women than economically secure women noted the role that difficult life events played in their own decision making: 63 percent of poor women experienced at least one disruptive event in the past year, whereas more economically secure women reported similar events at a 49 percent rate. The incidence of disruption also increased as income decreased.[30] For some women, these events are difficult enough to manage without adding the very real stress of a new baby. One married, low-income woman with two children described her situation: "Me and [my husband] are going through some problems right now, and I figure, what if I had to [do] it by myself? I cannot, like, nowadays daycare cost . . . people charge you too much. . . . So I was just thinking about [having the baby] . . . but right now my life is not good."[31]

While many people are aware that abortion rates are higher among poor women, fewer people consider the particular difficulties that women with fewer resources often face when managing various disruptions in their lives. For several women, losing their jobs meant losing their health insurance and, with it, their access to hormonal contraception. Others reported that they simply couldn't afford contraception, even when it was offered through a publicly funded health clinic. Even women who could afford contraception sometimes found it difficult to visit the clinic to stay up-to-date on their birth-control methods. Another low-income woman living with her boyfriend explained: "You go and get them [Depo-Provera shots] like every 3 months, and it had been, like, five, and I just took over a new business, and I am working, like, 90 hours a week. I mean, I am not making any money from my business, but I am working, like, you wouldn't imagine. So, I completely didn't even think about it."[32]

Not only are poor women disproportionately represented among abortion patients, but the percentage of poor women obtaining abortions has grown in recent years even as the rate of abortion among economically secure women has fallen.[33] This troubling trend was noted as early as a 1994–2000 study, which found that the rates of abortion among poor and low-income women had increased by 15 percent.[34] In 2001, the proportion of abortion patients below the poverty line was 27 percent, and this number rose to 42 percent in 2008 and increased again in 2014 to 49 percent. This means that although rates of abortion have been declining overall, they are rising substantially among disadvantaged women.

The structures of our society reflect our values. Too many jobs today do not pay a living wage, and high-quality childcare is either unavailable or outside the means of poor women. Affordable housing supply does not meet demand, public education is failing our poorest students, and effective public transportation is frequently nonexistent. These inadequate social structures more accurately indicate what we truly value as a country than does any rhetoric about freedom, equality, or justice. Or at least they indicate who we believe deserves to be free, and to be treated equally and justly. It is increasingly apparent that we have collectively built a country where the working poor cannot afford to pay their bills. We have failed as a human community to shape a country that truly reflects the values that we profess. The dominant cultural narratives about success in this country speak of perseverance, hard work, and pulling yourself up by your bootstraps. They imply that everyone can succeed if the person just works hard enough. But individuals cannot solve the structural problems that contribute to poverty in twenty-first-century America.

The working poor exist within the structures of society. They can't individually address the lack of affordable housing, childcare, strong schools, and public transportation. Yes, some people running the gauntlet of poverty in our country may pull themselves out of it, but if we look more closely at their stories, people rarely overcome unjust structures on their own. They are helped by friends or families or faith communities. Or their lottery number is drawn for one of the few affordable housing allocations in their town. Or they cobble together several jobs that allow them to pay their bills. The reality is that poor people exist and must make choices within the unjust structures of our society. Those who succeed in achieving the so-called American Dream of upward class mobility and economic stability are commended for their hard work and perseverance in the face of so many impediments. And they have worked hard and persevered. But this narrative belies the daily reality of millions of other people who also work very hard every day but are unable to escape the social structures that impede their success. And the structures that I have named are only those that relate to social infrastructures. When we consider how racial prejudice, misogyny, heterosexism, ableism, and other forms of oppression continue to shape cultural attitudes, societal institutions, and individual behavior, the obstacles that poor women face, particularly poor women of color, are almost overwhelming.

Economic inequality today is approaching the levels that existed during the era of the robber barons. That era required a constitutional amendment to institute a progressive tax structure ensuring that money continued to flow through the whole of our economy. Before then, money was concentrated in the pockets of wealth that served the needs and desires of a handful. For almost 40 percent of our population, wages cannot cover the basic costs of living. In this situation, additional mouths to feed represent a serious moral dilemma, particularly for women who already have children. Is it surprising that in this social context, both unplanned pregnancy rates and abortion rates continue to rise for poor women? In a country where poor women can't find jobs that pay a living wage, housing they can afford, or schools to properly educate their children, can we really say that their reproductive-health needs are being met?

In 2010, of the more than 19 million US women who needed publicly supported contraceptive services, 30 percent, or 5.8 million, were uninsured.[35] Many of these women either went without contraception or used methods with higher failure rates. Long-acting, reversible contraceptive (LARC) methods, like intrauterine devices (IUDs) and birth-control implants, have failure rates that approach zero but are often inaccessible for women without insurance. Unless we are seriously suggesting that poor women shouldn't have sex if they can't afford contraception, the issue of unplanned pregnancies is a public problem rooted in poverty and inequality. While the pregnancy risk of any given sexual encounter is only 3 percent, the annual pregnancy rate for sexually active women who don't use contraception is 85 percent.

Public invocations of "responsibility" are often laden with racial and class undertones associated with particular expectations about what constitutes responsibility, as well as moral judgment that abortion is not a responsible choice. Drilling down into the realities that shape the lives of women with unwanted pregnancies demonstrates that they are making reasonable and informed moral decisions to end their pregnancies. These difficult, real-life moral decisions stand in contrast with the insistence by predominantly white, middle-class politicians and anti-choice crusaders that women who have abortions need to take more responsibility. When we consider the situations of many poor and working-class women, the decision to have an abortion is often an imminently responsible decision made in the midst of trying to make ends meet. As they care for the children they already have, as they strive to work enough hours to pay their bills, as they seek to finish a degree to better their lives, or as they struggle with addictions, homelessness, or other chronic problems that prevent them from being able to mother a child (or another child), having an abortion is a responsible decision.

Furthermore, social-scientific studies that examine why women have abortions offer clear evidence that women do not casually or accidentally undergo terminations of their pregnancies in the United States; nor are they coerced to have an abortion. One study found that fewer than 1 percent reported influence from parents or partners as their primary reason for obtaining an abortion.[36] The same study showed that 89 percent of women gave at least two reasons for the abortion, 72 percent gave at least three reasons, and the median number of reasons given was four.[37] Seventy-four percent of the women cited interference with their education or job/career or responsibilities for existing children or other dependents. About half of the women indicated either relationship problems or an unwillingness to be a single parent, and 38 percent indicated that they had completed their childbearing. Not surprisingly, economics also plays a large role in women's decision-making, with 73 percent indicating that they could not afford to have a baby at that point in their lives.[38] This assessment is borne out by another recent study of *turnaways*, women who visited clinics for an abortion procedure but were turned away for having passed the gestational limit of that clinic. The study, which included women who procured an abortion elsewhere and those who carried their pregnancies to term after the initial turnaway, reported some enlightening financial results. Although the women across both categories were in comparable economic positions when they were pregnant, one year later, 76 percent of the turnaways (86 percent of whom were living with their babies) were receiving federal assistance, compared with 44 percent who had received abortions.[39]

The demographic data on who is having abortions and the empirical data about women's reasons for having abortions show clearly that childbearing is a deeply socioeconomic issue. The public rhetoric that insists women must justify their abortions represents a thinly veiled racial and class bias that does two things. It attempts to impose white, middle-class values about marriage, sexual activity, and childbearing on everyone—even those who do not have white, middle-class social and economic structures to support them. And it focuses on individual women's behavior while effectively obfuscating the complexity of their day-to-day lives and the viability of their various choices.

THE COMPLEXITY OF SECOND-TRIMESTER ABORTIONS

More than one-third of abortions occur by six weeks, and 91.6 percent happen in the first trimester.[40] This means that second-trimester abortions are rare, making up only 8.4 percent of abortions, with just over 1 percent of all abortions nationwide occurring after twenty-one weeks and only 0.08 percent after twenty-four weeks.[41]

Much is made in this country of second-trimester abortions. They are often used as an emotional wedge to try to sway public opinion about abortion more generally. Calling these abortions "late-term," for instance, is part of a rhetorical strategy designed to influence popular opinion about these procedures. Indeed, political battles over these procedures dominated the abortion wars throughout the 1990s and 2000s. Starting with opposition to the medical procedure known as *intact dilation and extraction* (intact D&E) in the mid-1990s, pro-life advocates labeled this procedure "partial-birth abortion" in a clear attempt to sway public opinion.[42] The intact D&E procedure is controversial because it involves reducing the size of the head, which is the largest part of the prenate, to ease its passage out of the cervix and vagina. By describing the surgical procedure in great detail, its opponents sought to shock the public into demanding (or at least accepting) that Congress ban this procedure. The reality is that surgery is often gruesome, and the removal of a prenate from a woman's uterus in a surgical procedure can evoke feelings of horror and disgust even for people who support abortion as a choice for women. It was this same evocative horror of "body parts" that the Center for Medical Progress, an antiabortion organization, tapped into in 2015, when it used heavily edited videos in an attempt to suggest that Planned Parenthood engaged in trafficking fetal tissue.

Individuals and groups that seek to restrict access to abortion often use sonograms, photos, and plastic models of prenates to play on people's emotional associations with newborn babies. As the prenate develops and grows, the exterior features begin to resemble a baby even as the interior organs and other systems are just beginning to take shape. A prenate *looks like* a baby long before it is viable, and our improved technological capacity in the last thirty years has brought prenatal images increasingly into our consciousness as a human community. The pro-life lobby attempts to capitalize on people's emotional responses to pregnancy and their ambivalence about abortion by labeling prenates as "unborn children" and by associating all second-trimester abortions with intact D&E. This strategy of emotional manipulation was nowhere more clear than in H.R. 36, the Pain-Capable Unborn Child Protection Act, which sought to ban abortions after twenty weeks except in cases of rape, incest, and the life of the mother. These exceptions are certainly essential, but many serious prenatal health issues often are not detected until after twenty weeks, and these situations were excluded from the bill.

The title of the bill itself illustrates the ideological nature of the legislation through its use of the three phrases "pain-capable," "unborn child," and "protection act." With its use of the term "protection," the legislation sets the state up as the defender and protector of the "unborn child" and, by implication, sets the pregnant woman up as the aggressor from whom the "unborn child" needs protecting. Since the term "unborn child" seems to have lost some of its emotional impact, the newest tactic to sway people's emotions is to tack on the idea that this innocent "child" is not simply "unborn" but also now "pain-capable." In six words, a safe and legal medical procedure has been transformed into an act of torture and child abuse perpetuated by an uncaring and ignominious monster, otherwise known as the pregnant woman.

The bill itself has nothing to do with the capacity of the prenate to feel pain. Nor is there any mention in the legislation of anesthetizing the prenate as a precaution to spare it pain. More importantly, scientific consensus indicates that although the biological pathways connected to pain sensation are beginning to develop at twenty weeks, the brain connections required to actually feel pain are not in place until closer to twenty-four weeks. Furthermore, even if the prenate can feel pain, at twenty weeks or twenty-four weeks, pain in and of itself is not a significant moral reason that would trump a pregnant woman's legal and moral right to terminate a pregnancy. When women terminate pregnancies for fetal and maternal health reasons, they have carefully considered their situations and made the difficult decision to end their wanted pregnancies. Qualitative research indicates that many of these women are influenced by their desire to be a good parent to existing and potential children.[43]

The legislation related to abortion, pregnancy, childbirth, and parenting shows undeniably that our legislators are far more focused on controlling pregnant women than they are on either reducing unwanted pregnancies or helping women gain access to earlier and safer abortions. Assistance with the latter would probably reduce the already small number of abortions performed in the second trimester. The complexities of women's lives and the realities of pregnancy, mean there will always be some need for second-trimester abortions. In a context that vilifies women who seek such abortions, we need a deeper, evidence-based understanding of women's lives and why they might delay their decision until the second trimester of a pregnancy.

The largest number of second-trimester abortions occurs among poor women and young women, two groups that face obstacles that push their procedures later into a pregnancy. People who aren't familiar with abortion and problem pregnancies may wonder why anyone would wait so late to have an abortion.

I was talking about this question with a friend of mine who had gotten pregnant at seventeen and decided to place her daughter for adoption forty years ago. She said, "Let me tell you, it's not at all hard not to know you are pregnant!" In her case, she went to the doctor with her mother after missing her period and had a false negative test. She went on to spend the summer riding her bike across the country. It wasn't until well into her pregnancy, when she was sitting on the couch one day watching TV and she felt the prenate move, that she realized she was pregnant.

Her experience is not uncommon. Statistics show that second-trimester abortion rates are higher for younger women, particularly for women in their teens, and most studies attribute this higher rate for young women to delayed confirmation of pregnancy. Of course, it's not only teens who have delayed confirmation of pregnancy: obese women and women who have few to no pregnancy-related symptoms are also more likely to be delayed in discovering their pregnancies. One study found that 88 percent of women who discovered their pregnancy at or before eight weeks had a first-trimester abortion whereas only 32 percent of women who found out after eight weeks had a first-trimester procedure. Overall, 43 percent of women reported that not realizing they were pregnant delayed their search for abortion care.[44] Another study found that nearly half of the women seeking second-trimester care had underestimated how far along they were by more than four weeks.[45]

While some critics have attempted to demonize women who seek second-trimester abortions in an effort to make them appear significantly different from women who have first-trimester abortions, qualitative social-scientific research has shown that by and large, women who seek abortions at any stage are remarkably similar.[46] Many factors can contribute to delays in seeking abortion care and, consequently, to significantly later abortion services. One study found that most women seeking abortions experience barriers to obtaining their abortions; 80 percent of women who had first-trimester abortions, and 94 percent who had second-trimester abortions, reported delays.[47] While the primary cause of delay was not knowing about the pregnancy, there were other significant factors as well. One study found that 37 percent of women reported that the difficulty of making a decision delayed their access to care, while another study found the same thing for 39 percent of women, and a third study found the rate to be almost 45 percent.[48] This data clearly challenges the image of pregnant women blithely deciding they simply don't want to be pregnant anymore and terminating late pregnancies after the point of viability. Fifty-eight percent of women who had second-trimester abortions indicated that they would have liked to have had an earlier abortion, again defying the stereotypes that demonize them.[49]

The data also clearly shows that women with limited financial resources face more significant barriers, particularly if they are uninsured or if their insurance doesn't cover abortion services. While many poor women are covered by Medicaid, federal legislation known as the Hyde Amendment was passed in 1977 prohibiting federal funds from being used to cover abortion services except in the case of rape, incest, or the life of the pregnant woman. Fifteen states have chosen to fund abortions for residents who have their procedures in the state. One study found that nearly two-thirds of the women said that their delay past twenty weeks was a result of raising money for the procedure and related costs.[50] Another study with similar results (36 percent of women having second-trimester procedures indicated that raising the money delayed their actions) showed that cost was the most significant factor for delaying access to abortion.[51] Many poor women rely on Medicaid to cover their healthcare, and without abortion coverage, it can often take them months to raise the money to pay for their procedure. Public policies that, like the Hyde Amendment, prevent the use of public funds for abortion function to delay rather than prevent abortions. Given that second-term procedures are significantly more expensive than first-trimester abortions, this increased financial burden often delays the procedure even more.

ENDING WANTED PREGNANCIES

So far, we have examined abortion in cases where pregnancy was unintended and unwanted. When the prenate is unhealthy and/or medically compromised, the pregnancy is also usually ended later. It is not a decision that pregnant women and their partners take lightly.[52] The grief and pain that women feel when they terminate wanted pregnancies has been shown to be very similar to the experience of perinatal death.[53] In 2003, I interviewed thirteen women who had had second-trimester abortions of wanted pregnancies. One woman told me: "I think of it as a death of a child. [Someone] said it's not like [having] a living child die. Which is worse? I've had people tell me it's worse if they're living first. I said I don't know. I said I would have liked to know his eye color, his hair color, and I said we'll never know."[54]

Abortions of wanted pregnancies fall into two categories—prenates that are incompatible with life, meaning that they cannot survive outside the womb, and prenates with disabilities or serious birth defects. There is far less social stigma associated with the termination of prenates that are incompatible with life. One woman referred to this form of pregnancy termination as choosing an "end-of-life care plan" for her prenate.[55] Let me share the story of one woman in this situation.

Jackie had two boys, aged fourteen and nine, from a previous marriage.[56] She and her second husband got pregnant immediately after they were married, and her life was so busy that she didn't get around to having an ultrasound until she was twenty-four weeks pregnant. She was thirty-three years old, and there was no reason to suspect anything was wrong with the pregnancy. She went for her ultrasound late on a Friday afternoon with her husband and her two boys. The technician discovered what appeared to be a brain cyst along with fluid on the brain. The obstetrician told her that he suspected that something might be wrong with the prenate's brain, but he wasn't sure. He wanted to send her to a specialist for further testing. Since it was Friday afternoon, she would have to wait until Monday. Imagine yourself, twenty-four weeks pregnant and having to wait four days before you could confirm whether your prenate's brain function was OK.

That night, Jackie called a friend whose husband was a radiologist. The friend and the husband suggested that they could sneak Jackie into his hospital for an ultrasound the next day. While the radiologist was not an obstetrician and not accustomed to analyzing fetal ultrasounds, he was able to confirm the presence of the cyst and the fluid and to establish that the fluid was blood—the prenate was hemorrhaging. He was the first person to mention to Jackie that she might want to consider an abortion. When Jackie got to her appointment with the specialist on Monday, she and her husband had had some time to think and talk about their situation.

At that appointment, she found out that the likelihood of severe brain damage was high. The staff told her that she and her husband would be lucky if the baby, a boy, could swallow and that he would probably never be able to recognize or respond to his parents. The doctors believed that her prenate had had a stroke in utero. Jackie decided to terminate her pregnancy.

She spoke with me about how this experience affected her faith. She had been raised Catholic and attended a Catholic church at the time of the abortion. She said that long ago, she had accepted the idea that there are good things and bad things that happen in life and that she was never angry with God throughout the whole experience. Nevertheless, she said she stopped going to church—mostly because of all the babies she encountered. In a terrible place of deep grief and pain, she didn't know whom she could confide in at her church. With the Catholic Church's official stance against abortion, she was afraid of being stigmatized and attacked for her decision rather than supported in her grief and healing.

Many women also decide to terminate after prenatal tests indicate serious chromosomal abnormalities that can cause conditions like Down syndrome, Tay-Sachs disease, or Triple X syndrome. Margaret's prenate had Down syndrome.[57] She had declined a screening for alpha-fetoprotein at fifteen weeks—a test that would have assessed if her prenate had any increased risk for either Down syndrome or neural tube defects. She had declined the test, she told me, because she thought that if her prenate had Down syndrome, it wouldn't matter to her—she would have the baby anyway. At nineteen weeks, an ultrasound revealed multisystemic abnormalities, including a cyst that took up one-third of the brain area, multiple heart defects, and bowels and kidneys that looked suspicious.

After deep soul-searching and long discussions, Margaret and her husband decided that the reality of Down syndrome that faced their son was much more complex and devastating than what they had imagined a child with Down syndrome might face. While many children with

Down syndrome can function quite well within a supportive community, there is a wide range of physical and mental capacities among people with the syndrome. As Margaret and her husband thought about what it would mean to continue the pregnancy, they considered a host of issues. They had only been married for four years, she noted: "We really hadn't even had the chance to have a really good solid foundation yet." They discussed the potential quality of life that faced their son and the risk of abuse at an institutional facility if they eventually had to move him to one. They considered the possible effects on their three-year-old daughter, as well as their other career and life choices. Ultimately, they felt that the best decision they could make in that situation was to terminate the pregnancy.

For women who terminate a viable pregnancy of a disabled or chromosomally nonstandard prenate, there is a strange mixture of social stigma and quiet acceptance. Two things must be noted before we discuss the moral implications of the choices made in these circumstances. First, people's initial reactions to the diagnosis as well as the quiet social acceptance of these terminations may very well be based on prejudice and a cultural misunderstanding of disability and birth defects. Second, parenting a special needs child is different from parenting other children. Depending on the diagnosis, the child might need extensive medical care, including multiple surgeries and medical procedures, hospital stays, and other medical care. Additionally, although many conditions can be diagnosed prenatally, the severity of the disability and the particular needs of that potential child cannot be known prenatally.

To say that women and couples who make painfully difficult decisions to terminate wanted pregnancies are suffering from the desire for a perfect child trivializes the very real and hard decisions these parents made. It is a particularly vicious form of social punishment for women and couples who decide to end the pregnancies of medically fragile prenates. Accusing women of wanting perfect children negates the serious prognosis that many of these potential parents face when confronted with the results of prenatal testing. They are often torn between the medical establishment's offer of more and more information about the potential child that they are carrying and an increasing social climate of hostility and judgment toward those who use that information to make moral decisions about the future health of their family.

Regardless of how much we might believe that "it takes a village" to raise a child or how seriously our communities take our common baptismal vows to support parents in the raising of their children, the parent or parents will ultimately be responsible for caring for and raising that child. In a country that provides limited support to parents of children with disabilities, the burden of raising differently abled or medically fragile children is significantly higher than that of raising healthy children. Many parents recognize that their choices will also have profound implications for their careers and for their other children. Rightly or wrongly, these parents must also grapple with a culture marked by prejudice and ignorance about disability. They are the only ones who can know the limits and capacities of what they can manage. Certainly, there are people who rise to the occasion, and of course, most parents do not know their children's abilities or disabilities until after the children are born. Most prospective parents examine the existing commitments to their partners, their other children, their parents, and others as they decide how to respond morally to an anomalous prenatal diagnosis.

Most women approach childbearing with a serious commitment to caring for and loving their children. They also have a reasonable expectation that there is a time limit on the intense caretaking responsibilities. These responsibilities usually diminish slowly through childhood and virtually cease once the child reaches adulthood. With children who have severe, incurable diagnoses, parents deserve the opportunity to reassess whether they are physically, financially, emotionally, and psychologically capable of providing the care that such a child requires. Philosopher Rosamond Rhodes argues that once women discover a serious fetal deformity, they are faced with a decision to either accept the responsibilities that parenting a seriously ill or disabled child might require or accept the responsibility of terminating the pregnancy.[58] In addition to concerns raised earlier, the lack of support services for disabled adults means that concerns about what will happen to one's child if it reaches the age of maturity are also relevant moral questions. Several women I interviewed spoke about their concerns for both their existing and their potential children and how these concerns factored into their decisions. One woman who had a two-year-old son at the time of her termination expressed it this way:

> It's hard enough looking after a normal two-year-old . . . discipline and, you know, all kinds of things. A big thing is the long term. If that child was to survive and be functioning to whatever degree, we may not be around and that child is still living. My husband's thirty-six now. I'm thirty-seven, and you know from our point of view, we didn't want to have a child . . . [who] at age forty—when we're near eighty—who's still behaving like a child, and that we are going to go to the grave worried about. And the responsibility for her would have fallen back on Mark [her son]. And I don't think that's fair on him. You know, I can't ask him now at the age of two if he's prepared to look after his little sister until the day she died. I don't think that's fair on him, and I don't think that's fair on anybody. Because you don't know to what degree the disability will be.[59]

The unknown factor of how severely prenates might be affected by their condition was a recurring theme in many of the women's narratives. One woman, an emergency room doctor, said, "I just can't imagine bringing a child into this world and immediately having open-heart surgery. . . . It just didn't make sense to me to do that to a child."[60] Many women shared this sentiment of terminating their pregnancy as the one act of love they could offer their potential child. They saw the option of abortion as a way of protecting it from the cruelties and other difficulties of the world. Several women also knew they would be the primary caregivers for their disabled or medically comprised children, and they spoke frankly about what this would mean for their ability to parent their existing or future children in addition to the potential child they carried. One woman I interviewed typifies the worries: "I mean, it was going to be so hard on my girls, who are biracial and adopted. They've got so many strikes against them already, and they're going to have to deal with a brother who requires all of my time. I'm going to have to quit my job, and I'm like, you know, so we'd just be doing it for him and we're not doing it for him, because he wouldn't even know who we were. I mean I thought if he had semi-quality of life, it would've been worth it, but I felt that he was going to have absolutely none."[61]

About half of the women I interviewed had prenates with conditions that were incompatible with life. The other half had prenates with variable prognoses, meaning that their doctors did not know if some of the prenates would survive childbirth and if they did, many faced surgeries and all faced an unknown range of mental and physical disabilities. Like the woman above, all the women whose prenates stood a chance of surviving were very clear about how the challenges of parenting a special needs child would affect their careers, their ability to parent their existing and potentially additional future children, and how the stresses of a medically fragile child might strain their marriages. For some women, this knowledge was based on volunteer or work experience with special needs children. Others knew from personal experience with disabled family members, and others knew from research and discussions with healthcare professionals who counseled them in the midst of their crisis pregnancies. As one woman stated, "I wasn't willing to give up my career, and neither was my husband."[62]

Within a polarized political debate about the morality of abortion, it is often difficult to communicate the very important nuances that shape women's experiences with abortion. The particular situation of women who decide to end wanted pregnancies offers surprising clarity into the nature of the debate. Women who terminate for prenatal or maternal health reasons are often excused or dismissed from the abortion debate because their reasons are accepted as "justified." In the context of an abortion debate that seeks to distinguish between "acceptable" abortions and "problematic" abortions, women who terminate for health reasons are generally not considered part of the problem.

In reality, the situation of prenatal and maternal health problems highlights the very heart of the real problem that we face as a country about abortion. Our collective social capacity to accept women's reasons for abortion in cases of prenatal and maternal health concerns illustrates our ability to recognize that context and circumstances matter. Because these women fit the traditional pronatalist narrative—they have wanted pregnancies and they desire motherhood—these women fit into traditional patriarchal narratives about women's sexuality and their role as mothers. In these circumstances, the majority of observers readily suspend any professed support for the prenate's "rights" in light of the obvious bodily integrity, health, and well-being of the pregnant woman. Women who conform to social expectations about pregnancy and mothering are deemed worthy of our support, our sympathy, and access to abortion services when something goes "wrong." These situations make it abundantly clear that abortion isn't the problem.

The stories in this chapter are intended to ground our conversation in the reality and voices of real women who have abortions in this country. Stories are important. They help us build relationships and teach us lessons. They generate empathy and invite listeners to think about the reality of other lives that might be different from our own. By offering examples of real situations, they help us think in new ways about a social problem. Real women's stories are particularly important in the debate about abortion, precisely because it is women's voices and lives that are often missing from the conversation.

With the silencing of women, the conversation about abortion in this country is often dominated by people who seek to speak on behalf of the primary constituency in the debate, namely, women who have abortions. The arguments put forth by these antiabortion actors are rooted in the same unexamined assumptions, prejudice, and disinformation that characterize the justification paradigm. Increasingly, this disinformation is being incorporated into state law through the actions of ideologically oriented conservative politicians, many of whom are affiliated with traditionalist interpretations of Christianity and Christian perspectives about women's sexuality, pregnancy, and abortion. In the following chapter, we will examine how conservative Christians are using public policy in this country to impose an authoritarian agenda that seeks to control women's sexuality and their fertility.

CHAPTER 3

Abortion Policy as the Public Abuse of Women

IMAGINE A SOCIETY WITH widespread stillbirths, miscarriages, and genetic deformities linked to sabotage and accidents at nuclear facilities, chemical and biological toxins leaking into the water supply, and the uncontrolled use of chemical insecticides and herbicides. Imagine now that in addition to dropping birth rates from this environmental apocalypse, a new strain of syphilis and rapidly increasing death rates from AIDS wipe out large segments of young, sexually active people from the reproductive pool. Could you imagine that in such a world, the fertility of the ruling class becomes so completely compromised by these disasters that many women can no longer conceive and bear children and the whole social order threatens to fall apart? This is the background of Margaret Atwood's iconic dystopian novel *The Handmaid's Tale*. In the story, a coup by patriarchal, right-wing Christians leads to the suspension of women's rights and the absolute control of the lives of fertile women.

Like all good dystopian literature, Atwood's tale is chilling because the social problem she describes is so plausible. The absolute social control of women and their bodies is neither fictional nor solely historical. Rather than inventing new horrors for her society, Atwood adopts aspects of the reality of women's lives around the world and incorporates them into her fictional society of Gilead. The shock value comes from seeing the US as a society where women are stripped of their legal and human rights and subject to the absolute authority of a fundamentalist Christian theocratic state. In this new society, sex is reduced to procreation and fertile women are forced to bear children for the elite members of society. The sexual servitude of the "handmaids" is justified by invoking the biblical practice of surrogacy, where matriarchs like Sarah, Rachel, and Leah "gave" their servants or handmaids to their patriarch husbands for the purpose of childbearing.

Though written more than thirty years ago, *The Handmaid's Tale* remains a cultural touchstone in the US. And no wonder: women's access to safe, legal, and affordable abortion is under siege by conservative Christian politicians who have had increasing success in using public policy to promote a patriarchal and pronatalist agenda. In the five years between 2011 and 2016, there were 334 abortion restrictions enacted at the state level, far exceeding the 189 enacted in the previous ten years.[1] The bulk of these recent regulations affect the most vulnerable women in our society, namely, poor, young, and minority women. In addition to restricting access to abortion services, the state has increasingly sought to legislate sexual morality through abstinence-only campaigns in public schools and by increasingly impeding women's access to contraception. In a country where pregnant women are being detained, arrested, and prosecuted for "crimes" related to their pregnancies; where some female prisoners are shackled during childbirth; and where pregnant women can be compelled to undergo surgery and other medical procedures against their will, we have to recognize how state and federal laws, judicial decisions, and law enforcement agencies are sanctioning and engaging in the public abuse of women. And the government's actions are often conducted at the behest of conservative Christian activists and politicians.

This abuse is possible because the justification framework has shaped a cultural atmosphere where the public tacitly accepts the idea of pregnancy as punishment for assumed immoral or irresponsible behavior. Let's stop and think about that for a moment, because the idea is quite remarkable—*pregnancy as punishment*. Having a child as *punishment*. As a Christian, a woman, and a mother, I find the notion of childbearing as punishment abhorrent. Parenting should be willfully and joyfully entered into. But in an atmosphere that accepts the idea of pregnancy itself as punishment for women's sexual activity, it is a short step to allowing, even encouraging the adoption of public policies that police, control, and punish women for their sexual activity and their reproductive decisions.

I would like to suggest that the reason poor women who seek to terminate their pregnancies are singled out for abuse, derision, and social shaming is because we *can*. Poor women's lack of social power contributes to their marginalization. These women represent the most vulnerable of the vulnerable, often lacking adequate financial and other material resources to care for their existing children, let alone any potential children. Lacking financial power, political strength, and social status, these women have become the collective scapegoats on which society heaps its discomfort with women's sexuality, abortion, poverty, and a host of other underexamined issues in the abortion debate.

In this chapter, I describe how conservative Christian antiabortion groups are using a sophisticated state-based strategy for reducing access to abortion services until they are able to recriminalize abortion at the federal level. I also show how this right-wing campaign manipulates public opinion to promote pronatalist policies that create a climate and culture of hostility, harassment, and control of women and their bodies—an environment that amounts to the state-sanctioned public abuse of women. I end with an argument for why our public policy ought to focus on addressing systemic social problems rather than attempting to police the behavior of individual pregnant women.

EXPOSING THE CONSERVATIVE CHRISTIAN POLITICS OF CONTROL

For several decades after abortion became legal in the United States, the antiabortion movement was led by the Roman Catholic–sponsored National Right to Life Committee (NRLC) and fundamentalist Christian televangelists like Jerry Falwell and Pat Robertson and their organizations—the Moral Majority and the Christian Coalition. The NRLC emphasized its theological perspective that life begins at conception and focused on pushing a political agenda oriented toward "fetal rights." Robertson and Falwell's brand of fundamentalist Christianity was more focused on promoting a patriarchal vision of Christianity that demonized gays and lesbians, abortion, single mothers, and feminists and promoted traditional domestic roles for women. This perspective was epitomized by Robertson in an infamous 1992 quote on the TV program *The 700 Club*: "I know this is painful for the ladies to hear, but if you get married, you have accepted the headship of a man, your husband. Christ is the head of the household and the husband is the head of the wife, and that's the way it is, period."[2]

While Catholics and evangelicals have sometimes approached the issue from different angles, their clear opposition to legalized abortion has often meant political collaboration in the public sphere. Anti-choice Catholics and fundamentalist Christians share a traditionalist Christian position toward sexuality and pregnancy: they not only believe that sex belongs exclusively within marriage and that anyone who has sex is obligated to accept pregnancy and childbirth as the "consequence" of their sexual activity, but also emphasize the sinful nature of sex outside marriage. For instance, a campaign in the early 1980s launched by Falwell to house single pregnant women emphasized the women's "fallen" nature. The director of the program said, "We all ought to be able to control ourselves and abstain from premarital or extra-marital sex. There were one and a half million abortions in this country last year—sin caused that. The act of fornication and adultery." While Falwell's program may have housed and fed the young women, it used shame and guilt to pressure them to place their babies for adoption into Christian families as a way of redeeming themselves.[3]

In recent years, a new and increasingly influential group of right-wing Christian antiabortion activists has been moving into positions of leadership in prominent antiabortion organizations like Americans United for Life, the NRLC, and Concerned Women for America and reshaping the political rhetoric of the antiabortion movement. Seeking to present a compassionate face, these young women emphasize their own motherhood and work to distance themselves from the harsh and judgmental attitudes of previous generations of antiabortion activists. Women like Charmaine Yoest, the former president of Americans United for Life (AUL), are quite candid about how they believe their work helps women. Yoest describes AUL's fight against Planned Parenthood as an attempt to "protect women": "When those babies aren't born, that is a loss for their mothers, and that's part of why they need a chance to live."[4]

Despite the antiabortion movement's shift in rhetoric from concern for "unborn babies" to concern for women, this new leadership does not represent a move away from the patriarchal attitude of the previous generation. Even couched in the cloak of "concern" for women, leaders of the movement are still pushing legislation that seeks to control women's lives and deny women's capacity to act as moral agents. The change in language is merely a strategic move calculated to garner increased political support for the elimination of legal abortion in the United States. Yoest told *Mother Jones*: "Repeatedly, the Supreme Court has turned away from the threat that abortion poses for the baby, because the Supreme Court has said repeatedly they're concerned about the woman. So we basically want to say to the court, 'We share your concern for women. You need to look at the fact that abortion itself harms women.'"[5]

In response to the 1992 *Casey* decision, in which the Supreme Court clarified its intent to use the standard of "undue burden" for evaluating state regulations of abortion procedures, antiabortion activists have pursued a short-term strategy of eroding access to abortion at the state level. In 2011, legislators across the country introduced more than 1,100 reproductive-health and rights-related provisions at the state level, many of which were prepared by AUL in its newest anti-choice strategy—drafting and circulating model legislation in statehouses across the country.[6] By year's end, 135 of these provisions had been enacted in thirty-six states, an increase from 89 and 77 in the previous two years.[7] More than two-thirds of these provisions (92 in twenty-four states) in some way restrict access to abortion services (the previous record was 34 adopted in 2005).[8]

"Concern for women" is nominally what holds these new regulations together. From waiting periods, mandatory ultrasounds, and restrictions on insurance coverage, to clinic regulations intended to close down facilities, to restrictions on the procedures for administering medical abortions, antiabortion forces are attempting to convince the public that abortion and abortion providers are a threat to women.[9] The legislation's portrayal of pregnant women as unable to recognize this threat not only undermines the public's ability to recognize women as capable moral agents but also reveals a fundamental distrust of women's decision-making abilities. Several overlapping strategies have had remarkable success in influencing public opinion about regulating abortion and in methodically reducing women's access to abortion services and contraceptives. The strategies I will examine here include the "women are stupid" approach and the "doctors are dangerous" approach, as well as the strategy of manipulation. These strategies illuminate the influence of Christian patriarchy and paternalism. They also reveal how conservative Christians are using the state to further their religious and ideological agenda.

Women are stupid

New legislation requiring counseling, ultrasounds, waiting periods, and other restrictions on medical procedures is rooted in a paternalistic presumption that pregnant women are not capable moral agents with the intellectual capacity to understand that a pregnancy, if carried to term, will result in the birth of a baby. This presumption is evident when we examine some of this legislation more carefully.

Counseling patients about impending medical procedures and obtaining informed consent is ethically and legally standard for all healthcare providers in the United States. Abortion providers, like all healthcare providers, already obtain informed consent and ensure that their patients receive counseling in preparation for their procedures. Nevertheless, thirty-five states have passed legislation requiring counseling before an abortion procedure can be performed.[10] Analysis of the content of the counseling makes clear that its intent is not simply to ensure that women understand the medical facts and consequences of the procedure, which is the goal of informed consent. Rather, in addition to information about the procedure, thirty-three states require that the woman be given information about the gestational age of the fetus, twenty-eight states include information about fetal development throughout pregnancy, and fifteen require that women be told that they cannot be coerced into having an abortion.

The most egregious aspect of this new legislation is that some of it is medically inaccurate. Five states assert a link between abortion and breast cancer in their mandatory counseling, a claim roundly debunked in medical literature, and four states offer inaccurate information about the risk of abortion to a woman's future fertility.[11] Thirteen states require that women be informed about the fetus's alleged ability to feel pain after twenty weeks, a claim disputed by the American College of Obstetricians and Gynecologists, and six states inform the woman that personhood begins at conception, a position that is a theological claim rather than a biological or medical fact.[12] The intent of these counseling sessions is clearly to intimidate women—to indicate that having an abortion will undermine her health and future, and to imply that abortion is immoral. If our state legislatures demonstrated an equivalent enthusiasm for accurate sex education programs in the public schools, undoubtedly the numbers of unplanned pregnancies (and thus abortions) would plummet.

Unfortunately, the state's paternalism does not stop with the need to simply educate "ignorant" pregnant women who are seeking abortion. Twenty-seven states also require a waiting period, usually twenty-four hours between the "counseling" and the abortion procedure, though five states now have a seventy-two-hour waiting period.[13] Implicit in the judgment that women need to wait twenty-four hours before they can know their own mind regarding their desire to terminate a pregnancy is the paternalistic belief that women have difficulty making complex moral decisions and must be given time to think about and process the information before they can be trusted to make a rational decision. These policies also assume that women seeking abortions have not thought about the decision before they arrive at the clinic. There are no similar state-mandated waiting periods for vasectomies (or any other medical procedure).

The draft legislation that AUL developed for mandatory ultrasounds, which it called the Women's Ultrasound Right to Know Act, embodies a similar attitude toward women. The description of this model legislation implies that women who have had abortions are victims who were ignorant of what was happening to them and in need of "adequate and accurate medical information," which AUL (a legal advocacy organization, not a reputable body of abortion providers or ob-gyns) define as an ultrasound. The only evidence the organization gives of how an ultrasound can contribute to "adequate and accurate medical information" about an abortion procedure is the claim that requiring a pregnant woman to see "her unborn child and hear the heartbeat" is a concrete step that can help ensure the woman's ability to give her fully informed consent to the procedure.[14]

Fourteen states currently have legislation that requires an ultrasound to be performed before an abortion procedure regardless of whether it is medically necessary, and four of those fourteen states require the provider to not only display the image but to verbally describe the image.[15] In Virginia, the stated reason for the required ultrasound was to accurately determine the gestational age of the fetus. An ultrasound, however, is not standard practice for determining gestational age. This use of ultrasonography is at odds with the American College of Obstetricians and Gynecologists, which has stated that ultrasonography should only be performed when there is a valid medical indication.[16] Not only do ultrasounds fail to provide medical information pertinent for every abortion procedure, but before eight weeks, ultrasounds can only be administered by inserting an ultrasound wand into the vagina. Given that 60 percent of abortions occur in the first eight weeks of pregnancy, requiring these women to undergo transvaginal ultrasounds when the procedure is not medically indicated is a completely unnecessary and invasive procedure.

That the real intention of these mandatory ultrasounds is to emotionally manipulate women into changing their minds about termination is evident by the medical "evidence" that AUL uses to support its recommendation. The organization cites a 1983 report showing that two pregnant women had an emotional response to ultrasound images of their potentially compromised prenates in wanted pregnancies. The authors of the report commented that the use of ultrasound is "likely to increase the value of the early fetus for parents who already strongly desire a child."[17] Clearly, antiabortion advocates hope that the use of ultrasonography will stimulate or increase an emotional bond on the part of the pregnant woman. Implicit in this legislation is the assumption that pregnant women do not understand what they are doing when they seek an abortion procedure and thus must be shown pictures.

Strategies like lecturing (mandatory information about fetal development), time-outs (waiting periods), corporal punishment (vaginal ultrasounds), and taking away privileges (insurance coverage) put the state in the role of parental authority figure and pregnant women in the role of minors. By definition, minors are children and young people who have not reached the age of legal majority, which is the age that the state treats individuals as responsible adults under the law. For obvious reasons, the state has a vested interest in protecting the health and well-being of minors, and the state thus interacts with minors in a different way than it does with adults. But nearly 97 percent of the women in the US who seek abortions have reached the age of majority and are adults in the eyes of the law.[18] Although these are adult women seeking to exercise their legal rights as citizens of this country, the public-policy directives that have increased the regulation of abortion in this country for the last forty years reveal an attitude of paternalism and control—an attitude more appropriate for children, not adults.

While these legal strategies ostensibly arise from the antiabortion lobby's express desire to "protect women," the tactics reveal a deep patriarchal interpretation of "protection" as social control. Such regulations position the state to restrict and control the behavior of a particular group of citizens (pregnant women) who are deemed incapable of making rational decisions about their own health and well-being. In this context, many recent laws passed to delay women's access to abortion services or to require medically unnecessary regulation of the procedure are not perceived as placing an "undue burden" on women, the standard required in abortion legislation. The overrepresentation of women of color among poor women (as noted in the previous chapter, 75 percent of those seeking abortions are poor or low-income) means that racial and class bias also make legislators and the public more comfortable in proscribing morality.

Doctors are dangerous

Another manipulative tactic currently being pursued in state legislatures is the attempt to villainize abortion providers and healthcare workers to undermine their credibility and again position the state as the protector of women. This tactic is clearly connected to legislation related to state-mandated counseling. The move not only to require counseling but also to mandate its content is based on the unfounded notion that women do not receive adequate information about pregnancy or abortion before having their procedure. The underlying assumption is that physicians and other healthcare workers who provide abortion services are pressuring women into the procedures. Sociologist Katherine Johnson argues that the scripts for these counseling sessions reveal an attempt to portray both physicians and biological fathers as untrustworthy actors who may not have a woman's best interest at heart.[19] For example, Alaska's script reads as follows: "Alaska law requires your doctor to discuss with you the information described in this website before performing an abortion. You must have a chance to ask questions and discuss your pregnancy decision before an abortion can be performed. It is illegal for a healthcare provider to perform any medical or surgical procedure without first obtaining the informed consent of the patient."[20]

The statement implies that doctors may seek to withhold vital information from their patients and may try to perform abortions illegally without obtaining informed consent, despite no evidence of such illegal practice. Under the alleged concern that women are being coerced into having abortions, five states include some version of the following paragraph: "No one can force you to have an abortion. It is against the law for a spouse, a boyfriend, a parent, a friend, a medical care provider, or any other person to . . . force you to have an abortion."[21]

While many women identify multiple reasons for deciding to terminate a pregnancy, peer-reviewed social-scientific research indicates that women are making this decision intentionally and with full knowledge of the implications of their decision. One study found that less than 1 percent of respondents mentioned influence of partners or parents as their most important reason for termination.[22]

In addition to targeting the credibility of abortion providers, abortion clinics have also been targeted with onerous and unnecessary regulations intended to close their doors. These regulations, known as Targeted Regulation of Abortion Providers (TRAP) laws, include provisions like requiring physicians to have admitting privileges at local hospitals and requiring clinics to meet the regulatory standards for ambulatory surgical centers or even hospitals. The Supreme Court dealt a severe blow to this approach to limit women's access to abortion services in 2016, when, in *Whole Woman's Health v. Cole*, it struck down the restrictive TRAP laws that had already closed twenty-one of the forty clinics in Texas that provide abortion services. In deciding in favor of Whole Woman's Health and other abortion clinics, the justices rejected the argument that requiring doctors to have admitting privileges at local hospitals and requiring clinics to meet the standards of ambulatory surgical centers were necessary for patients' health. Both arguments had been roundly debunked by leading public-health experts. The American Medical Association, the American College of Obstetricians and Gynecologists, the American Academy of Family Physicians, and the American Osteopathic Association all signed an amicus brief arguing that these requirements not only were inconsistent with accepted medical practice but also offered no benefit to patient care or health outcomes.[23]

The new spate of legislation sweeping the country and attempting to position the state as the trustworthy authority figure and protector of pregnant women brings up a question: Who is the state supposedly protecting women from? What these regulations betray is an explicit ideological agenda as they invariably seek to convince the pregnant woman that she ought not terminate her pregnancy. Increasingly, it looks like what women need to be protected from is the state.

Employing a strategy of manipulation

The debates about new legislation at the state level also reveal remarkable levels of dissembling as right-wing activists seek to exploit and manipulate both the news cycle and public opinion through the strategic use of red-herring issues meant to mislead the public about the facts related to abortion. These red-herring campaigns are always sensationalist attempts to rile up the American public in an attempt to soften its resistance to some new form of legislation intended to whittle away at women's access to abortion services and other forms of reproductive healthcare.

A similar legislative tactic was launched in the early 2000s, when the movement rebranded the intact dilation and extraction (intact D&E) procedure as "partial-birth abortion." Opponents of intact D&E provided graphic descriptions to secure support for a legislative ban on a medical procedure that has no greater risks than other procedures do and that has documented benefits.[24] Other diversions meant to provoke public sentiment include objections to abortion for sex selection and attempts to portray the pro-choice movement as advocating abortion on demand. This diversionary tactic was used most recently by Donald Trump in the 2016 presidential debates, when he described babies being "ripped from the womb" in the ninth month. With only 0.08 percent of all abortions in the US occurring after twenty-four weeks, the idea of abortion on demand is clearly a red herring meant to provoke an emotionally negative response to abortion and the women who have them. Rational, healthy women don't simply decide to end their pregnancies at will during their last trimester. And it is pure fiction to suggest that licensed, practicing physicians would acquiesce to such requests even if women made them. The women who terminate their pregnancies after twenty-four weeks are those whose health is at risk by the pregnancy or who received information about a fatal or severe fetal anomaly very late in their pregnancy. The fact that such a tiny proportion of pregnant women need to terminate their pregnancies this late should be regarded as a public-health success. It is a testament to both earlier detection of prenatal health problems and better ability to manage pregnant women's healthcare.

The persistent campaign to defund Planned Parenthood demonstrates that the right-wing's agenda is not just to criminalize abortion but also to reduce access to contraception. Eighty percent of Planned Parenthood's patients receive contraceptive services, and an estimated one in five women visits Planned Parenthood at least once in her life.[25] Planned Parenthood clinics are on the front lines in communities across the country, helping to provide access to reproductive healthcare to women and men, many of whom do not have regular physicians. The attempt to smear Planned Parenthood's reputation and defund its essential healthcare and contraceptive services in communities across the country could only contribute to a rise in abortion demand in the long run. The smear campaign is certainly not intended to promote the health and well-being of women.

In addition to cultivating and exploiting red herrings, the current right-wing strategy displays a disturbing lack of attention to basing public policy on evidence. The North Carolina legislature's treatment of a 2015 bill requiring a seventy-two-hour waiting period between a patient's counseling appointment and the procedure shows instead how people's stories and experiences are used in public debates and how legislation is being enacted on the basis of emotion, speculation, and paternalistic attitudes.

During the North Carolina floor debate, state representative Michele Presnell stated, "Seventy-two hours is only three days. I think that's a good amount of time. These young girls, when they go in there—very abrupt, very quickly—they make that decision that they're going to get rid of this baby." Presnell's argument is full of assumptions that are patently wrong. Her first assumption is that it is primarily young girls seeking abortions. In 2014, only 12 percent of US women seeking abortions were in their teens, and two-thirds of these were eighteen or nineteen years old. Teens between fifteen and seventeen account for approximately 3 percent of abortions nationwide, whereas teens younger than fifteen account for .02 percent.[26] The vast majority of women who seek abortions are sexually active adults, and 61 percent of them already have at least one child. These observations challenge Presnell's second assumption—that women are making snap decisions to have abortions. Social-scientific data affirms not only that women are clearly aware of what it means to have an abortion but that they also overwhelmingly feel confident that they made the right decisions both at the time of the abortion and after the fact.[27]

Blatant disregard for an informed debate was also evident in the North Carolina house committee hearing the day before Presnell made her remarks. During the hearing, committee chair Brian Brown apparently only allowed one opponent of the bill to speak, whereas he granted supporters a half hour of testimony. Refusing to allow opposition testimony from the doctors and other experts who came to testify about the problems associated with longer waiting periods, not to mention the new requirements for physicians who perform abortions, is outright manipulation of the political process to further an ideological agenda. In addition to the abuse and harassment of women, the integrity of our political process has evidently suffered in the ongoing politics of the abortion debate. Public policy should be based on reasoned argument supported by reputable evidence and facts, not on speculation, opinions, and the manipulation of emotion.

If concern for women were at the heart of public policy around abortion, these policies would seek to support women by addressing the factors that women themselves have identified as contributing to their decisions to seek abortions. As we saw in the last chapter, poverty, contraceptive failure, inability to parent a small child, the need to work or finish schooling, and demands of current children are the self-reported reasons that women identify for seeking to terminate their pregnancies.[28] Developing public policy that would address the expressed reasons that women find themselves unable to embrace an unplanned pregnancy is a more effective strategy to lower abortion rates than waiting periods.

We have seen how recent public policy embodies a paternalistic attitude toward women. Now let us examine how right-wing Christians are using the state to promote pronatalist policies.

PRONATALIST POLICIES

Although the government has not directly forced women to bear children since Emancipation, in a country where abortion is legal, the cultural expectation that women must provide sufficiently "acceptable" reasons to end a pregnancy reveals a persistent cultural bias toward continuing a pregnancy. Further evidence of this bias is obvious in the recent legislation we have been discussing. All the public policies we have examined express the position that states have a vested interest in encouraging women to continue their pregnancies. This pronatalist position is strongest in many of the same states that fail to provide adequate healthcare, housing, food, or education for many of the poor children in their states. The states seem far more focused on making sure women continue their pregnancies than on the well-being of the actual children who are born as a result of their policies.

The states' pronatalist positions are troubling enough on their own, but even more disturbing are the tactics legislators are using to influence women. As we have seen, the texts that states are drafting to be read to pregnant women under the guise of counseling—texts drafted by legislators with no training in prenatal or medical counseling—are ideological scripts. They seek to tell women what women ought to think about the moral status of the prenate and their "relationship" to it. These questions are not only theological and philosophical but questions about which people of goodwill continue to disagree.

South Dakota's law, which was the first of these "mandated counseling texts" to pass, offers evidence that they are written with the express intent of discouraging women from having abortions. The bill instructs women that the South Dakota legislature has found that abortion terminates the life of "a whole, separate, unique, living human being." The legislature goes even further to tell women that they have an "existing relationship" with the prenate, a position clearly reflecting a particular belief about the ontological status of the prenate and about the legislators' (and thus the state's) expectations that women ought to continue their pregnancies.[29] The law also requires that women be told that having an abortion will place them at risk of depression, psychological distress, and suicide, claims that are not supported by any reputable scientific data. Such laws are clearly intended to either persuade women to continue their pregnancies or simply interfere with women's access and thus force women to continue them. The underlying assumption is that women have a moral obligation to have a baby when they get pregnant.

Women legislators have sought to highlight the flagrant gender bias fueling recent pronatalist legislation by introducing similar sorts of legislation that would regulate men's access to healthcare, particularly men's access to drugs for erectile dysfunction like Viagra. In 2012, Ohio lawmaker Nina Turner introduced Senate Bill 307, which would require men to see a sex therapist, get a cardiac stress test, and provide a notarized affidavit from their sexual partner before receiving a prescription for Viagra.[30] Four years later in Kentucky, Mary Lou Marzian introduced a similar bill that also required that a man seeking drugs for erectile dysfunction be married, have two office visits on two different days, and make a sworn statement on a Bible that he will only use the prescription when having sex with his current spouse.[31] Clearly these bills are intended to demonstrate the absurdity of the current approach to regulating women's access to reproductive health care. But even these bills fail to demonstrate the truly unequal expectations about how women are expected to sacrifice their very bodies in the service of motherhood in ways that are not parallel for their male partners.

So far, no one has dared to introduce a bill requiring fathers to donate a kidney to save the life of their dying child. In fact, the very thought of requiring someone to undergo such an invasive procedure is anathema. But it is far easier to recognize the altruistic nature of a father offering his child a kidney than to recognize that pregnancy and childbirth are also fundamentally altruistic acts that many women willingly accept. Altruism, by its very definition, cannot be forced. We can readily see this in the case of a kidney donation, where even the thought of requiring someone to forcefully have a kidney removed against the person's will generates a visceral revulsion. Our lack of this same visceral response to the idea of controlling women's bodies demonstrates the gendered nature of this debate and of the continued power of misogyny to render the control of women's bodies not only culturally acceptable but culturally necessary.

Forced pregnancy would have a chilling effect on women across the country. We saw such a policy of forced breeding of enslaved black women in the nineteenth century. The coercion of women to bear children cannot be tolerated in any society that values human dignity and that claims to support the equal rights of women and men. While abortion remains legal in the US, the moralism associated with the justification paradigm is increasingly translating into the incarceration and abuse of pregnant women.

POLICING THE PREGNANT BODY

In June 2015, twenty-three-year-old Kenlissia Jones was arrested in Georgia on suspicion of murder after she took medication and self-induced an abortion to end her twenty-two-week pregnancy. The charges were dropped three days later (and Jones was released from jail) after authorities clarified that women could not be prosecuted for abortions involving their own pregnancies.[32] In Indiana, Purvi Patel was not so lucky. Just weeks earlier, in April, Patel was sentenced to twenty years in prison for her self-induced abortion under that state's feticide law. Then, six months later in December, Anna Yocca used a coat hanger to self-induce an abortion at twenty-four weeks in Tennessee. After her extensive blood loss, Yocca's boyfriend took her to the hospital, where she delivered a 1.5-pound baby boy via C-section. In January 2017, after serving one year in jail and having two sets of charges dismissed without her release, Yocca agreed to plead guilty to a nineteenth-century law criminalizing any "attempted procurement of a miscarriage."[33]

These three cases represent high-profile public stories. They do not, however, represent the majority of women who have abortions or even most women who have second-trimester abortions.[34] These women were clearly desperate and unable to access safe and comprehensive medical care, including legal abortion procedures. Despite claims by proponents of feticide laws that the laws are not intended for putting women in prison, the Patel and Yocca cases demonstrate the very real threat that feticide laws pose to pregnant women.[35]

Women attempting to self-induce abortions are not the only ones who have been under scrutiny in recent years. In December 2013, Bei Bei Shuai, a Chinese immigrant who was eight months pregnant and living in Indiana, ate rat poison in an unsuccessful suicide attempt. A week later, she gave birth to a daughter. When the baby died three days later, prosecutors charged Shuai with murder and feticide. The case was eventually settled when Shuai pleaded guilty to the lesser charge of criminal recklessness after it was revealed that drugs she had received at the hospital might have played a factor in the baby's death.[36]

In 2010, Christine Taylor fell down a flight of stairs in her Iowa home while pregnant with her third child. After voluntarily going to the hospital to check on the health of her prenate, she confided in the nurse that she had been thinking about either abortion or adoption because of the stress of her separation from her spouse and the prospect of raising three children as a single parent. When the nurse promptly told a doctor that she suspected Taylor had thrown herself down the stairs, the doctor called the police, who arrested and jailed Taylor on charges of "attempted fetal homicide."[37]

Several states, including Virginia, Georgia, and Kansas, have proposed legislation that would require women to report *and explain* their miscarriages to police within twenty-four hours. While none of these bills have yet been enacted into laws, the bills, and the cases above, are a further indication of increased suspicion of pregnant women and increased public tolerance for monitoring and controlling the behavior of pregnant women. In some places the negative public-health implications of other laws that seek to punish women for problems like drug addiction are slowly being recognized, but only after serious damage has already occurred. In 2016, Tennessee legislators allowed a 2014 fetal-assault statute to expire after legislators recognized the profound damage the law inflicted on pregnant women and their newborn babies, as many women avoided prenatal care rather than risk incarceration.[38]

If we accept that public policy ought to set broad moral guidelines for society, then the goal of that policy ought to be justice and the common good. While public policy sets the boundaries that shape our moral lives together as a society, public policy is not usually used to monitor or control individual citizens' moral choices.

The US government is built on the principle of social contract theory as developed in the seventeenth- and eighteenth-century philosophical tradition of Thomas Hobbes, John Locke, and Jean Jacques Rousseau. The idea of the "social contract" begins with a recognition that nature is a primitive state without any laws or morality. Human capacity for reason, cooperation, and organization has allowed us to create governmental systems that provide for a more orderly state of existence for humankind. The principle behind the social contract is that citizens agree to give up some measure of freedom or individual liberty to secure a more civil and safe social environment. Most of our contemporary political debates are about the nature of the social contract: First, how much individual liberty should we concede to the government in return for security? And what role do we collectively agree is acceptable for the state to play, particularly in issues that begin to encroach on personal liberty? US citizens have generally rejected perceived infringements of civil liberties, including actions like mass surveillance or attempts to curtail free speech or the right to bear arms. Despite this rejection, women's ability to exercise their legal rights to abortion has increasingly fallen victim to the patriarchal desire for control of women's sexuality and women's bodies.

Public policy about controversial social issues is fraught with the difficulty of creating legislation that reflects the public's best sense of moral good for society in the midst of differing perspectives. Since 2011, AUL and its conservative allies in state legislatures across the country have had some success in pushing through various laws that ultimately restrict women's access to abortion in the United States. However, the public also bears some responsibility for this shift, either for electing these politicians or for accepting the argument that these laws are reasonable and that they function to protect women. While the *Whole Woman's Health* decision was a critical victory for women's health, the public's interest in the morality of abortion will not be resolved through the courts. As a nation, we must attend to deeper questions related to the morality of abortion—questions that go beyond the questions of legal access. Our public-policy struggles reflect an anxiety about the issue of abortion, and this anxiety confounds productive public debate and often allows us to accept restrictive policies that we would not tolerate under other circumstances.

The most important factor for many people in assessing the morality of abortion is the reason why a woman wants to end her pregnancy. This focus, in and of itself, is evidence that how we think about abortion is shaped by our judgment of women and their motivations. If a woman wants to end her pregnancy because her life is in danger or because she was raped, it is deemed tragic but acceptable and this woman is viewed as a victim in need of support. If a woman wants to end her pregnancy because she cannot afford a child or she wants to finish school or it's not a good time for her professionally to have a child, she is viewed as selfish and is scorned by society. If she is addicted to drugs or didn't use birth control, she is judged irresponsible and shamed for her careless attitude and behavior. But a woman who seeks an abortion for sex selection is condemned in the most hostile terms of all.

While some people may find the decision to have an abortion for sex selection repugnant or the decision to terminate a pregnancy in order to finish school selfish, the reality is that women are basing their decisions to terminate for countless social reasons. Women consider abortions within a complex set of social factors that include the individual woman's life circumstances (including her health, mental state, financial situation, intimate relationship with the father, existing responsibilities, and the actual or potential health of the prenate) and the sociopolitical and cultural circumstances in which she lives. Denying individual women the ability to control their fertility and make decisions to positively affect their future is a punitive and harassing strategy that only succeeds in punishing women (and their existing or future children). It does not address the larger social problems that often prompt women to seek abortions.

Social attitudes that compel women to desire a child of a particular sex, so much that they are willing to terminate a pregnancy of the "wrong" sex, is a larger social problem that needs to be addressed.[39] Likewise, if 73 percent of women obtaining abortions indicate that they cannot afford a child (or another one), we could enact social policies to assist women in having and caring for these children. However, as we know from public-policy debates about welfare, there is very little political will and public support of financial assistance for poor women and their children. If women are deciding to abort because of social pressures they face, those pressures need to be addressed rather than sanctioning women who are basing their personal decisions on the social climate that they inhabit.

If we are truly concerned about the health and well-being of pregnant women and their children, then we ought to be addressing through our public policy the social problems that women cite as contributing to their decisions to terminate a pregnancy. We have seen that these problems relate to many aspects of a woman's life: affordable housing and daycare, free and dependable access to reliable birth control, a culture of racism that threatens the health and well-being of black and brown children, prejudice against people with disabilities, and social attitudes that cause families to prefer boy children over girl children. Whatever problems women are facing, we need to tackle the social problems themselves rather than punishing women for the responsible decisions they make within their social worlds. Although abortion is legal, the majority of public-policy decisions related to abortion since *Roe v. Wade* are rooted in a basic distrust of women. The patriarchal desire to control women prevents us from trusting women's ability to assess their circumstances and make good and moral decisions about their families and their futures.

MORAL HAZARD, OR THE DANGER OF TRUSTING WOMEN

The major problem with building a social policy based on trusting women is that we would first have to trust women. In a culture built on second-guessing women's choices, questioning their capacity to understand pregnancy (even women who already have children), and controlling their behavior, trusting women to make good decisions for themselves and their families is a hard sell. Trusting women as moral agents means that the state needs to recognize women's capacity to know what is in their best interest and to act accordingly. While trust may be a challenge when some women make decisions that others disagree with, social policy must create the conditions for social flourishing, not police individuals' moral choices.

Furthermore, social policy should not punish women whose decisions are shaped by the limitations of their social reality. Women in poverty who cannot afford another child should not be punished for being poor. The primary issue to be addressed in that situation is not a woman's decision to abort but the social reality of poverty, which constricts some women in ways that lead them to decide that abortion is the only tenable option.

The real challenge of public policy on abortion is that a pro-choice position legally affirms the fundamental claim of women's equality as full moral agents. *Roe v. Wade* established a woman's right to abortion for any reason or no reason through the first two trimesters and only then required a "compelling reason" for abortions in the third trimester. This stance recognizes the legal right of women to make fundamental decisions about themselves and their families or potential families' well-being independently, without the oversight and control of any external factors, including their partners, physicians, religious leaders, or the state. The sheer power of women to make these kinds of life-and-death decisions about their bodies and their future is simply untenable for some people. After all, what if they make bad decisions? Decisions that we don't agree with? Decisions that don't reflect our values or our religious beliefs?

Certainly, some women will make bad decisions. Some will choose to abort for reasons that we don't agree with or that we find morally unacceptable. How many women will do so? We will never know. We cannot know. But that is beside the point. When we create social policy, we must do it for the right reasons and then work as a society to empower women to make the best moral decisions possible. For women who are addicted, mentally ill, or destitute and struggling to feed the children that they already have, terminating a pregnancy is the least of their problems, from a moral and material perspective. When we begin our moral analysis from the perspective of women's lives, the questions about what is moral and what is immoral look different.

When we shape social policy, we must also do so in light of our aspirations for society, not according to a least-common-denominator morality. Social policy that is coercive is the beginning of a police state. Our unwillingness or inability to recognize the morally coercive impact of current abortion legislation reflects how readily the public accepts deep-seated misogynist expectations about women's sexuality, women's moral obligations, and state control of women's bodies. Moreover, when we make social policy, there will always be those who will game the system, disregard the intentions of the laws, or simply act in ways that some of us find morally reprehensible. That is the nature of a free society, human nature, and democracy. But social policy must always begin with our aspirations for who we want to be as a society.

As this chapter has shown, current public-policy efforts to restrict abortion are rooted in traditionalist ideals about women's sexuality and fertility—ideals that are more than a bit misogynist. But where did these attitudes come from, and why are they so firmly ingrained in, and accepted by, our culture? In the next chapter, we will examine how misogyny and patriarchy have developed throughout Western culture and how they have shaped ideas about women, sex, and power.

Why Misogyny and Patriarchy Matter

CHAPTER 4

Misogyny Is Exhausting

WOMEN'S DESIRE TO CONTROL their fertility is not new. A nearly four-thousand-year-old Egyptian papyrus contains a prescription titled "Recipe Not to Become Pregnant."[1] Whether or not the recipe (which calls for crocodile dung to be mixed with fermented dough and placed in the vagina) works, it is extraordinarily early written evidence of the practice of contraception. Another papyrus, known as the Ebers Papyrus, records a recipe "to cause a woman to stop pregnancy in the first, second, or third period [trimester]: unripe fruit of acacia, colocynth, dates, triturate with 6/7th pint of honey; moisten a pessary of plant fiber and place in the vagina."[2] The recipe might seem magical or at least questionable regarding its efficacy in preventing pregnancy, but it contains two plants long connected with contraception. An even older fragment of a Sumerian tablet appears to contain the recipe for an abortifacient, and ancient Assyrian women apparently made pessaries of pomegranate on wool and inserted them in their vaginas, probably to prevent pregnancy.[3]

The Greeks, Mesopotamians, Egyptians, Assyrians, and Romans have texts that identify various herbs and plants (rue, pennyroyal, silphium, artemesia, Queen Anne's Lace, myrrh, pomegranates, and figs, among others) as effective for controlling fertility.[4] While some folklore evidently suggested that some women relied on amulets and other charms in their attempts to control their fertility, modern research has found that many of the plants identified as possessing contraceptive and abortifacient qualities do demonstrate efficacy in controlling fertility. Demographic evidence of fertility rates in various societies in the ancient world corroborates the hypothesis that at some times and in some places, women regularly controlled their fertility.

Yet despite these remarkable records of women's needs and desires to control fertility, the historically dominant view of women's reproductive lives, including fertility, pregnancies, childbearing, and practices of contraception and abortion, has been primarily shaped by official versions of history recorded in religious teachings, laws, history books, and other "authorized" sources. These histories, primarily written by men, tell a different story, one about the social control of women's bodies, sexuality, and moral agency through laws, cultural attitudes, and religious narratives that seek to define and constrain women's behavior. Throughout Western history, from Aristotle's argument that women are merely "misbegotten" males to Tertullian's naked hostility toward women to the witch hunts of the medieval church, the misogyny of male philosophers and theologians has shaped cultural attitudes about women.

Misogyny is defined as the hatred of women. To say that elements of our history and our culture actively express a hatred of women is a bold claim. This claim may seem especially surprising in the United States and other countries where women have the right to vote and are increasingly represented in politics and the business world. In these environments, many people find the term *misogyny* too extreme and would prefer softer language—*discrimination*, *prejudice*, *condescension*, *disregard*, or perhaps even *objectification*. Yet this attempt to soften, through language, the abusive treatment of women is dangerously misleading. There is nothing soft about the sentiments expressed by many male philosophers and theologians. Nor is there anything soft about the social control of women that often accompanies misogynist and patriarchal attitudes.

When theologians and church leaders use scripture and Christian tradition to argue that women's subordination is not only divinely inspired but also *divinely ordained*—meaning that God intended for women to be subservient to men—the core Christian value of justice is distorted and

Christianity itself is damaged. The inferiority of women forms the ideological foundation of the paternalism that has shaped how men have treated women in Western societies for centuries. Certainly, misogyny is not exclusively Western or Christian, but it is very much a part of these cultures.

If misogyny is about cultural attitudes and beliefs, patriarchy is about power and authority. Within Western patriarchal history and culture, it was widely accepted that external forces (husbands, the state, the church, religious authorities, etc.) had the right to control not only women's sexuality but also their very bodies. Misogynist attitudes—about women's nature, mental and psychological capacities, decision-making abilities, and sexuality—justified the control.

Identifying how contemporary forms of discrimination against women are rooted in a history of misogyny and patriarchal control of women helps explain the persistence of gender discrimination. By examining both official attitudes toward sex and birth control as represented by legal codes and religious and political positions and unofficial stances denoted by fertility rates and other evidence of people's behaviors, this chapter offers a complicated corrective to the dominant Christian narrative that abortion has always been viewed as immoral. Additionally, given the continued scorn aimed at women who have abortions in our culture, we need to identify and expose how patriarchy and misogyny have shaped attitudes about contraception and abortion if we are to build an alternative theology of reproductive justice.

ANCIENT CIVILIZATIONS

Historical records indicate that fertility control was widely practiced in the Greco-Roman world. Plato states that there were "many devices available; if too many children are being born, there are measures to check propagation."[5] Socrates clarifies these "devices" in his reference to "midwives, [who] by means of drugs and incantations, . . . cause abortions at an early state if they think them desirable."[6] In his *Politics*, the manner in which Aristotle discusses population control not only indicates widespread acceptance and usage of contraception for birth control but also goes as far as recommending abortion as a more appropriate form of population control than infanticide (which he refers to as exposure): "No child is to be exposed, but when couples have children in excess, let abortion be procured before sense and life have begun, what may or may not be lawfully done in these cases depends on the question of life and sensation."[7] And of course, an oath ascribed to Hippocrates includes the pledge not to provide women with pessaries that will produce abortion.[8] The oath, however, is silent on oral contraceptives and abortifacients, pessaries to prevent pregnancies, and surgical abortions, all of which were options during Hippocrates's era.

One small Greek colony in North Africa became synonymous with birth control around the seventh century BCE. Soon after settling the small town of Cyrene, the inhabitants discovered a plant that they named silphion (and the Romans called silphium) that was so successful at controlling fertility that it become a major export crop and even ended up on Cyrenian coins as the distinctive mark of the city. As demand for silphium across the Roman Empire increased, prices increased and supplies began to dwindle. The preferred use of silphium is graphically illustrated on one coin. It depicts a woman sitting next to a stalk of the plant, indicating the plant with one hand while the other points to her genital area. The Greek physician Soranus details the exact amount of the herb that should be ingested (one chickpea amount once a month), with the notation that silphium can both prevent conception and "destroy any already existing." Attempts to domesticate the plant failed and high demand led to such overharvesting that silphium had become extinct by late antiquity.[9]

While the records are scanty, we can make several observations about ancient attitudes toward the practice of contraception and abortion. The first is that even 2,500 years ago, people were divided about their support of contraception and abortion. The earliest records, from the fifth century BCE, represent the opinions of Socrates, Plato, Aristotle, and, reportedly, Hippocrates. Their discussions seem to indicate widespread usage and acceptance of fertility control. In fact, for Aristotle, who is interested in the proper ordering and control of the state, the ability of the people to control their fertility—increasing or decreasing births as the state needs—is generally represented as a social good. The Hippocratic oath, as noted above, does contain a contrary statement: "I will not give to a woman a pessary to produce an abortion."[10] But modern scholarly consensus is that the oath was probably written by a member of a fringe group, given that the attitudes toward both abortion and suicide in the oath do not reflect Hippocrates's other writings or the Greek attitude toward either of those actions more generally.[11] Historian John M. Riddle notes that the acceptance of suicide was one marker that divided the Greeks from many of their neighbors, whom the Greeks considered barbarians.[12]

Two centuries later, both Polybius and Musonius Rufus associate the practice of fertility control with a growing selfishness and greed among the Greek population; they claim that these attitudes are contributing to the downfall of the state. Both these philosophers, while documenting the widespread practice of women controlling their fertility, do so in the midst of diatribes that chastise the people for these very same practices. Their denouncement of this practice does not indicate any moral outrage at the actual practice of contraception or abortion but rather at the consequences of those actions: population decline. Moreover, fertility control, through contraception or abortion, appears to be legal until very late in the Roman Empire.

It was not until the reigns of Septimus Severus (193–211 CE) and Antoninus Caracalla (211–217 CE) that abortion was classified as one of the *crimina extraordinaria*.[13] These were crimes punished outside a formal system and without a fixed penalty. Documents from the time indicate that concern over abortion was related to upholding the rights of men as husbands and fathers as "it might appear scandalous that she should be able to deprive her husband of children without being punished."[14] Another woman was exiled for having an abortion to deprive her former husband, whom she reportedly hated, of a child.[15] The earliest clear legal principle comes from the third-century CE jurist Paulus, who wrote: "Because the thing is a bad example, lower-class people who give a drink to cause an abortion or to excite passion (although they don't do it deceitfully), are to be condemned to the mines, and more distinguished persons to be relegated to an island and deprived of a part of their wealth. If by this drink a woman or a man has died, they are condemned to capital punishment."[16]

Two things seem clear from the historical records of the ancient world. First, women in the ancient world used both contraception and abortion to control their fertility. Second, the male elites (philosophers, physicians, and politicians) held varying opinions about whether women should be *allowed* to control their fertility through contraception or abortion. The witness of women is in their actions—many women in the ancient world sought to control their fertility. The witness of men is in their writings and in the law—elite men sought to control the actions of women. This behavior continued into the Christian era as many of the early church fathers were heavily influenced by Greek and Roman thought.

Aristotle's ideas about sexual reproduction played a critical role in the development of Christian attitudes and theological thinking about pregnancy and prenatal life. To fully understand Aristotle's attitudes about procreation, we need to examine his attitudes about gender. He notoriously held women to be inferior to men and described women as "misbegotten males," a category informed by his belief that male children were the result of "good" seed while "weak" seed malformed a developing prenate into a female. In *The History of Animals*, he gave an extensive comparison of the sexes: "Woman is more compassionate than man, more easily moved to tears, at the same time is more jealous, more querulous, more apt to scold and to strike. She is, furthermore, more prone to despondency and less hopeful than the man, more void of shame or self-respect, more false of speech, more deceptive, and of more retentive memory. She is also more wakeful, more shrinking, more difficult to rouse to action, and requires a smaller quantity of nutriment."[17]

Many qualities Aristotle associates with women and the supposed differences that he cites between men and women are familiar to modern readers because many of these stereotypes continue into the present day. The real damage here is not in pointing out differences that exist in the human community; it is in associating those differences with particular genders and then lifting up the qualities of one gender over another. Anyone, of course, can be jealous or despondent or deceptive. But like many Greek philosophers, Aristotle created binary, oppositional divisions between males and females, privileging male traits while denigrating female ones. This sort of classic dualism shaped cultural attitudes about women well into early Christianity.

MISOGYNY IN THE CHRISTIAN TRADITION

Despite later restrictions on women's roles in Christianity, there is strong documentary evidence of women's leadership in the early church.[18] In Romans, Paul greets Junia, a woman, as an apostle, and he refers to Priscilla and her husband, Aquila, as "fellow workers in Christ Jesus." The widely circulated apocryphal text of *The Acts of Paul and Thecla* relates the active ministry of Thecla, a woman who cut her hair and wore men's clothing when she traveled as a missionary, preaching and baptizing in early Christian communities.[19] Other women in the early church followed the examples of these women leaders and led local congregations, engaging in public acts of ministry.

These Christian women leaders in the early church threatened traditional Roman notions of appropriate female behavior. Good Roman women were expected to be chaste and to reserve their activities for the private sphere of the Roman household. They wore white clothing and avoided makeup and jewelry. If and when they appeared in public, they were chaperoned and their bodies were covered.[20] Women who defied cultural expectations of chastity, silence, and obedience by appearing in public without a chaperone, engaging in public activities, or not dressing modestly appeared to threaten the social order that marked Roman rule.[21] While there were some Roman women who held public roles in business or government positions, they were wealthy women whose private virtues of devotion to husband and children were also extolled as evidence of their chastity and sexual fidelity.[22] The public profile of Christianity's women leaders was an identifiable aspect of how Christianity threatened traditional Roman social norms as the Christian church began to gain political and social power in the third century CE.

In response, male Christian theologians sought to make their religion acceptable by demonstrating that Christian morals were aligned with Roman morality. Given the predominance of women's leadership in the early church, once male leaders decided to curtail it, significant steps had to be taken to undermine women's authority. One way to do this was to demonstrate that Christian attitudes toward appropriate gender roles mirrored the Roman approach. Paul's attempts to circumscribe women's behavior in the Corinthian church by first instructing them to wear veils when speaking in church (1 Corinthians 11: 1–16) and later emphasizing that they should stay silent in church and subordinate themselves to their husbands (1 Corinthians 14:34–35) reflect dominant Roman gender role expectations that Christian women were clearly defying. Increasingly, dismissive and hostile attitudes toward women and their leadership in the church became more prominent.

One of the earliest and most outspoken Christian leaders to restrict women's leadership and position was Tertullian. In the early third century CE, Tertullian openly challenged the right of Christian women to lead churches and to engage in other acts of ministry like teaching and baptism. He attacked one woman who had been baptizing followers by calling her a "viper" and sought to undermine the authority that women had been claiming from *The Acts of Paul and Thecla*. He invoked Paul's own words that women should keep silent and ask their husbands for instruction at home as evidence to undermine the text's authenticity.[23] At the time, in the North African church at Carthage, there was also a movement of young women who embraced celibacy and rejected the convention of marriage. Identifying as "virgins," they redefined their social status as a third gender class that transcended male and female. In this sanctified role, they sought to create a new locus of authority in the church, where they were not bound by the traditional expectations of male or female and thus they refused to veil themselves in the manner of Christian women of the time. These women, who were teaching, preaching, and baptizing, sought to establish a place for themselves in the evolving leadership of the early church.

But Tertullian was interested in more than simply removing women from positions of leadership in the church: his agenda was to establish within Christianity a gender hierarchy in which men were dominant and women were subordinate. This objective required more than simply appealing to Paul. Tertullian looked deeper into the tradition and focused on using the creation narrative in Genesis to establish the inferiority of women and the superiority of men. Commenting on the importance of modesty in female dress, he invoked Eve: "And do you not know that you are (each) an Eve? The sentence of God on this sex of yours lives in this age: the guilt must of necessity live too. *You* are the devil's gateway: *you* are the unsealer of that (forbidden) tree: *you* are the first deserter of the divine law: *you* are she who persuaded him whom the devil was not valiant enough to attack. *You* destroyed so easily God's image, man. On account of *your* desert—that is, death—even the Son of God had to die."[24]

It is not incidental that Tertullian invoked Eve while instructing women on the necessity of modesty in their dress. Besides believing that men were superior to women, he also thought that women, and most particularly their bodies, were the root of sin in the world. Not only did Tertullian perpetuate Aristotle's negative attitudes toward women, but these negative attitudes (misogyny) now start to be used as a lens by Christian theologians to interpret scripture. Tertullian's interpretation of the Garden of Eden story condemns Eve for eating the apple and offering it to Adam. Then, not only does he proceed to blame Jesus's death on Eve, but he also interprets Eve's actions as condemning all women in perpetuity to suffer for Eve's "crime." This interpretation of Eve as the "devil's gateway," the temptress, and the author of original sin becomes a dominant tradition throughout the history of Christianity.

The depth of Tertullian's disdain for women as women is manifest in his attack on the virgins of Carthage. In response to their argument that their virginity allows them to transcend the limitations of their gender, Tertullian argues that nothing, not even baptism or celibacy, can "sever" a woman from the ontological reality of her femaleness.[25] Beyond describing sexual allure and magnetism as the essence of what it means to be female, Tertullian argues that it was virgins who incited lust so powerful that it tempted angels into their beds.[26] He seeks to put these young virgins right back into what he sees as their proper role: subordinate to their fathers and husbands.

Many of these early male Christian theologians are referred to as the "church fathers," and their writings, *patristics*. Throughout the patristic period, influential male theologians continued to present interpretations of scripture biased by their negative views of women. This bias helped shape misogynist theologies that reinforced and sanctified the inferiority of women while also developing church structures that excluded women from leadership in the church. Augustine interpreted Paul's injunction that women but not men must cover their heads through a similarly negative interpretation of the Genesis creation story: "The woman does not possess the image of God in herself, but only when taken together with the male who is her head, so that the whole substance is one image. But when she is assigned as a helpmate, a function that pertains to her alone, then she is not the image of God. But as far as the man is concerned, he is by himself alone the image of God, just as fully and completely as when he and the woman are joined together into one."[27]

These interpretations say far more about what Augustine thought of women than what God does. However, given Augustine's status in the church, his belief that women are not created in the image of God equally with men and that women's roles were ordained by God to be wife and "helpmate" has had enormous influence on cultural and religious attitudes toward women even into the present day.

The theologians of the Protestant Reformation certainly contributed their fair share of unflattering ideas about women, including Martin Luther's views on how male and female bodies are designed for different tasks: "Men have broad and large chests, and small narrow hips, and more understanding than women, who have but small and narrow breasts, and broad hips, to the end they should remain at home, sit still, keep house, and bear and bring up children."[28] Even the highly regarded twentieth-century Swiss theologian Karl Barth exhibited rigid opinions on gender roles: "Just as God rules over creation in the covenant of creation, so man rules over woman. He must be A; he must be first. She is B; she must be second. He must stay in his place. She must stay in hers. She must accept this order as the right nature of things through which she is saved, even if she is abused and wronged by the man."[29]

Conservative Christians still preach similarly misogynist interpretations of scripture to justify narrowly proscribed roles for women in society and in the church. The Southern Baptist Convention, which promotes narrowly defined gender roles, holds that "a wife is to submit herself graciously to the servant leadership of her husband even as the church willingly submits to the headship of Christ."[30] People who promote this sort of narrow biblical interpretation of gender roles refer to it as "gender complementarianism." Many contemporary Christian promoters of this theology will argue that men and women are equal but that they have different roles in society. We see this theology more fully expressed in megachurch pastor Mark Driscoll's comment (which echoes Pat Robertson's patriarchal theology from the previous chapter): "Women will be saved by going back to that role that God has chosen for them. Ladies, if the hair on the back of your neck stands up it is because you are fighting your role in the scripture."[31]

This theological position of gender complementarianism is rooted in a traditionalist interpretation of Paul's first letter to the Corinthians, in which he says, "I want you to understand that Christ is the head of every man, and the husband is the head of his wife, and God is head of Christ." And then he continues: "For a man ought not to have his head veiled, since he is the image and reflection of God; but woman is the reflection of man" (1 Corinthians 11: 2–4, 7). Paul's commentary, of course, is not the only biblical text that expresses an attitude of social inequality. After all, the patriarchs of the Hebrew Bible were often heads of large tribal communities, which included not only multiple wives but also concubines, slaves, servants, and other dependents. The scriptures, a product of their cultural period, clearly lift these men up as moral and political leaders; the stories are the men's stories, not those of their servants and concubines or even of their wives, sisters, and mothers. Likewise, Paul's letters are a product of his time, and they largely reflect dominant first-century Roman attitudes toward women. The cultural boundedness of the scripture is an important factor in reading and interpreting it.

The danger of these patriarchal Christian attitudes toward women goes beyond the personal attitudes of individual men about women. As leaders of the church, their belief in women's inferiority to men shaped theological perspectives about the social superiority of men. Such beliefs allowed for the abuse and neglect of women and supported the ecclesiological superiority of men as the official and ordained spiritual leaders of the Christian community. These ideas—that women are the root of sin and evil, that women must be subservient to their husbands, that women must accept their inferior status in life—are rightly understood as part of a misogynist tradition in Christianity, a tradition that has contributed to larger social attitudes and behaviors in society that collectively express a serious hatred of women.

One way this hatred of women shows up is in the double standard about sexual behavior. While some churches still preach against sex before marriage and 30 percent of Americans think it is not morally acceptable, culturally it is only women who are truly expected to comply.[32] Women who have sex outside marriage are labeled in many ways—whore, slut, tramp, harlot, strumpet, bimbo, floozy, hussy, tart, trollop, and jezebel, to name just a few. Sexually active women who are not married are regularly described as promiscuous, loose, or fallen. Despite the increasing numbers of women who are sexually active outside marriage, these tropes still dominate popular culture and continue to influence public opinion. By contrast, male sexual promiscuity, including sex outside marriage, is alternatively celebrated (Casanova, stud, ladies' man, gigolo, playboy, rake, horndog, tomcat, lady-killer, wolf, heartbreaker) or dismissed as an expected and natural aspect of male sexuality ("boys will be boys"). Although expressions like *philanderer, womanizer,* and *adulterer* are more euphemistic terms that may express a certain ambivalence or even disapproval of male sexual activity, the celebration and expectation of male sexual conquest remains rampant in contemporary culture.

The idea that women are monogamous and selective about their choice of mate and the corresponding idea that men are naturally promiscuous is so dominant in scientific circles that it even has a name. In a 1948 study of the sexual behavior of fruit flies, scientist A. J. Bateman demonstrated that male survival is enhanced through impregnating as many females as possible, whereas female survival is enhanced by choosing the male with the most advantageous genes (such as physical strength, intelligence, and beauty). As it turns out, a recent attempt to replicate his findings in 2012 demonstrated a strong confirmation bias that tainted Bateman's original study. Namely, Bateman's belief in the evolutionary basis of the sexual double standard (that females are monogamous and selective and males are polygamous and promiscuous) biased his interpretation of the data in ways that confirmed his original hypothesis.[33] Given that his data reinforced what he believed to be true, Bateman missed a fundamental flaw in his data set, a flaw that led to the promulgation of the so-called Bateman principle. In other words, the idea that men are hardwired for multiple sexual partners while women are hardwired for monogamy has no credible scientific basis. Not only has this cultural trope persisted for millennia, but for the past sixty-five years, scientists have attempted to lend this misogynist cultural belief scientific credibility.

My interest in this question is not so much with the possibility that humans may not be monogamous or even that males may be promiscuous. I want to understand better why the idea that humans (and particularly male humans) are not "biologically inclined" toward monogamy is so trenchant in human culture. A second question is whose interests this belief serves. From an ethical perspective, decisions about whom we have sex with, when, and under what circumstances ought to involve a process of moral discernment. Our sexual behavior is only partly biological and physical; it is also a question of moral behavior, what we choose to do and why. Monogamy is a moral choice that humans are capable of making, not a biological propensity. We are moral creatures who can act morally. What is misogynist about the Bateman principle and the cultural attitudes that it supports is the idea that male sexual behavior is fundamentally, biologically different from female sexual behavior in ways that validate male promiscuity while implicitly condemning female promiscuity. If male promiscuity, according to the Bateman principle, is natural, female promiscuity is unnatural. This double standard reflects the misogyny of our culture, validating and excusing male promiscuity while simultaneously judging and shaming women for the same behavior.

Identifying misogynist social structures and attitudes can help us understand larger social problems. Determining that various aspects of society, like the cultural debate about abortion, function in misogynist and patriarchal ways doesn't mean that the people who hold particular opinions themselves hate women; they probably don't. Very few individual people in modern America are truly misogynist (though there are some), but misogyny continues to function in society in ways that can damage women and girls. Feminist Christian ethicist Beverly Harrison's insight that the "social control of women as a group has totally shaped our deepest and most basic attitudes toward sexuality" helps us understand the foundational problem in contemporary ethical conversation about abortion.[34] Abortion politics can only be understood within the larger social and historical framework of misogyny as the social control of women, particularly the control of their sexual and reproductive behavior.

Given that the early Christian church grew out of and developed as a new religious movement within the Roman Empire, it is not surprising that it was influenced by Greco-Roman attitudes. Indeed, the most influential Christian beliefs about embryology and ensoulment were taken directly from Aristotle and adopted almost without revision by Christian theologians. So how did attitudes and beliefs about contraception and abortion shift so radically with the advent of Christianity?

SHIFTING FROM SHAME TO SIN

Historian Kyle Harper argues that the most significant difference between the Greco-Roman era and the Christian era is that the cultural framework for sexuality and sexual mores shifts from one of shame to one of sin.[35] While sin and shame were both operative concepts in each era, Harper argues that the meaning and role of each idea shifted with the emergence of Christian theology. This new theology created a different understanding of how the world works. Harper argues that the framework of shame that functioned in the Greco-Roman world was rooted in the social approbation of one's peers within one's community. Consequently, the dominant feelings of shame in the Greco-Roman era came from the disapproval of one's moral community for having transgressed accepted moral norms. In this way, shame was primarily a social concept.[36]

In the hands of the emerging Christian community, however, sin became the defining framework. Sin is a theological concept that moves the moral assessment of the action from the community to the cosmos or the divine. No longer is a moral act deemed wrong or inappropriate merely by one's peers; the early Christian community held that moral conduct was expected by the divine being. This divine being was imagined as perfect and without sin, a far cry from the pantheon of Greek and Roman deities who, though powerful, were also rife with flaws that resembled human sinfulness. These theological shifts, in the understanding of both the nature of the divine and the locus of morality, transformed the cultural understanding of morality. Although some of the codes and expectations might have remained similar (the sexual activity of women of good standing was still expected to be contained within lawful marriage), the consequences of breaching these expectations shifted from moral accountability before one's neighbors to moral accountability before God. And the social consequences paled in comparison with the divine ones.

The earliest Christian theologians used the genre of *apologia*, or "apologies," which are texts written to defend Christianity against its critics. As we have already seen with the writings of Tertullian and Augustine, many opinions of these early church fathers formed the foundation of developing theological ideas that would eventually become accepted as orthodox, or *right belief*. At this early stage, however, there was a diversity of ideas about a range of theological issues, including sexuality. Tatian, a second-century apologist, lumps together "those who marry, those who violate children, and those who commit adultery" in a list of sinners who seek worldly pleasures.[37] While the church eventually denounced the idea that marriage was as sinful as heresy, the fact that a group of early Christians, known as the Encratites, included marriage as part of their definition of sexual immorality demonstrates the diversity of ideas about sexuality in second-century Christianity. It also highlights how far second-century Christian ideas about sexuality are from twenty-first-century Christian ideas.

The more dominant position on marriage in the early church followed Paul's teaching that marriage was a necessity for those who were unable to resist the temptations of the flesh, but that virginity and celibacy were the ideal. As the early church moved further and further away from the time of Jesus, the expectation of his immediate return began to lessen. Some Christians sought to elevate the status of marriage so that it was on par with that of celibacy. Hoping to redeem sexual activity within marriage, church leaders reframed the purpose of sexuality from pleasure to procreation. Once sex was reconceived within the framework of procreation, the divine injunction represented by the command "be fruitful and multiply" was reinterpreted. While sexual intercourse was regarded as necessary to fulfill this command, any association of sex with physical pleasure was suppressed.

Justin Martyr, a second-century convert and influential apologist, portrayed the Christian practices both of marrying to raise children and of remaining single and celibate as forms of sexual purity. He contrasted this purity with a description of the pagan world as rife with prostitution and other forms of sexual excess. While the Greco-Roman world also recognized the importance of the institution of marriage as the proper location for procreation, Justin adapts the pagan belief that children should be raised within the institution of marriage into a Christian position that the purpose of marriage is for procreation.[38] This subtle shift marks a significant turning point in the development of Christian attitudes about marriage and sexual intercourse. It was a short leap from there to the position that dominated the Christian church for centuries—that sex without the possibility of procreation is sinful.

This theological belief—that sex without the possibility of procreation is sinful—is the root of Christian prohibitions associated with contraception and abortion. If procreation is what removes the sinfulness from sexual activity, then any human action that interferes with the possibility of procreation in any given sexual act is deemed sinful. Abstaining from vaginal-penal sexual intercourse was acceptable for those who didn't want more children, but contraception, anal or oral sex, or other forms of sexual activity that did not allow for the possibility of procreation were deemed sinful.

This brief introduction to the origins of the influential Christian belief in the procreative necessity of sexual intercourse is essential background as we consider contemporary Christian ethical attitudes toward abortion.[39] A history of sexuality within Christianity or even a review of all the references to abortion in Christian tradition lies beyond the scope and purpose of this book. Nor is such scholarship necessary here. Despite the prominence of contemporary pro-life rhetoric that seeks to establish an univocal and authoritative history of Christianity as resolutely against abortion, abortion simply has not been a major theological concern until very recently in Christian history.[40] And even though theologians have addressed abortion throughout Christian history, abortion itself did not become a major ethical concern within Christianity until the twentieth century. As we will see in the next chapter, even when there was a major secular fight to criminalize abortion in the United States in the nineteenth century, the churches largely stayed out of it.

Little was written about abortion in the early centuries of the church. Some early references to abortion in the *Didache* (late first century), the *Apocalypse of Peter* (early second century), and Clement and Tertullian (third century) refer to abortion as killing. But abortion is more often lumped in with other sexual sins as part of a general denouncement of sexual immorality and licentiousness, specifically, where texts denounce women's failure to adhere to broader sexual and social norms of patriarchal societies associated with the control of women's sexuality. Harper's observation of how the cultural framework of early Christian thought about sexuality—be it marriage, sexual intercourse, masturbation, contraception, same-sex relationships, or abortion—shifted from shame to sin shows us that the framework was intended to control the sexual lives and behavior of early Christians.

Writing in the late fourth century, Augustine shows no particular interest in condemning women for their abortions and only discusses the topic at all when it bears on related theological questions. His matter-of-fact description of the surgical removal of a prenate from a pregnant woman's body to save her life indicates that this practice was not only familiar but, since he doesn't condemn it, apparently accepted as a normative practice.[41] Augustine's interest seems to be not so much in the morality of ending a pregnancy as in the theological question of whether prenates have eternal souls that will be resurrected. In discussing this question, he makes a clear distinction between prenates that are "fully formed" and prenates that are "undeveloped." He compares the undeveloped prenate to a seed that failed to germinate and speaks of it as perishing or simply ceasing to exist. Augustine does not imagine an eternal status for the souls of these undeveloped prenates, even though his doctrine of resurrection is one that promotes God's ability to provide bodies "free from blemish and deformity" at the time of the resurrection.[42] From this position, it is clear that Augustine did not consider these unformed prenates as possessing eternal souls. In Augustine's discussion of prenatal life, he has revived the Aristotelian concept of delayed ensoulment, which holds that male prenates receive their "soul" forty days after conception, and females receive theirs at ninety days.

Theological attention to the developmental progress of the prenate and the idea of delayed ensoulment was prominent from Augustine up until the seventeenth century. During this period, most theologians made a distinction similar to the one that Augustine makes between prenates that were "formed" and "unformed." This idea of ensoulment is also associated with the terms *animation*, or *quickening*, which refer to the prenate's first movements that a pregnant woman can feel. For most of human history, it was not until quickening occurred that pregnancy could be definitively confirmed. In the early fifth century, Jerome wrote that abortion was not to be considered as homicide until the prenate had a recognizably formed human appearance and limbs.[43] In the thirteenth century, Pope Innocent III and Aquinas both expressed their belief that terminating a pregnancy before the prenate was "ever animated" was also not considered homicide. This notion of prohibiting abortion only after the soul is "animated" has been the dominant position throughout the majority of Christian history. Even within the Roman Catholic Church, abortion was not completely prohibited until 1889.[44] In fact, not until the Second Vatican Council issued *Gaudium et Spes* in 1965 did official Roman Catholic teaching completely shift its concern over abortion from the concealment of sexual sin to the protection of life.[45]

Christian scripture is completely silent on the topic of abortion. Jesus never once addressed it, and abortion is not a major topic of concern in the church until the late twentieth century. Although some theologians throughout history have addressed abortion, it was often included in a longer list of sexual sins, which, as we have noted, often included contraception and sexual activity without a procreative intent. Furthermore, abortion is often only mentioned in passing, and no theologian or church leader before the twentieth century devoted much attention to either contraception or abortion.

To understand Christian thinking about contraception and abortion, we must examine it within the dominant cultural, medical, and historical contexts of the theologians who addressed these issues. To this end, we must recognize the importance of the social control of women throughout this same history, a control focused consistently on women's bodies and their sexuality. In order to truly understand what various theologians believed about abortion, then, their work must be studied within the larger body of their writings and situated within their theological and cultural understanding of women, sexuality, and sin.

This critical intellectual task offers important background on a wide variety of contemporary Christian attitudes about women's bodies, women's sexuality, and gender expectations more broadly. However, because I am a social ethicist, a historical study is not my task here. Regardless of what we might discover about the history of Christian theologians' attitudes toward women's sexuality, these attitudes should not determine contemporary Christian attitudes about women's sexuality, women's bodies, and women's moral agency. The misogynistic and patriarchal history of the Christian tradition confirms the need for new and healthy ethical models for sexuality—models that commit to justice, partnership, respect, and integrity in relationships of sexual intimacy.

To summarize, although history can help us better understand how contemporary attitudes and expectations are related to the past, and it can help us see what purpose these arguments served in their own context, history has its limitations. We should not search our history for answers and models of how to think about abortion any more than we should do so for issues in medicine, science, or even contemporary society. Our relationship and attitude toward history is not deterministic.

Christianity significantly influenced our cultural attitudes about pregnancy, abortion, and the sacredness of life (among other things); therefore, we must recognize how the Christian tradition and its theological ideals have been influenced by misogyny and patriarchy. While misogyny is deeply embedded in the development, history, and theology of Christianity, the religion is not *inherently* misogynist or patriarchal. We human beings shape attitudes and beliefs about human nature, the sacred, and religions through our teachings and our practices. And it is human beings who have created patriarchal church structures and misogynist theologies. The real danger of these misogynist theologies lies in the way that they shape attitudes about how women can and should be treated. In the next chapter, we will look at how the mechanisms of patriarchy were set up to control women's reproductive power in the late nineteenth and twentieth centuries in the US and some of the ways women sought to exercise some control over their lives and their future.

CHAPTER 5

Patriarchy as Social Control

ABORTION HAS NOT ALWAYS been controversial in the United States. In the mid-nineteenth century, not only was abortion legal but married women regularly used abortion as a means of birth control. One prominent physician of the time noted that "there is *not one married female in ten who has not had an abortion, or at least attempted one!* . . . I have met with women who have had respectively eight, ten and thirteen children, and *as many abortions!*"[1] That there was widespread social acceptance of this practice is confirmed by testimony of physician Andrew Nebinger in 1870. He said that his professional inquiries into the subject of abortion found that respectable, married women regularly sought out abortions. Moreover, he said, they did not believe that the prenate was alive but only that it possessed the "capacity for living, and hence that, to destroy it was not homicide, and hardly more criminal than to prevent conception."[2] Women across the social classes recognized that abortion offered them the means to have a measure of control over their lives by spacing their pregnancies and limiting the number of children they had. Evidence suggests that women embraced this possibility enthusiastically as the abortion rate rose from an estimated one abortion for every twenty-five to thirty live births at the beginning of the 1800s to a likely high of one abortion for every five to six live births by midcentury.[3]

The political and social establishments of the newly formed United States were almost exclusively male and often dominated by educated, wealthy white men. Like most patriarchal social structures, the laws and social codes of the early US functioned to order, contain, dictate, and control the "proper" behavior of women. An intersectional analysis of the patriarchal desire for social control demonstrates that expectations for various social roles were not only gendered, but also raced. For the white women who were the cultural partners of these ruling-class males, this meant embodying moral roles like that of the Victorian "true woman," who was regarded as "delicate, refined, and chaste" and "perfectly suited to the home, where she served as mother and wife."[4] Legal scholar Dorothy Roberts describes how these attributes were exactly the opposite of those that characterized stereotypes of black women at the time.[5] Even as white women were being constrained by the narrow expectations of "true womanhood," this same trope was used to demonize black women, whom Roberts describes as being marked as the bearers of "incurable immorality" and considered unfit to be mothers.[6] Whether that "unfitness" was defined as hypersexuality, negligent mothering, dominance and control, or dependency, racist attitudes about black women have continued to drive public accèptance of the social control of black women's reproduction.[7] The different moral and social standards applied to the fertility of different groups of women illustrate the complex way in which attitudes about race, class, and immigrant status have intersected with dominant cultural ideas about which women should reproduce and why. The historical connection in the United States between a woman's perceived worthiness and cultural attitudes about whether she should have babies is an important consideration in contemporary debates about women's reproductive power.

The history of the control of women's reproductive bodies in the United States offers important context for understanding what is at stake in the contemporary debates. And those who think *Roe v. Wade* will never be overturned should know how quickly a small and committed group of male physicians in the late nineteenth century transformed public attitudes about abortion and criminalized it. However, this history is complicated. As historian Rickie Solinger has noted, there is no single history of women's reproduction in the US.[8] Not only is the history different for different groups of women—Protestant, Catholic, immigrant, US-born, black, white, married, unmarried—but attitudes and opinions about which women should have babies and under what conditions have changed dramatically over time.

One consistent aspect of public policy related to women's fertility has been the attempt to control their fertility to solve variously defined "social problems" facing the country.[9] From the "breeding" of enslaved people and the promotion of white women's fertility in the nineteenth century to the coercive and widespread sterilization of women deemed "unfit to reproduce" (including women labeled "feeble-minded" in the 1920s and 1930s, Puerto Rican women from the 1930s to the 1970s, unwed mothers in the 1950s and 1960s, and Native American women since the conquest), the control of women's fertility epitomizes an agenda of social control deeply marked by attitudes of racism, racial purity, and eugenics.

This chapter outlines the patriarchal threads that consistently shape the evolution of ideas about contraception and abortion in the United States, from the revolutionary period through the physicians' crusade of the nineteenth century and into the racialized reproductive politics of the twentieth century. Examining the transformation of public opinion about pregnancy and abortion over the years offers insight into the development of the justification framework that shapes the contemporary cultural climate of abortion conversations in the United States. Recognizing how and why public opinion has changed over time helps disrupt the compelling dominant narrative that women have always had to justify the termination of a pregnancy.

Like many cultural norms, the justification framework reflects a particular history, ideology, and set of assumptions that will be examined more closely in the next chapter. For now, let us remember that while popular opinion traces effective family planning back only to the late eighteenth century, recent scholarship indicates that women's ability to control their fertility has waxed and waned throughout recorded history, often reflecting cultural attitudes and practices that either contributed to or reflected acceptance or condemnation of these practices.[10] Just as certainly as pregnancy and childbirth are biological facts, women's desire to control their fertility is far from a modern invention.

REVOLUTIONARY IDEAS AND FERTILITY CONTROL IN THE EARLY UNITED STATES

Despite the Catholic Church's denunciation of abortion and contraception during the Inquisition, there is ample evidence that women in the West quietly continued using both contraception and abortion from the Middle Ages through the modern era. During the period of the American Revolution, new attitudes toward childbearing and women's self-understanding began to develop. Historian Susan Klepp argues that many women in the revolutionary era were inspired by the rhetoric of freedom and liberty and began to rethink traditional roles and responsibilities that they had inherited from Europe. Although the precise details are unknown, within a single generation, from the colonial families of the mid-1700s to their children's generation just after the Revolutionary War, average family size dropped notably. The period of the Seven Years' War (1756–1763) saw the peak of fertility in the US; by 1760, crude birth rates had begun to drop in both the black and white free populations.[11] While there is no documentation of efficacy or usage rates, ample evidence suggests that women were practicing various methods of birth control to limit the number of children in their families. In addition to the marked drop in fertility rates, physicians' writings and lectures from the time acknowledge the practice of abortion, and the presence of home health literature and advertisements aimed at women document the use of various pills and potions to "regulate" menstruation.

Mary Wollstonecraft's *Vindication of the Rights of Women*, published in 1793, reflects the radical idea of "*women's* rights" as a new and necessary category of civil discourse. Wollstonecraft also promoted the idea that women could "control" their fertility through limiting the number and spacing of their pregnancies, capturing in writing an idea that was already beginning to be put into practice by women of her era.[12] In addition to improving the quality of women's health, Wollstonecraft also noted that responsibilities for fewer children would leave women with more time to "improve their minds through the study of literature, science, and the fine arts."[13] While these pursuits reflect only one understanding of the benefits of limiting the number of children in a household, Klepp argues that a broad cultural shift was taking place among women regarding their self-identity and their purpose in life. Women were beginning to reject expectations of abundant fertility and multiple births in favor of planned and limited fertility. This change was part of a revising of marital expectations as women and men began to think of marriage in terms of companionship rather than obligations. Klepp also argues that it was not the elite that led this revolution in reducing the number of children per family but rather what she refers to as the "urban middling sort," or what we might call the middle class.[14]

While the paucity of records pertaining to contraception and abortion makes it impossible to know exactly how widespread the practice of birth control was in the eighteenth century, there is ample evidence that both contraception and abortion played increasingly important roles in the control of women's fertility.[15] Several factors contributed to this interest in decreasing family size across all classes. In addition to the growing embrace of freedom and liberty inspired by the American Revolution, it was increasingly expensive to raise children, particularly in urban areas. The increasing availability and desirability of consumer goods had an impact on household economics and contributed to a growing cash economy in the United States. As people replaced handmade items with manufactured ones or supplemented their diets and homes with luxury items, the role of children in the family shifted from workers and contributors to the family economy to consumers. Of course, a shift in attitude does not necessarily translate into behavioral change, particularly if the means to control fertility are unavailable or unreliable. Misunderstanding of women's menstrual cycles meant that women who sought to employ "natural family planning" by avoiding sexual intercourse during their most fertile periods were actually having sex when they were most fertile.[16] Although it was not uncommon for women in the American colonies to bear a child every eighteen months to two years, meaning that eight to twelve children would not have been unusual, that number dropped to seven by 1800, five by 1850, and three and a half by 1900.[17]

Up until the middle of the nineteenth century, the domain of pregnancy and childbearing was largely the realm of women and the midwives and folk healers who cared for them. The lack of public interest in interfering with activities related to women's pregnancies is evident in colonial trial histories from the seventeenth and eighteenth centuries. There, reference to abortive practices emerges in a handful of cases for other types of crimes, namely, infanticide, rape, fornication, adultery, assault, perjury, and slander.[18] Though trial depositions indicate widespread knowledge of abortive drugs among young and old, rich and poor, the only incidents that reached the courts involved transgressions of white (Protestant) patriarchal boundaries. These court cases include relationships between women and men of different social classes and races, a Jewish doctor working in a Protestant settlement, servant women who acted out of their place, and men who forced abortifacients on unwilling women to hide sexual transgressions.[19]

The legal perspective toward pregnancy and the termination of a pregnancy in the colonial period reflected the inherited common-law tradition, a tradition that continued to govern much of the newly formed United States in the early days after independence. Common law, which had been practiced for several hundred years in Britain, reflected the practical moral wisdom that quickening marked the existence of the prenate as separate from the pregnant woman and was therefore subject to some moral consideration. Given the lack of reliable means of confirming pregnancy, quickening was generally regarded as the official recognition of a confirmed pregnancy. Up until this point, many of the other physical indications of a possible pregnancy could, presumably, have alternative origins.[20] Although quickening usually happens in the later fourth or early fifth month, it varies not only among women but also among pregnancies. Notably, this diagnostic tool is also fully and solely within the control of the pregnant woman: only she can feel the movement and verify the existence of her pregnancy. With a standard of quickening as the marker for the recognition of a pregnancy, women retained a certain amount of control over their situations. Before quickening, there was no recognized pregnancy, and any actions that brought on the flow of blood were not regarded as immoral and certainly not as criminal. Prenatal life was simply not recognized as beginning until the point of quickening, a practice that has a long tradition throughout history.

The term *abortion* was only used *after* quickening, and British common law reflected this widely accepted cultural norm. In 1812, the Massachusetts Supreme Court dismissed charges against Isaiah Bangs for providing an abortifacient drug to a pregnant woman, because it could not be proved that the woman was "quick with child at the time."[21] As no legislation that governed contraception and abortion had been passed anywhere in the United States, the actions of the Massachusetts Supreme Court were in keeping with the British common-law tradition that had governed such cases since the colonial period. The reluctance of courts to criminalize abortion prior to quickening was based on the logic that there was no way to prove intent on the part of either the woman or the person providing her with potential abortifacients if quickening had not occurred.[22]

Quickening continued to shape legislation dealing with pregnancy and abortion from 1821 to 1841, a period that historian James Mohr identifies as the "first wave of abortion legislation" in the United States. During this period, ten states and one territory passed laws specifically intended to regulate abortion procedures.[23] The earliest legislation seeking to criminalize abortion was largely framed as a poison control measure to protect women from the potentially lethal ingredients of some of the so-called medicines that were widely advertised and available for purchase. Statutes like these were aimed toward apothecaries and physicians who were knowingly marketing potentially lethal substances.[24] The inclusion of each of these provisions in larger omnibus revisions of criminal codes indicates that there was no particular social demand to curtail the practice of abortion. Neither did these new laws affect any significant change in the practice. Half of them merely codified the existing common-law tradition criminalizing abortion after quickening, and the remaining five were virtually unenforceable, given the impossibility of proving the existence of a pregnancy (and thus the intent to terminate it) before quickening.[25]

The general acceptance of quickening not only as the predominant cultural way of confirming pregnancy but also as the common-law definition of pregnancy suggests that women's perspectives on this issue largely determined public opinion. Thus, both culturally and legally, women were regarded as the experts on pregnancy and childbearing. Early techniques to "restore the menses" were not regarded as either an abortion or as morally suspect in any way. People widely believed that any emptying of the contents of the uterus before quickening was *not* abortion.[26] Home health guides of the time, which would have been present in many homes, offer some indication of the ideas and practices that governed women's behavior with regards to maintaining their own health and the health of women in their families. Amenorrhea, or the absence or interruption of a woman's menstrual cycle, was referred to alternatively as lost, blocked, hidden, obstructed, or suppressed menses, and any number of problems were cited as the potential cause of such an interruption.[27] The idea that women's wombs could be obstructed dates back at least as far as the Greeks. "Remedies" for amenorrhea were widely recognized and shared publicly through home medical manuals and medical textbooks and lecture notes from professors in medical schools.[28] From bloodletting, pulling teeth, bathing, jumping, horseback riding, and vigorous exercise to teas, extracts, purgatives, and douches—the possibilities for clearing women's "blockages" and returning their monthly menses ranged from dangerous to ridiculous to potentially quite effective.[29]

The marked drop in birth rates from the 1700s through the 1800s demonstrates that women were increasingly effective in exercising control over their fertility. Evidence suggests that these shifts were due to a combination of behaviors, including marrying at a later age, lengthening periods of breastfeeding, abstaining from sexual intercourse, and increasingly ending childbearing by the age of thirty-five.[30] The ubiquitous knowledge and presence of emmenagogues, or medicines or procedures to restore menstrual flow, in healthcare literature, pharmacies, drugstores, and medical chests prepared for rural families of the time, not to mention the growth of advertisements for "female pills" and other birth-control paraphernalia, indicates that both contraception and abortion played a prominent role in dropping fertility rates, particularly by the mid-nineteenth century.[31]

While little is known on precisely how women of the time understood the use of these medications, it is important to consider women's desire to regulate their menstrual cycles within the larger social and historical context of medical ideas that were prevalent at the time. Absent scientific knowledge of biological systems, viruses, and germ theory, medicine was an inexact science. Women's reproductive cycles and illness more broadly were something of a mystery. A missed period was often referred to as "taking the cold" and was considered as likely to indicate the onset of consumption or some other malady as it was to indicate pregnancy.[32] Medical literature from the eighteenth and nineteenth centuries indicates that physicians often considered women's emotional state one of the strongest indications of the origins of a missed menstrual cycle, with hysteria, grief, depression, anxiety, and fatigue noted as possible indications. Descriptions in medical literature that associate hysteria with "an inflated belly, perceived motion, vomiting, and colic" bear a noticeable resemblance to descriptions of early pregnancy.[33]

Abortion became increasingly more common in women's attempts to control their fertility in the middle decades of the 1800s. It was gradually more visible in public life as advertisements for emmenagogues and doctors specializing in "married women's health" proliferated in newspapers and magazines. Marketed under names like Hooper's Female Pills, Hungary Water, Dr. Ryan's Worm-Destroying Sugar Plombs, Madame Restell's Female Monthly Pills, Madame Drunette's French Lunar Pills, and Dr. Peter's French Renovating Pills, these remedies were advertised in daily papers and popular magazines and were widely available from apothecaries, physicians, and pharmacies. Likewise, popular health materials instructed women on methods of aborting themselves, including providing recipes for restoring menstrual flow as well as instructions for the use of "French syringes" and other implements intended for douching. While it is likely that this commercialization of the practice functioned to increase demand for services, abortion was clearly coming into the mainstream in a new way, and married women began to incorporate abortion into their birth-control practices—much to the chagrin of a group of physicians in the newly developing medical profession.

THE PHYSICIAN'S CRUSADE AGAINST ABORTION

Given the colonial history of the US and the democratic spirit of the new republic, no formal guild system oversaw the medical profession until the establishment of the American Medical Association (AMA) in 1847.[34] Before then, anyone could claim the title of doctor and set about offering medicine and treatments to anyone who would pay. Those physicians who were formally trained and understood their profession as a scientific and rational pursuit called themselves *regulars*. They were markedly distinct from their colleagues who either lacked formal training or whose training was deemed inferior to these regular physicians.[35] Some of these "irregulars" were self-taught or had apprenticed with another healer; others had attended medical schools that Mohr indicates were often degree mills that lacked standards or any other semblance of the professionalism associated with modern medical training.[36] As the nineteenth century wore on, the self-proclaimed healers and physicians from this irregular category were increasingly the ones who provided emmenagogues and other gynecological treatments. Women's use of these healers often diverted paying customers from regular physicians, a practice that could have long-term implications, particularly if these women began to rely on the irregulars for other family medical needs.[37]

Although these two groups of practitioners were separated by very real differences in their training and in their understanding of the causes of disease, many scientific advancements that improved the practice of medicine—advancements like antisepsis, anesthesia, and bacteriology—would not be widely acknowledged or practiced in the United States until near the end of the nineteenth century. Consequently, the medical outcomes of treatments from regular physicians were not markedly different from their competitors. It was hard to prove that the practices of the regular physicians were superior to those of other healers by simply looking at the medical results of their patients. The regular physicians, who by and large came from more elite families and engaged in training that often included study in European universities, developed an avid interest in differentiating themselves and their approach to medicine from the irregulars.[38]

By midcentury, a group of regular physicians associated with the newly organized AMA had seized on the issue of abortion as a way to establish the group's moral and intellectual credentials and thus support its demand for the licensing of medical professionals and the regulation of certain medical procedures. The AMA's crusade for the criminalization of abortion had the added benefit of challenging and discrediting their rivals, effectively cutting them out of the lucrative market of reproductive services. It also shifted normative ideas about pregnancy and reproduction from the control of women to the control of professional physicians, at least in the eyes of the law.

Horatio Storer was one of these physicians. He argued that the prenate was a living human being that deserved protection—a markedly different social understanding of its status. This position was based on the consensus within the nascent professionalized medical community regarding prenatal development as a continuous process that began with conception. In 1857, he turned his personal crusade against abortion into a national campaign by convincing the AMA to form a Committee on Criminal Abortion to investigate the incidence of abortion in the US and to recommend professional action.[39] The committee's report cited widespread public ignorance about quickening as a stage of gestation, laxity in the medical profession, and "grave defects of our laws" as the primary causes of what it called the increasing problem of abortion in society.[40] These physicians worked assiduously throughout the 1860s and 1870s to criminalize abortion. Given the widespread cultural acceptance and practice of abortion, the AMA crusade to criminalize abortion required that physicians generate a wholesale transformation of popular opinion about pregnancy, quickening, and the moral status of the prenate.

The first strategy of the AMA doctors was to discredit the prevailing doctrine of quickening as the start of a pregnancy. Arguing that a scientific understanding of pregnancy demonstrated prenatal development to be a biologically continuous process, they denounced quickening as merely one recognizable stage of that process. For the physicians, this observation meant that there was no point during a pregnancy or childbirth when the prenate was more alive than any other. Therefore, they held that the termination of a pregnancy at any stage must be understood as immoral, equivalent to the killing of a newborn baby.

Recognizing that it would take time to change public opinion about the morality of abortion, a second strategy was to curtail the practice by attempting to frighten women about the potential dangers associated with the procedure. In a book he wrote to convince married women not to have abortions, Storer enumerated a host of potential consequences of the procedure, intending to frighten women away from terminating their pregnancies. These included sterility of the mother, deformation or ill health of subsequent children, likely death from the procedure, insanity, and the mother's future ill health, including cancer, diseases of the uterus, back pain, headaches, and impatient bladders.[41] He also said that the risk of these various conditions was increased when abortion was "criminal" (i.e., intentional) rather than a spontaneous abortion, or a miscarriage.[42]

Because the physicians were also in the difficult position of potentially offending the public (particularly their female patients) by accusing them of murder, they sought to soften this message by portraying women as unwitting victims of their own ignorance regarding the moral status of the prenate. Here the perspective of Winslow Ayer, a physician of the time, is representative of this prevailing attitude: "The *crime* [of abortion] is wholly inconsistent with the purity of women's nature, and revolting to her moral sentiments. It is generally the act of those who know not what they do."[43]

Storer supplemented his argument by additionally casting women as incapable of rational thought because of the destabilizing impact of their hormones. Here is Storer's response to why women should not be allowed to decide for themselves whether to end a pregnancy:

> Woman's mind is prone to depression and, indeed, to *temporary actual derangement*, under the stimulus of uterine excitation, and this alike at the time of puberty and the final cessation of the menses, at the monthly period and at conception, during pregnancy, at labor, and during lactation. . . . During the state of gestation the woman is therefore liable to thoughts, convictions even, that at other times she would turn from in disgust or dismay; and in this fact, that must be as familiar to herself as it is to the physician, we find her most valid excuse for the crime.[44]

Portraying women as ignorant and irrational was an important aspect of the physicians' strategy to both change public opinion about the moral status of the prenate and wrest control of women's reproductive care from women and hand it over to the protection of the learned physician. Storer also argued that women are "physiologically constituted" for pregnancy and motherhood and that any attempt to prevent pregnancy, other than by total abstinence, is "disastrous to a woman's mental, moral, and physical well-being."[45] The tactics used by these physicians to fabricate a need for the social control of women is a classic example of how misogyny functions in society.

In fact, Storer's objections to any form of birth control other than abstinence led him to argue that it was morally preferable for a husband to have sex with a prostitute than for his wife to have an abortion. This stance explicitly encouraged couples who wished to limit their fertility to stop having sex together while encouraging husbands to sleep with prostitutes to "save" their wives from the evil of abortion.[46]

REFRAMING ABORTION FROM FERTILITY CONTROL TO JUSTIFIABLE KILLING

While the AMA crusade clearly played a significant part in a larger effort to bolster the credibility and authority of regular physicians amid a medical landscape rife with charlatans, physicians no doubt understood this campaign as part of their duty to protect human life and educate the public. However, the idea that pregnancy was a biologically continuous process was not a new scientific development in the mid-1800s, when these physicians began their campaign. The idea had been represented in a popular 1809 obstetric textbook that was widely read in the United States.[47] Furthermore, although the evidence indicates that more women were incorporating abortion into their fertility control, the practice of abortion was hardly a new phenomenon.

It seems that what motivated the ire of the physicians was *who* was having the abortions. As long as abortion was perceived to be a practice that single women resorted to in dire situations, the prevailing attitude seemed to be one of pity and tolerance rather than criminal liability.[48] However, as it became increasingly evident that married women were using abortion as a normal method of fertility control, physicians across the country began to elevate their rhetoric and seek out more popular ways of conveying their concerns to the public. Members of the medical community had rejected quickening as a viable marker since the early 1800s, and some had spoken out against abortion.[49] Yet, they had failed to sway public opinion. It wasn't until the physicians began to push for criminalization of the procedure in much more public forums that they began to shift public attitudes about abortion.

Their campaign was portrayed as an attempt to educate the public that the development of the prenate was a continuous biological process. The aim was to convince people that the prenate ought to hold an equivalent moral status to that of an infant. Their claim, however, that women didn't understand prenatal development as a continuous process is questionable.

Through their own and other women's miscarriages and abortions, some women would have been familiar with the various developmental stages at different points in a pregnancy. After all, many of these women would have seen the prenates that they had miscarried and would have easily recognized the developmental resemblance to full-term babies they had seen. Beyond personal experience of pregnancy, miscarriage, and abortion, a popular home medical guide from 1817 meticulously described monthly prenatal developments beginning seven days after conception.[50] Moreover, there is no evidence that anyone thought that a baby suddenly appeared inside a woman in the fourth or fifth month of pregnancy when she began to feel its movements. On the contrary, the doctrine of quickening marked recognition of the *social* nature of the prenate, that point at which its independent movement was recognizable and its existence as an independent entity was acknowledged. It was only at this point that the prenate gained a moral status that warranted consideration. In attempting to change the public's attitude toward abortion, then, the physicians sought an ideological shift—a change in the public understanding and recognition of the social and moral value of the prenate.

Not all physicians shared the absolutist position represented by Storer and his colleagues. Most physicians did recognize some moral distinction between prenatal life and the life of the pregnant woman. This distinction commonly appeared in medical literature, including many obstetrical textbooks of the day. One of these books noted that "the life of the child was 'incomparably small' when pitted against that of its mother," and another concurred: "Whenever a clear indication for the sacrifice of the tender embryo exists, no evil is done in procuring the greater good of the mother."[51] Indeed, much of the legislation that was passed to criminalize abortion continued to reserve the right to abortion when it was deemed necessary to save the life of the mother. This guideline was presented as standard medical practice in textbooks.[52] Abortion, then, was not wrong in an absolute sense; even the physicians recognized that there were times when it might be necessary.

The physicians did not simply want to shift public understanding of the biological continuity of the prenate. They wanted to reframe the question of the morality of abortion from a fertility-control measure to an issue of justifiable killing. These are two very different moral questions with very different moral frameworks. When abortion was understood as a fertility-control issue, the moral emphasis and starting point was the life and health of the potential mother, and how many children a family wanted or could manage was a morally relevant factor. From this perspective, the question was deeply rooted in the lives and circumstances of women and their families, women who presumably engaged in serious moral discernment as part of their family planning. By transforming the public's social understanding of the prenate, the physicians effectively changed the nature of the debate. If the prenate was now presented as having a moral status equivalent to that of a newborn baby, the question of abortion moved from the concrete, material questions of women and their health and well-being to the abstract question of how to weigh the value of one life against another.

In addition, the language of the physicians' crusade to criminalize abortion indicates that revoking women's control of their bodies and their decision-making about their reproductive capacities was no small part of the impetus for their campaign. At the time, US law was governed by coverture laws inherited from the English common-law tradition, which held that husband and wife were one person and that the husband held all legal rights.[53] Within this legal framework, there was a certain logic in moving control of women's decisions about their bodies. Under coverture laws, married women were unable to sign contracts or own property. Husbands could decide whether their wives could pursue an education or work, and women's wages legally belonged to their husbands. These legal codes reflected a larger cultural attitude that women need to be protected. Of course, this protection was really just a euphemism that established and codified male authority over the women in their lives.

As the abortion debate shifted from material questions about the shape and quality of women's lives and families to an abstract question about the morality of terminating a pregnancy, pregnant women as moral agents were effectively erased, even as their bodies and the most intimate details of their private lives were made hypervisible and subject to public debate. While an abortion could still be sought to save a woman's life, she was no longer deemed competent to judge when this action was necessary.

Women became pawns, vessels, objects to be treated, managed, and controlled. In the abstract, abortion was wrong but justifiable under certain, very limited circumstances. Physicians were elevated to a new social role that recognized their authority to judge just what these conditions were. Establishing the need for regular physicians to confirm the necessity of an abortion helped bolster their professional authority and supported the AMA's desire to establish formal control over the medical profession through licensing requirements. This move also shifted decision-making control over most abortion issues from women to their doctors.

For the physicians, the decision to terminate a pregnancy was approached abstractly as a theoretical question: Is it morally acceptable to interrupt a pregnancy? This approach is not, however, how women of the day framed or approached the question. Rather, as we have seen, women in the nineteenth century sought increased control over their fertility and recognized that abortion was one avenue for establishing that control. The ability to control their childbearing was valued as a social good that allowed them the time and energy for other aspects of their lives, including increased attention to self and to their existing children. Decisions about family size reflected the financial and social circumstances of individual families and were an example of ethical reasoning based on concrete circumstances.

The physicians' success in reframing the debate is evident in the shift in the cultural framing of the issue from accepting abortion as a form of fertility control to requiring justification for the "killing" of prenatal life. Clearly, if abortion were murder, it could have no justification, but we have already seen that many physicians routinely chose to save the life of the pregnant woman when her life was endangered by a pregnancy. This very fact establishes that the physicians' crusade was interested in establishing abortion as *killing* rather than murder. Within such a framework, there are circumstances under which it can be justifiable to "kill" the prenate to "save" the pregnant woman. The result of this crusade was a cultural shift from a recognition of abortion as part of the broader experience of women's life and health to a framing of abortion as an abstract philosophical phenomenon in which the prenatal life was elevated to a moral status equivalent to the pregnant woman's.

Women's legitimate concerns about controlling their fertility were dismissed, and recognition of their capacity for moral agency and rational thought eviscerated in the process. "If each woman were allowed to judge for herself in this matter," Storer said, "her decision upon the abstract question would be too sure to be warped by personal considerations, and those of the moment."[54] Women's "personal considerations" were deemed selfish and portrayed most unfavorably by physicians in many lectures and tracts intended to turn public opinion against abortion. Women were accused of seeking abortions in order to engage in "excessive expenditures," pursue a "fashionable life," indulge their "extravagance of living," and indulge in their "lust."[55] Given that the most significant drops in birth rates seemed to be occurring in white Protestant families, there were also outcries that these "native born" women weren't bearing enough children.[56] Such protests emphasize the racist and anti-immigrant sentiment that undergirded much of the objection to abortion at the time.

RACE, CLASS, PURITY, AND THE SPECTER OF EUGENICS

Although the criminalization of abortion in the nineteenth century was largely focused on white America, the history of abortion in this country is also shaped by how the fertility and reproductive rights of minority and other vulnerable communities have been persistently managed, controlled, and abused throughout US history. These varied histories are not tangential to the larger history. Rather, their variation illustrates the pernicious nature of patriarchy at work. Patriarchy always represents the control of an elite group of ruling-class men. In different eras and different contexts, different characteristics determine who is allowed to belong to that ruling class. Ruling-class men in the nineteenth-century United States differed in how they sought to control the sexuality of various groups of women. The sexuality of ruling-class white women was seen as distinct from the sexuality of working-class and immigrant white women, which was viewed quite differently again from that of black women (enslaved or free). The intersecting realities of race, gender, class, disability, sexual identity, and other facets of identity mean that different groups of women experienced patriarchal control of their sexuality in different ways. The differential impact on various groups of women is a constant feature of patriarchal power throughout history. A closer examination of nineteenth and twentieth-century US shows how these differences are associated with various forms of prejudice and racism and how the desire to control women's behavior is the thread that weaves through the varied experiences of women.

Native American women have specifically been targeted for destruction and control since the earliest days of European contact. Andrew Jackson argued that after state-sanctioned massacres, US troops should systematically kill any remaining Native women and children to complete the extermination of the Native peoples.[57] The blatant disregard for Native American dignity and autonomy marks US history and is evident in much more recent times as well: Indian Health Services, a division within the US Department of Health and Human Services, forcibly sterilized Native women in the second half of the twentieth century. Although the full extent of these practices was never fully documented, the Women of All Red Nations, a Native women's advocacy organization, has estimated that the rates of sterilization were as high as 80 percent on some reservations.[58] Approximately 42 percent of Native women were sterilized between 1968 and 1982, compared with a 15 percent rate among white women during the same period.[59]

State control of black women's fertility shows a similar disregard of women's autonomy. The injustice began with the "breeding" programs of slave owners. During slavery, some enslaved black women were targeted for reproduction and treated like farm animals, valued primarily for their ability to have healthy babies and increase their owners' wealth. Thomas Jefferson remarked, "I consider a woman who brings a child every two years as more profitable than the best man on the farm; what she produces is an addition to capital."[60] The economic interest in black women's reproductive capacities increased after Congress outlawed the importation of slaves to the US in 1807. Since no new slaves were allowed to be brought in on slave ships, slave owners and traders focused their attention on the existing slave population. Black women were subjected to the whims of their owners, and often the owner's sons; both groups raped and otherwise used these women's bodies with no regard to their dignity and their humanity. Enslaved women and men were forced into marriages against their wishes as well as subject to coerced sexual relations between enslaved people handpicked to produce the best offspring. Our country's history of control of black sexuality and black women's bodies cannot be overemphasized in the current politicized and racially charged debate about abortion.

Racist attitudes about the value of black children have continued to shape public opinion about black women's pregnancy and childbearing. After Emancipation, blacks began to be viewed by some as a drain on society rather than an economic asset. Such attitudes were crystalized in 1965 in a report titled *The Negro Family: The Case for National Action* (known as the Moynihan Report). Written by then assistant secretary of labor Daniel Patrick Moynihan, the report attempted to pathologize black families and specifically black women by blaming high rates of poverty among blacks on single-mother families and the "matriarchal structure" of black culture. Moynihan's report signaled a sea change in the public-policy approach to poverty and ushered in a new era of anger and blame directed toward unmarried black women who had children.

This history also lays bare the racism within the physicians' campaign: many of the ideas and justifications embedded in it reflect an attempt to promote the fertility of the "right" women to provide citizens for the state. The emergence of the eugenics movement, which sought to improve the genetic foundations of the human race through selective reproduction of the "right" people, amplified this idea and gave it a scientific veneer. This movement arose in the wake of several publications by Sir Francis Galton, who emphasized the role of heredity or nature in social achievement and success. Galton, who coined the term *eugenics*, rejected the idea that people could be taught moral behavior. He sought to apply Darwin's theory of natural selection to improve the gene pool of the species.[61] The violent nineteenth-century history of attempting to control the fertility of women of color to match the needs of the capitalist state combined with the "scientific" legitimacy of the eugenics movement in the early twentieth century to shape a powerful racist agenda of reproductive control. Like many other members of the white ruling class, Theodore Roosevelt, a prominent eugenicist, worried about "race decay" and "racial death" and the "insufficient breeding of Anglo-Saxon women."[62] The eugenic desire to "improve the species" by controlling who reproduced contributed to immigration quotas, anti-miscegenation laws (laws prohibiting interracial marriage or sexual activity), and state-enforced sterilization abuse aimed at criminals and those labeled as "feeble-minded."[63]

Henry Goddard, a prominent psychologist and eugenicist, proposed to keep the United States a white-dominant country by dividing people into categories of the "fit" and "others." With regard to the "others," Goddard wrote, "we need to hunt them out in every possible place and take care of them, and see to it that they do not propagate."[64] It is estimated that more than sixty thousand men and women were sterilized under state laws across the country under the belief that "degeneracy" was inherited.[65] Of course, many people who were labeled feeble-minded or degenerate were simply poor or uneducated. In the landmark 1927 Supreme Court case known as *Buck v. Bell*, Carrie Buck was sentenced to compulsory sterilization in Virginia after she gave birth "out of wedlock" in a state institution. The "evidence" presented in the case consisted of the fact that she was one of several children born to an unmarried woman and that Carrie herself was a foster child who got pregnant and gave birth to a baby of low intelligence. One witness for the state began his history of the Buck family with these words: "These people belong to the shiftless, ignorant and worthless class of anti-social whites of the South."[66] The text of the decision is worth quoting at length:

> We have seen more than once that the public welfare may call upon the best citizens for their lives. It would be strange if it could not call upon those who already sap the strength of the State for these lesser sacrifices, often not felt to be such by those concerned, in order to prevent our being swamped with incompetence. It is better for all the world, if instead of waiting to execute degenerate offspring for crime, or to let them starve for their imbecility, society can prevent those who are manifestly unfit from continuing their kind. The principle that sustains compulsory vaccination is broad enough to cover cutting the Fallopian tubes. Three generations of imbeciles are enough.[67]

Carrie Buck was sterilized. Historians later discovered that Buck had been raped by a member of her foster family and was likely sent to the institution to hide the crime. While forced sterilization may seem like the opposite of draconian antiabortion laws, both efforts are rooted in identical assumptions about women's autonomy and moral agency—assumptions that respect neither. During the twentieth century, sterilization became increasingly linked with abortion as "punishment" for women who had abortions. After World War II, crackdowns on largely female abortion providers across the country drove hospitals to create hospital abortion committees that met to weigh individual cases and decide whether women could receive an abortion. By midcentury, more than 53 percent of teaching hospitals and 40 percent of all US hospitals required women to undergo a simultaneous sterilization with her abortion. One physician at the time described the requirement for sterilization as the equivalent of saying to women, "All right, if you do not want this baby, you are not capable of having any."[68]

One of the most noteworthy aspects of the history of women's fertility and abortion in the United States is the remarkable malleability of public opinion. As described earlier, public campaigns have managed to transform the legal status of women's reproductive health care, including access to contraception and abortion. Moreover, the public has readily accepted the social control of women's bodies through forced reproduction and sterilization rooted in appeals to deep-seated racial, ethnic, class, and ableist prejudices. The influence of "experts," whether they were psychiatrists, other physicians, or psychologists, has been paramount in influencing public attitudes and public policies related to pregnant women and their fertility.

After World War II, unwed mothers were increasingly characterized not as feeble-minded but mentally defective and morally weak. Particularly within white communities, getting pregnant outside marriage was viewed as a reflection of a woman's (or a girl's) moral failings, which marked her social standing in the community and confined unmarried women and their children to a permanent underclass of society.[69] Psychiatrists argued that unmarried mothers were mentally ill and in need of treatment. Given that unwed mothers were generally regarded as social outcasts, mental health professionals determined that only women who were irrational and deeply mentally ill could possibly put themselves in a situation where they would end up unmarried and pregnant. Solinger points out that this "diagnosis" stripped women of their moral agency and transformed them into children who needed to be cared for.[70] Homes for unwed mothers from the postwar period through the 1960s were filled with unmarried white women who were diagnosed as deeply psychologically disturbed (often attributed to family dysfunction). Interestingly, public attitudes, again influenced by the psychologists, psychiatrists, and social workers who worked most closely with these women, held that if these young women experienced remorse and gave their babies over for adoption, they would be somehow cleansed and might move forward with a more proper script for their life: respectable marriage and children of their "own" in the future.[71] Unmarried pregnant black women, on the other hand, were much more likely to keep their babies and to find support in their communities.[72]

This reminder that women's experiences of fertility and reproduction are deeply marked by their race, class, ethnicity, immigrant status, and other factors underlies our ability to understand the complexity of women's lives, fertility, and autonomy and the idea of reproductive justice. Despite the differences that have attended social attitudes toward women's fertility, society has consistently believed that it is socially, culturally, and politically acceptable for external forces to control women's fertility—whether through the encouragement or discouragement of (or the permitting or prohibiting of) pregnancies and abortions. In short, the idea that it is OK for the state or other cultural forces to control the reproduction of women from all different social circumstances has been culturally normative.

The connection between the social and moral acceptability of abortion and contraception and a woman's race, class, ability, or mental health status strongly suggests that the social control of women's fertility in the United States has not been a consistent moral narrative of concern for life—as the dominant contemporary pro-life account would have it. Rather, the history of women's fertility in this country has been one of using shame, guilt, legal measures, and coercion to control which women get pregnant, carry a pregnancy to term, keep a child, or place it for adoption.

The very fact that the attitudes about which women should bear and keep children and which women should not are racially and economically marked offers frightening insight into the depth of the misogyny and racism that has shaped public attitudes and public policies about women's fertility and reproduction since the earliest days of this country. Questions about reproduction—issues that are arguably some of the most fundamental questions women face about identity, autonomy, family, community, and faith—have long been subject to oversight and control by public forces that seek to shape the population in particular ways.

ABORTION IN THE TWENTIETH CENTURY

Although the changes to the legal codes in the nineteenth century criminalized most forms of abortion, it was never completely illegal. The administration of legal abortion procedures was governed by medical professionals, first by individual physicians in the early twentieth century and increasingly by hospital ethics committees in the post–World War II era. Sociologist Carole Joffe documented the struggle of doctors to provide safe abortions during the era of criminalization. She reports that one doctor who practiced during the early years said, "Every doctor—let's put it frankly—who wanted to help people had to have an abortionist he trusted."[73]

Demand for abortion did not evaporate simply because it was criminalized in the 1860s. Rather, the practice was forced underground. Though largely illegal, abortions remained widespread and continued to be largely performed by physicians. There was a tremendous increase in the demand for abortion services during the Depression; studies indicate that working-class women from all races and ethnic groups had abortions at the same rate, whereas affluent women had higher rates.[74] A Kinsey study estimated the abortion rate for white upper- and middle-class women at almost 25 percent, with 84 percent of abortions for white, urban women being performed by physicians.[75] A de facto truce between law enforcement and abortion providers meant that arrests and prosecutions were only triggered by maternal deaths that resulted from unsafe abortions.[76]

When the post–World War II era ushered in a pronatalist sentiment as well as a resurgence of traditional gender roles, women were urged back into the domestic sphere and away from the paid work they had undertaken during the war effort. The abortion truce evaporated as social pressures for (white) women to return from the factories to the home expressed themselves in public crackdowns on illegal abortions during the 1940s and 1950s, and raids of illegal abortion providers became more common.[77] Although the raids largely focused on female abortion providers, fewer and fewer physicians of any gender continued to provide abortion services as the risk of losing their licenses to practice medicine increased with the crackdowns. Solinger describes the highly publicized and sensationalized public trials of abortion providers as "drenched in sex" and intended to simultaneously titillate the public and demonstrate women's moral obligation to have babies when they got pregnant, regardless of their circumstances or desires.[78] The 1950s also saw the rise of hospital review committees that acted as gatekeepers for legal abortion. Historian Leslie Reagan describes how the review was designed to embarrass women and discourage abortions.[79] Whether the discouragement, the shaming, or the crackdown on illegal providers was the cause, abortions dropped from an estimated thirty thousand in 1940 to closer to eight thousand in 1964.[80]

Particularly in the era of the hospital review committees, access to legal abortion often depended on who you were, who you knew, and what the local medical community's opinion was on abortion. One physician described the situation this way: "As long as you were the banker's daughter, the doctor's daughter, the golf buddy's daughter, it was always taken care of."[81] Access to safe abortions became a privilege of the white, wealthy, and upper middle class, as they were the ones with the connections and the money to travel to Europe or Mexico if necessary. Since the physicians who had quietly performed abortions in their offices through the first half of the century were now closed down, the alternatives available for poor and working-class women were increasingly dangerous. Access to these unsafe procedures became part of a network of underground abortion care. The often unsanitary conditions and questionably trained providers contributed to an increase in complications to what is normally a safe and relatively easy procedure. As access to illegal but safe procedures diminished, poor women bore the brunt of the burden. Sick, injured, and dying women started pouring into hospital emergency rooms, where the medical staff struggled to repair the damage caused by botched abortions. In 1967 alone, ten thousand women were admitted to New York City hospitals for complications from illegal abortions.[82]

Physicians again took up abortion as a crusade—only this time, they sought to decriminalize the procedure, to provide safe and sanitary healthcare to women. As the ones responsible for caring for women after their bungled procedures, many physicians spoke out about the unnecessary damage that was being done across the country to young women who saw abortion as their only option. Clearly, given the conditions, the risk, and the expense, women who sought out abortions were desperate to end their pregnancies. In 1962, the American Law Institute drew up model legislation that aimed to reform the existing legal code to allow for limited access to legal abortion for "conditions that threatened the physical or mental health of the woman, in cases of severely deformed fetuses, and for rape or incest."[83]

Despite the law organization's purported intention to seek meaningful reforms to the country's abortion laws, its proposed reforms had several drawbacks. Not only did the reforms conform to the justification framework of abortion by seeking to establish additional reasons that would justify abortion, they also failed to address the primary reason that women were seeking abortions in the 1960s and the primary reason that women seek abortions today—birth control. In 1967, an estimated one million women had had abortions, and the majority were married women with children. As is the case today, disadvantaged women of color bore the brunt of the abhorrent and misogynist abortion policies in effect before *Roe v. Wade*. In New York in 1967, some 42 percent of all maternal deaths were the result of illegal abortions. Of those maternal deaths, half were black, 44 percent were Puerto Rican, and only 6 percent were white. Of the legal abortions performed that same year in New York hospitals, 93 percent were white women who could afford a private room.[84]

The criminalization of abortion clearly presented a grave public-health threat. Arguments over the proper response appeared to waver between reforming the existing laws or repealing them. Legislation rooted in either a reform or a repeal tactic was introduced in state houses across the country. Groups that promoted a feminist or women's health agenda like Planned Parenthood and the YWCA supported repeal when it became clear that the reform agenda was simply going to leave too many women without access to legal abortion services. Members of the mostly male

AMA still thought physicians needed to be the ones to sign off on whether a woman's request was justified—though they did advocate expanding the reasons to include social and economic issues.[85] In April 1970, the first bill to make it through a state legislature was a compromise bill in New York. It kept abortion in the penal code but allowed women to decide whether to have an abortion through the first twenty-four weeks of pregnancy, after which time abortion was banned unless it would save the mother's life.[86] The New York bill became the model legislation for other states and ultimately the model for the Supreme Court's decision in *Roe v. Wade* less than three years later. *Roe v. Wade* nullified all existing state laws on abortion and stood as the law of the land for almost twenty years, until *Planned Parenthood v. Casey* in 1992 opened the door to the possibility of state regulations and the checkerboard of access and services that women across the country now face.

As this brief history shows, making abortion an illegal activity also made it a de facto immoral activity. Throughout the nineteenth and twentieth centuries, the arguments of the physicians' campaign have been woven together with Western Christian assumptions about women's sexuality to shape a framework that requires women to justify their desire to end a pregnancy. This framework has disordered our ability to think and talk thoughtfully and ethically about abortion's important role in helping women achieve some measure of order and control in their lives. In the next chapter, we will examine the flaws of this framework more deeply.

CHAPTER 6

The Tragedy of Flawed Moral Discourse

AS WE'VE SEEN, the justification framework that shapes the current abortion debate in the United States is a direct inheritance of the nineteenth-century physicians' crusade to criminalize abortion. While this campaign was almost entirely secular and neither churches nor religious leaders played any coordinated role in it, the ideas it put forth about women's place in society and women's obligations as wives and mothers were a legacy of the patriarchal interpretations of Christianity that dominated Western history. Connections to patriarchal, Christian attitudes about gender are explicit in the way that the primary crusaders described their task. Horatio Storer, the primary force behind the crusade, advocated that not only was it a married woman's responsibility to "occasionally" bear children, but pregnancy and childbearing were also "the end for which they are physiologically constituted and for which they are destined by nature."[1] This position represents neither science nor medicine but theology.

In criminalizing abortion, the physicians succeeded in codifying the moral position that abortion was a prima facie illicit action. From here on out, women and their physicians would be required to offer adequate reasons why abortion was necessary. Whereas previous centuries had seen abortion denounced for its association with sexual sin, these physicians weren't concerned with prohibiting abortion because it might hide fornication or interfere with the purpose of sexual intercourse. Instead, the moral focus of Storer and his colleagues was explicitly on their perceived expectations about how "good" wives should behave. Considering that it was largely married women who were securing abortions, the moral issue at stake was clearly not the desire to hide sexual sin. The moral issue for women was the capacity to limit their family size and to have more control over their families and their personal lives. The criminalization of abortion changed the moral framework. By making abortion an illegal activity, the decision also made it a de facto immoral activity. But on what grounds had abortion been deemed illegal and immoral? If it was no longer an issue of sexual sin, what was the moral basis for this shift?

This chapter examines the justification framework that shapes public discussion of abortion in the United States. I will describe the assumptions the framework is predicated on and its intrinsic flaws. I will also show how this flawed framework has disordered contemporary discussions about abortion.

THE FLAWED FRAMEWORK OF JUSTIFICATION

Framing abortion as a prima facie illicit action is based on two key assumptions that women who get pregnant are obligated to have a baby and that the prenate is a person. Let's examine each of these assumptions in turn.

Moral obligation of women

The deeply rooted belief that women have a moral obligation to bear children can be traced back to the creation narrative in the first chapter of Genesis. In that story, God creates humankind, male and female, in God's image. Because this feat was the last act of creation and because humans were said to be created in God's image, tradition has often described humanity as the crowning glory of creation. The story ends with God offering a blessing to the newly created humans, just as God had blessed each part of creation.

The blessing God offered to each group of living creatures was the promise of fecundity, which God also gave to the human creatures: "Be fruitful and multiply" (Genesis 1:28). From this original benediction, humans who hold these scriptures sacred have cherished the idea of having children as a blessing from God. In the early centuries of Christianity, as the new sect struggled with its developing identity in the midst of Greco-Roman culture, this idea of God's blessing of fecundity became the basis for the newly developing Christian sexual ethics.

I have already discussed how the early church fathers established the idea that sex without the possibility of procreation was sinful. The possibility of a child, understood as a blessing from God, made sexual intercourse acceptable in their eyes. This belief that the purpose of sex is childbearing also shapes a corresponding belief that women have an obligation to bear children. It is a short distance from that belief to the idea that when women get pregnant, they have a moral obligation to continue the pregnancy. The idea that childbearing and motherhood are women's proper role has played a deep and abiding role in Christian history.

Culturally and theologically, women are marked as mothers. Classically, within Christianity, women have been assigned three roles—virgin, mother, or whore. Virgins and mothers are exalted and praised for the right use of their sexuality, as defined by male religious authorities, while women who defy these religio-cultural expectations are marked as whores. Within Catholicism, Mary, the mother of Jesus, is crowned with the ultimate female power of being a virgin mother, a position that garners the sacred purity of virginity and avoids any association with the sinful act of sexual intercourse while simultaneously fulfilling women's sacred role as mother. The veneration of Mary as the paragon of women has shaped cultural expectations about women's behavior and the sacrificial nature of motherhood for centuries. These cultural expectations hold for both Protestants and Catholics because the attitudes have their roots in the early church, far before the Reformation. The cultural and theological belief that women's destiny is to be mothers can also be traced back to the story of Eve, in which traditional interpretations hold that she is punished by God with increased pain in childbearing. Her very name, in fact, denotes that she is "the mother of all living."

The expectation that women ought to desire motherhood is so deeply ingrained in our psyches that we are almost unable to recognize that our public discussion around limiting women's access to abortion is really a conversation about forced pregnancy and childbirth. In the midst of a pronatalist logic that sees women's appropriate social role as mother, our capacity to recognize the bodily integrity of women as free and autonomous human beings is eclipsed by our cultural expectation that women will and should bear children when they are pregnant. In 1984, sociologist Kristen Luker argued in her book *Abortion and the Politics of Motherhood* that the abortion debate was so deeply charged "*because it is a referendum on the place and meaning of motherhood.*"[2] Luker describes the issue as a debate between two social worlds that hold radically different visions about the meaning of women's lives.

In addition to religious and cultural expectations for women to become mothers, some Christian scholars also argue that the existence of the prenate generates a moral obligation on the part of the pregnant woman to gestate. Catholic social ethicist Lisa Cahill represents this position when she argues that people sometimes have obligations that bind them to others "in ways to which they have not explicitly consented."[3] She argues that the relationships we have with significant others in our community and social circles embody reciprocity; they require give-and-take. She understands certain relationships, such as the parent-child relationship, as being defined by nature with particular obligations. This position represents a more contemporary version of natural law theology.

While it is curious that she considers these obligations binding regardless of whether people have consented to them, she makes an enormous leap when she applies obligations implicit in a parent-child relationship to pregnancy. In so doing, Cahill is imbuing the prenate with a moral status that elicits from the pregnant woman an obligation parallel to the obligation that a mother owes to her child. Such a position assumes a false equivalency between the prenate and a child.[4] However, as we will see in a later chapter, there is no consensus about the prenate's moral status in our contemporary social, cultural, and legal world. In the absence of adequate moral categories that represent the complicated relationship between the pregnant woman and the prenate, Cahill has adapted what she sees as the most closely analogous relationship and transferred the moral obligations from one relationship to the other. There are certainly similarities, the most obvious being if the pregnant woman–prenate relationship comes to fruition, it will transform into the parent-child relationship, but there are also very real differences in these two relationships.

One way in which these relationships differ is corporeal. While both relationships include two entities, in a pregnancy, the prenate occupies the body of the pregnant woman in a way that is not analogous to any other human relationship. Philosopher Margaret Olivia Little describes the experience of being pregnant as an experience of being "inhabited." She describes the pregnant woman–prenate relationship as one so intimate that the prenate "shifts and alters the very physical boundaries of the woman's self."[5] Given the complete bodily surrender required by a pregnant woman for the gestation of the prenate, Little challenges the assumption that a pregnant woman has an obligation to continue to host the prenate. Rather than the woman owing any obligation to the prenate, the circumstances of surrendering one's whole body to the process of gestation are so absolute that it requires a woman's consent. To those who would argue that a woman's consent to having sex is tantamount to her consent to gestate a child, Little has this response:

> It's just false that consent to sex means consent to gestate. If I consent to sexual intercourse and I'm informed of the risk of impregnation (my partner hasn't claimed a phantom vasectomy, say), we can say that I consent to sexual intercourse knowing the risk of impregnation; but this doesn't mean I then consent to gestate should I become pregnant. For one thing, it's the wrong party: to consent to a man for him to have sexual intercourse with me doesn't mean I consent to the fetus for it to occupy my body. . . . Moreover, it confuses the assumption of risk with commitment about what one will do if the risk is realized. To assume the risk of impregnation is not the same as consenting to gestate rather than abort if I do become pregnant.[6]

In vitro fertilization offers another insight into the underlying misogyny of the cultural expectation that pregnant women are morally obligated to have a child. While there is much debate about what we should do, legally and morally, with the thousands of fertilized human embryos that are created through in vitro fertilization, there is no cultural presumption that the couples who created those embryos have a moral obligation to carry them to term. The primary difference between those embryos and the thousands of women who seek early medical or surgical abortions is the location of the prenate. When a prenate is physically located inside the body of a woman, the state increasingly finds it acceptable to exercise pressure on pregnant women to remain pregnant and give birth. It does not instruct the putative parents of frozen embryos that they have an obligation to give birth to the embryos that they willingly created.

The assumption that women who get pregnant have a moral obligation to bear a child reflects deeply unexamined theological attitudes about women, pregnancy, children, and parenting. Even though the idea that pregnant women ought to give birth has been the predominant moral code throughout much of human history, the idea's longevity is not evidence of its moral rightness. The corollary assumption is that women who have sex have tacitly agreed to accept the possibility of pregnancy as a consequence of their choice to be sexually active. Attempts to enforce this perceived moral obligation to carry a pregnancy to term presuppose that external forces (husbands, the state, the church, religious authorities, etc.) have the right to control women's sexuality and women's very bodies. In a twenty-first-century context, biology is not destiny and the fact that fertilization of an egg by a sperm can lead to the birth of a child does not mean, prima facie, that it will lead to a birth, that it should lead to a birth, or that a fertilized ovum or zygote has moral standing.

Fetal personhood

The second assumption supporting the justification framework is that the prenate is a person from the moment of conception and thus holds equal moral standing with the pregnant woman. In chapter 4, we saw the historical development of this position as well as the theological disagreements associated with it at different points in Christian history. More than any other idea associated with the moral position that women must justify their desire to end a pregnancy is the fundamentally theological argument that the prenate is a person. The question of personhood relates to the moral status of the prenate and is what is referred to in theological terms as an *ontological* question, or a question about what it means to be human. Ontological questions have traditionally grappled with human understandings of being, of what *is*. Much of philosophical and theological discourse has been an attempt to theorize, discuss, and to a certain extent understand the ontological reality of what it means to be human. For Christians, this conversation is deeply shaped by an understanding of covenant community and humanity's relationship with the divine.

In the latter half of the twentieth century, as scientific advancement allowed for increasingly safer and more reliable abortion procedures, these ontological concerns were directed toward questions about prenatal life (as we saw with the shift in the Roman Catholic position on abortion in 1965). People who disagreed with the decriminalization of abortion in 1973 by the Supreme Court developed an abortion-fighting strategy that hinged on the theological belief that a prenate is a person. This belief, also referred to as *fetal personhood*, holds that life or personhood begins at conception. The fetal-personhood argument is based on the theological belief that once the egg and sperm join, the prenate becomes a full member of the human community. With this membership come certain rights that need to be protected, most specifically, the prenate is viewed as having a right to life. This concept of a right to life is supported by the natural law tradition, which holds that elective abortion interrupts the natural progression of a pregnancy. Natural law also believes that pregnancy is the natural and right outcome of sexual activity, that sexual activity is only moral when located within a marriage, and that people engaging in sexual activity ought to welcome any possible pregnancy and child as part of God's intention for their life and the world.

The modern abortion debate after *Roe v. Wade* elevated attention to the moral status of the prenate in ways that have reshaped how women must respond to the question of whether their desire to end a pregnancy can be justified. While many contest the claim that abortion is not justifiable because the prenate is a person, the justification framework lends credibility to this antiabortion position by the very fact that culturally, women who have abortions are judged on their reasons for ending a pregnancy. This judging happens daily through media coverage of legislative debates, on billboards and bumper stickers, and, for many women, in their churches, in their workplaces, and even in books and movies. A framework that did not position the prenate as morally equivalent with a pregnant woman would have no reason to require women to justify their actions. The presumed status of the prenate as a person and any attendant rights associated with this status are at the heart of the requirement that women justify their desire to end a pregnancy.

The question of the moral status of the prenate is the linchpin of our collective discomfort about abortion in the United States. If the moral status of the prenate is accepted as equivalent to a pregnant woman from the moment of conception, then justifying the killing of the prenate would be a reasonable approach to thinking about the situation of abortion. If the moral status of the prenate is equivalent to a bunch of cells, then abortion requires no more thought than does a haircut.[7] For most Americans, however, our relationship with the prenate falls somewhere between affording it the status of a full human being and dismissing it as merely a bunch of cells. The difficulty is in determining how to classify and understand the moral status of the prenate. This task is complicated by several factors that are often fodder for the pro-life and pro-choice camps in the abortion debate. The three most trenchant debates revolve around whether the prenate is human, whether it is alive, and whether it is a person.

Prenates, of course, are human. Clearly their tissue is human and they grow to fullness inside a human woman's body. But even though they are human, they are not human beings in the same way that pregnant women are human beings. While we regularly claim that the prenatal heart begins to beat at four weeks and that prospective parents can listen to the heartbeat at ten weeks, this observation is inaccurate, given that the prenatal heart is not a heart in the sense that you or I have a heart. The prenatal heart is still in development, as is the rest of the prenatal body.[8] Evidence of a beating heart is one of the primary signs that people use to argue that the prenate is alive and that ending a pregnancy is tantamount to killing. But before viability, prenates cannot exist outside a woman's womb. If it cannot exist independently, can it be said to be "alive"? This brings up the question of what we mean by *alive*. In tautological fashion, to be alive is, perhaps, not to be dead, but still, this language and these concepts just don't seem to apply in the situation of pregnancy, where the prenate is still in formation. Perhaps even more importantly, before birth, prenates are still dependent on a woman's body for life. Until they have drawn breath, expanded their lungs, and activated all their own vital bodily functions—prenates are utterly dependent and utterly *not-yet*. These questions of when life begins and ends and what constitutes personhood are primarily theological and philosophical questions, not biological. We will take up these theological and philosophical questions more fully in the next chapter, but for now, we should recognize how the justification of abortion is contingent on the positioning of the prenate in a status that is morally equivalent to, or even higher than, that of the pregnant woman.

Acknowledging the theological and philosophical nature of the moral status of the prenate will only become more important as medical technology increases the capacity to care for prematurely born infants and the measure of viability is pushed further and further back. The possibility of gestating a prenate outside a woman's body, a process known as *ectogenesis*, is no longer a question of science fiction but one of technological innovation. In a world where prenates can be gestated outside women's wombs, the human community will need to grapple with the profound ethical question of whether we should do so just because we can. Even more pointedly, in those circumstances, does the state (or any other outside force) have the authority to harvest fertilized eggs or prenates from women's bodies and gestate them against a woman's will?

Within a rhetorical framework of fetal personhood that frames abortion as an issue of killing—and killing an "innocent," no less—the requirement that women justify their abortions seems reasonable. However, for people who reject the idea that a prenate at any stage is morally equivalent to a pregnant woman, the moral calculus shifts. When we decenter the prenate from the equation and approach the situation from a neutral perspective, we can see that the moral dilemma is not whether abortion is justified, but what to do in the face of an unwanted or problem pregnancy. My analysis is not intended to ignore or reject the question of the moral status of the prenate, but rather to show how the moral conversation changes when we challenge the assumptions in the current abortion debate and are empowered to ask different moral questions.

DANGERS OF A JUSTIFICATION FRAMEWORK

Considering its assumptions that women have a moral obligation to carry any given pregnancy to term and its belief in fetal personhood, the justification framework is inherently biased against women and toward the prenate. It is thus intrinsically flawed as a logical argument: it presupposes the wrongness of a particular action instead of examining the moral evidence before making a judgment. Equally problematic, the justification framework has disrupted our public conversation about women's health and fertility in at least four ways. It has distorted our public moral discourse, denied the complexity of the decisions that women make, misrepresented the nature of the moral problem, and harmed women in the deepest and most damaging ways. Let us now examine the harmful consequences of these disruptions.

Distortion of public moral discourse

By framing the issue of abortion as a question of whether women have legitimate reasons to terminate their pregnancy, the justification framework generated the contemporary political divisions that we refer to as pro-life and pro-choice. Sociologist Gene Burns describes these positions as two competing frames dominating the contemporary abortion debate in the United States.[9] The media certainly employ this binary framework when covering the topic in the news. It is also how legislators talk about the issue in their speeches and on the floor of statehouses across the country. And the binary framework is used by the two sides that are fighting to influence the public's mind on the issue.

Conventional wisdom holds that public opinion polls gauging whether people identify as pro-life or pro-choice can indicate how Americans feel about the morality of abortion. In the mid-1990s, when Gallup began surveying for this question, 56 percent of the population identified as pro-choice, whereas only 33 percent identified as pro-life. These numbers quickly began to approach an equilibrium, and although the majority position has shifted back and forth by degrees in the years since, the 2016 poll showed 47 percent of respondents identifying as pro-choice and 46 percent identifying as pro-life.[10]

Determining public opinion about abortion is a tricky thing, given that responses to polls can be manipulated by how various questions are posed.

For abortion, the social framing of the issue as a binary framework divided between the pro-choice and pro-life camps is reinforced by the very options offered to the public in polling questions and in public discussions of abortion. When the issue of abortion is framed as a debate, we are reduced to binary thinking. We are forced into taking one of two sides. The pollsters ask, "Are you pro-choice or pro-life?" when they call or send out questionnaires. Of course, the pollsters are simply reflecting the larger public framing of the topic. Within the dominant discourse, you are either pro-choice or pro-life. In this framework, you are either for women or for babies. The divisive nature of this framing is evident in the false struggle cast between the rights of a pregnant woman for self-determination and the prenate's right to life.

The pro-choice and pro-life frames offer a glimpse into the different moral worlds of the people who use these frames and how they understand and define the problem. On the pro-life side, the emphasis on life demonstrates that the issue is framed primarily as one of the moral status of the prenate. For this side, the issue is the protection of "innocent life." On the pro-choice side, the language indicates a focus primarily on the autonomy and moral agency of the pregnant woman. For this side, the issue is about pregnant women's ability to exercise control over their bodies and what happens to them. Although many other issues arise as the debates develop, examining these two frames allows us to see that abortion is primarily about protecting babies for the pro-life side and primarily about protecting women's rights for the pro-choice side. This artificial divide into two dominant camps forces people to choose a side.

These categories have never adequately represented the complexity of the ethical nature of the abortion debate, not least because the categories and terms themselves are incommensurable: one category is a theological position, and the other a legal position. The pro-life frame refers to a moral position based on the theological belief that the personhood of the prenate begins at fertilization and therefore that all prenates possess equal moral status with pregnant women. This moral position then informs its adherents' approach to the question of whether abortion should be legal. Because this position is rooted in a theological belief about the ontological status of the prenate, pro-life becomes an absolutist position. It is impossible for this group to compromise on the question of abortion, and thus, very few people in this camp simultaneously identify as pro-choice.

The pro-choice frame refers to the attitude that its proponents hold toward the legal status of abortion in a democratic society. Given the implications of making abortion illegal (forcing women to be pregnant, the danger of illegal abortions, the threat to women's health, etc.), people who hold this position believe that a society that supports freedom and respect for women's lives must continue to maintain legal access to abortion. However, because the pro-choice position is oriented toward addressing the legal question, it does not address the morality of abortion. This focus on legality helps explain the seeming contradiction between polls showing that three-quarters of people believe that abortion needs to remain legal while roughly half think that abortion is immoral.[11] A 2013 Pew poll identified 18 percent of the population who thought that abortion was immoral but that *Roe v. Wade* should not be overturned.[12] That is about one-fifth of the country who identify both as pro-choice (regarding the legal question) and as pro-life regarding their moral position. Many pro-choice Christians consider their support of both pregnant women and a woman's decision to terminate a pregnancy an expression of supporting life, namely, the life and dignity of the pregnant woman. This group rejects the pro-life lobby's hijacking of the value of "life" in this debate.

The inadequacy of these terms and the binary framing of the issue are being contested in two ways. First, religious leaders on both sides of the aisle challenge the inadequacy of the binary framing of public discussions of the most trenchant moral and social issues that need to be addressed. Sister Joan Chittister, a prominent Roman Catholic Benedictine nun, addressed the inadequacy of our terminology: "I do not believe that just because you're opposed to abortion, that that makes you pro-life. In fact, I think in many cases, your morality is deeply lacking if all you want is a child born but not a child fed, not a child educated, not a child housed. And why would I think that you don't? Because you don't want any tax money to go there. That's not pro-life. That's pro-birth. We need a much broader conversation on what the morality of pro-life is."[13]

On the other side of the aisle, Frances Kissling, cofounder of Catholics for Choice, said, "The fetus is more visible than ever before, and the abortion-rights movement needs to accept its existence and its value. It may not have a right to life, and its value may not be equal to that of the pregnant woman, but ending the life of a fetus is not a morally insignificant event."[14] Both of these religious leaders give voice to the gut feelings of broad sectors of the public who are frustrated with the polarization of the debate and a perceived extremism underlying each of the sides. Chittister is interested in deeper ethical debates about what it means socially and politically to say that we support life and children, and Kissling wants more meaningful discussion of the moral status of the prenate. Developing both these areas of moral dialogue rejects the dualistic nature of the justification framework and seeks a different way of thinking ethically and morally about the issues at hand.

The second challenge to this binary frame comes from individuals who reject both labels as inadequate for describing their beliefs and attitudes about abortion. When given the opportunity, people increasingly identity as both pro-choice and pro-life. A recent poll by the Public Religion Research Institute found that 70 percent of Americans say that the term *pro-choice* describes them somewhat or very well, and the same poll found that two-thirds of the same group also identified somewhat or very well with the term *pro-life*.[15] A research firm studying focus groups on abortion on behalf of Planned Parenthood found that people rejected the labels because neither label fit. "I'm neither pro-choice nor pro-life, I'm pro-whatever-the-situation is," said one woman in a focus group. Another said, "There should be three: pro-life, pro-choice and something in the middle that helps people understand circumstances. . . . It's not just black or white, there's grey."[16]

The binary framing of the abortion debate arose in the post-*Roe* era as a response to the justification framework. In its most extreme form, the pro-life response is a resounding no to the question of whether abortion can be justified. For people who approach the question of abortion through a pro-life frame, justification is impossible when you consider abortion the murder of innocent children. On the pro-choice side, the response is a resounding yes to the question of whether abortion can be justified. When the issue is framed as a violation of women's bodily integrity and forcing women to bear children against their will, there can be no doubt that women must be allowed to decide whether to continue a pregnancy. The extreme positions demand either that pregnant women must sacrifice themselves to save their "babies" or that they have the right to abortion on demand at any point of gestation. In their most extreme forms, the pro-life frame's emphasis on the "unborn baby" supplants any meaningful recognition of pregnant women as worthy moral actors, and the pro-choice frame's singular attention to women's rights to bodily integrity eclipses recognition of any potential moral worth of the prenate. These frames are inadequate for dealing with the moral complexity of abortion and distort our public conversation.

Universal appeals that deny the complexity of abortion decisions

The binary nature of the justification frame also pushes each side to stake out a universal claim: One side says abortion is always wrong, because of a prenate's right to life. The other side says abortion is always right, because of a woman's right to control her own body. The reality of abortion is much more complicated than this framework allows. Abortion is a moral situation where the circumstances of women's lives define what is at stake morally.

Because the justification frame creates two oppositional and absolute moral positions, it precludes the sort of critical and rigorous analysis that ought to characterize our approach to social problems as Christian social ethicists, people of faith, citizens, and legislators in a modern democratic state. Making sense of our world and the social problems related to pregnancy—planned and unplanned, wanted and unwanted—requires more sophisticated and nuanced moral, philosophical, and theological thinking than the current terms of the debate allow.

Women don't have babies in the abstract; they bear them in the real-life circumstances of a complicated and imperfect world. There are some who have criticized women and their partners for seeking perfection in their children and attempting to play God by intervening in pregnancies or by terminating pregnancies where the prenates are not perfect. This attitude not only trivializes the very serious physiological problems of some prenates, but also implies that the parents making these very difficult decisions are doing so casually and thoughtlessly. In an imperfect world, women must consider the circumstances of their lives and whether they could meet their parental obligations if they accepted a particular pregnancy. Furthermore, in any pregnancy, financial issues, domestic violence, education level, and emotional readiness for motherhood are morally relevant factors a woman needs to consider when deciding whether to have a child.

Decisions about whether to terminate a pregnancy or to carry a pregnancy to term are made within the context of individual women's lives and are the embodiment of their hopes and dreams. For many women, terminating a pregnancy is a positive moral step within the story of her life. The social and moral meaning of pregnancy, childbirth, abortion, and parenting can only be examined and understood within the whole of a particular woman's life, which includes her family, her community, her faith, and her calling, all of which represent overlapping and intersecting relationships and obligations. A more appropriate starting point for considering the legal and moral status of abortion, then, is within the larger context of women's reproductive lives.

Misrepresentation of the moral problem

The justification framework distorts the discourse in another substantive way. Requiring women to justify their decision not to have a child defines an unwanted pregnancy as a moral dilemma. While certainly any woman with an unwanted pregnancy would rather that she had not become pregnant in the first place, framing the decision as a moral dilemma indicates that a woman with an unwanted pregnancy must choose between two bad options. This framing of abortion as the sad, unfortunate, tragic, or even forgivable choice that women might make in some circumstances contributes to the ongoing assault of women who choose abortions in our culture today.

If there were not a presumption of an obligation to carry to term, a woman would be free to make a *decision* about whether to continue the pregnancy. For some women, this decision might very well be a moral dilemma. For these women, it is important to provide resources to help them make responsible moral decisions and to provide the necessary material support (financial, emotional, physical, etc.) to enable them to have an early abortion or to carry their pregnancy to term. Only when women have access to the resources they need to support a decision to continue a pregnancy and raise a child, and to the resources they need to have an abortion, will they be able to fully exercise their moral agency in uncoerced ways.

But abortion is not necessarily a moral dilemma. What makes abortion a moral dilemma for some women is their attitude about the moral value of the prenate. For these women, the decision to continue or terminate a pregnancy may be a moral dilemma. In such cases, women must carefully weigh the competing moral obligations they face, including obligations to existing children, to themselves, and to partners, parents, or significant others in their lives, as well as various other considerations unique to their own circumstances. But these women may still decide to have an abortion in ways that are morally good.

For other women, an unwanted pregnancy does not present a moral dilemma. For these women, the decision to terminate their pregnancy is the obvious moral choice. In circumstances where pregnancy or parenting a child, or an additional child, represents undue physical, financial, or psychological hardship, the possibility of an abortion represents a moral good that secures a woman's well-being and often the well-being of her existing family. For many women, abortion is *not* a moral dilemma. It is not a dilemma, because they do not want to be pregnant (for any number of reasons), the procedure is legal in this country, and we have the medical knowledge of how to safely terminate their pregnancy. These women feel no moral obligation to carry every pregnancy to term. They are simply sexually active women who have gotten pregnant.

In fact, in many situations, it might even be considered immoral to carry a pregnancy to term. Women who are addicted to drugs or seriously mentally ill may have deep-rooted physical and medical problems that are potentially dangerous to a developing prenate. Most women in these circumstances are in no position to maintain a healthy pregnancy, much less to raise a child. Women who are already struggling to care for one or more children because of economic deprivation, an abusive spouse or partner, or other challenges may very well decide that bringing another child into those circumstances is immoral. It bears repeating, however, that only the women themselves are in a position to assess their circumstances and evaluate the moral nature of the options that they face. Many poor women embrace unplanned or unexpected pregnancies and welcome the child into their lives. As we consider what sort of framework should replace the justification framework, we should remember that it must not only respect women and their moral agency but also provide the necessary support that women need to make positive moral decisions about whether to continue their pregnancies.

Harm to women

When I began working on this project, I talked with a number of pastors to get a sense of how they have encountered the issue of abortion in their ministry. The most vivid response came from an African American pastor who answered immediately with a single word. "Shame," she said. "I hope your work will address the deep shame that many Christian women feel when they have an abortion." Studies on abortion stigma indicate that two-thirds of women who have had abortions think that other people would look down on them if those people knew about the abortions, even when the women feel comfortable about their own decisions.[17] One woman said, "You're supposed to feel totally ashamed and you're supposed to feel alone and you're supposed to feel like you murdered someone and you're supposed to punish yourself. And I was just like not prepared for that. I don't feel that that is true for myself. I don't have the experience that I murdered anything but I do feel like I'm supposed to feel that way."[18]

The fear of negative responses to the knowledge of their abortions leads many women to keep their experiences a secret, often from family and close friends who they think will disapprove, perhaps sharing their experiences with only one or two people in their social circles. While studies show that 95 percent of women do not regret their abortion decisions, this secrecy can exacerbate the clandestine feeling of abortion and contribute to the internalization of shame, a dominant emotion in the justification framework.[19] In her study of abortion stigma, sociologist Kristen Shellenberg found that many women, even those who felt confident about their decisions to have an abortion, were deeply affected by the opinions of their families and friends. One of the women she spoke to explained that if her family members found out about the abortion, they would be disgusted and disappointed in her. The woman said this reaction would make her feel ashamed and worthless, and that being around them afterward would cause her to feel disgusted with herself.[20]

Our moral sensibilities are shaped by the very rhetoric of the conversation. Too often, rhetoric around abortion is predicated on deeply misogynist notions about women, mothers, and mothering. The trope of the uncaring, abusive, self-absorbed, selfish, hateful, jealous (take your pick) mother is deep-seated and vicious in our culture. These adjectives are often used in relation to women who end their pregnancies, as we saw clearly in earlier discussions about cultural assumptions undergirding the public's antipathy toward "abortions of convenience" and "abortion as birth control." This denunciation of women who run counter to the cultural script of mothers as selfless, caring, and tirelessly devoted to their children is a part of the right-wing attempt to define the norms and characteristics of motherhood, parenting, and family in the US.

When we allow our thinking to be shaped by the presupposition that abortion is wrong *unless* we can offer adequate justification, we have created a cultural climate in which the decisions and behavior of all pregnant women are subject to public moral scrutiny. Ultimately, a justification framework supports and promotes the ongoing judging and policing of women's sexual activity and the enforcement of biased gender expectations about sexuality, family, bodies, bodily integrity, and moral obligations.

JUSTIFICATION AS SOCIAL CONTROL

We have seen both the intrinsic flaws in the logic of the justification framework and evidence of how this framework has disordered our public moral discourse and public understanding of the issues associated with women's sexual behavior, fertility, pregnancy, and abortion. We have also seen many ways in which women's behavior is controlled within this model. But is this control simply a consequence of this paradigm, or is it the logic on which the entire system depends?

To answer this question, let us begin by examining the ramifications of what it means to say that abortion can be justified. If abortion is a prima facie moral wrong, then there are some circumstances where this moral imperative can be set aside. What is the logic by which some abortions are considered allowable? As we have seen, there is widespread social acceptance that prenatal health, rape, incest, and the life of the mother (the PRIM reasons) can justify abortions. This social norm raises two important questions: What makes these reasons justifiable? And what exactly does *justified* mean in these situations? The case of a woman's health is a bit different from the other three, so let's set it aside for the moment. The three remaining grounds for abortion—prenatal health, rape, and incest—have a common focus on the psychological impact of these pregnancies and births on the pregnant woman.

Let's begin with rape and incest. The logic behind allowing women to have abortions in the case of rape or incest is that the emotional burden of daily living with a pregnancy that resulted from a rape or incest is too traumatic and abusive to require women to continue pregnancies under these circumstances. In these situations, the termination of a pregnancy is seen as justified when it is weighed against the psychological harm inflicted on the woman who was required to carry and bear the child of her abuser. This compassionate response to the survivors of sexual crimes fits into the larger cultural narrative about women's sexuality outlined in chapter 4. The idea that women should be responsible for their consensual sexual activity is code for the expectation that women who get pregnant have a moral obligation to have a baby. The fact that women who experienced rape or incest did not engage in consensual sex allows the public to accept these abortions as justified. The allowances for rape and incest highlight how normative expectations about female sexuality and behavior dominate how we think about what qualifies as adequate justification to terminate a pregnancy. The public continues to demand these exceptions in any legislation that seeks to regulate or diminish women's access to abortion services.

In the exception for prenatal health-related issues, there are two broad categories to consider. The first category are those labeled *incompatible with life*. This phrase is a sanitized way of saying that if the pregnancy in question were carried to term, the baby would not be able to live outside the womb. Little is known about many of these health problems or their causes. Prenates in this category often have a range of developmental anomalies whereby various parts of their body have failed to develop in healthy and functional ways. These prenates will die either during the pregnancy, during the birth process, or within several hours after birth.

Certainly, it is a personal decision for women about whether they wish to continue such a pregnancy. Some women choose to continue these pregnancies with the full knowledge of their prenate's terminal prognosis. However, much like the public response to rape and incest, compassion for the psychological burden of carrying a pregnancy to term knowing your child will die during or immediately after birth has resulted in broad public acceptance of abortion in these cases. Compelling a woman in such a case to carry a pregnancy to term is recognized as a cruel punishment that would, in many cases, cause prolonged grief and emotional pain to the woman for no apparent gain. Likewise, forcing a woman in such a case to terminate the pregnancy is equally cruel. Different women will respond to the terminal diagnosis of their prenate in different ways. In these situations, compassion for the pregnant women drives the desire to let them decide whether they wish to continue or terminate their pregnancy.

A second set of exceptions are prenatal diagnoses of chromosomal abnormalities, genetic disorders, and other situations in which the potential child might have a range of physical and mental disabilities. These conditions range in severity from Tay-Sachs disease, which usually results in the death of a child by age four, to sickle cell anemia, which has a longer survival rate (about half the people with sickle cell live into their fifties) but results in a life filled with acute and chronic health problems. Additionally, the severity of impairment can also range within a particular diagnosis. Down syndrome, for instance, has a range of severity from mild to profound, and no existing prenatal tests can confirm the level of impairment. With some exceptions, the social consensus related to termination of pregnancies for a wide range of prenatal health issues has been to respect the right of pregnant women and their partners to decide whether to continue a pregnancy in these situations. While some of this attitude undoubtedly reflects unacknowledged prejudices against people with disabilities, it also recognizes the physical, mental, and economic challenges posed by parenting a child with a severe disability as well as a respect for parental rights in assessing potential quality-of-life issues. In these cases, in addition to recognizing the emotional and psychological burdens that parenting a severely disabled child might pose, the public also allows issues of economics and quality of life to enter into the equation.

The public's willingness to accept abortion in these situations demonstrates its practical acknowledgment of the different moral statuses of the prenate and the pregnant woman. Here we begin to see the answer to the second question posed above—what exactly does it mean to say that abortion is justified in these circumstances? If people believed in the equivalent moral status of the prenate and the pregnant woman, then no circumstances would justify the killing of one to save the life of the other. The idea of infanticide is not even on the political spectrum of possibilities and is unlikely to be supported in the United States. While philosopher Peter Singer has argued that newborns should not be considered persons until thirty days after birth so that the practice of infanticide might become more common in the case of severely disabled babies, this position has not found any traction in the public sphere.[21] Widespread support for retaining legal abortion in this country alongside a clear and evident state interest in protecting babies indicates cultural recognition of a moral distinction between prenatal life and neonatal life. The public, the state, and the courts clearly distinguish between the termination of a pregnancy and infanticide.

The saving of a woman's life as the final commonly shared acceptable reason for termination further illustrates the general belief that there is a difference between prenatal and neonatal life. The predominant belief and practice in this country is that abortion is justifiable to save the life of a pregnant woman. In no other moral situations is it acceptable to kill one human being to save the life of another. This, in fact, is the position of the Roman Catholic Church. Because the official Roman Catholic position on abortion is not only that human life begins at conception but that the prenate possesses full moral status, the church opposes any action intended to end a pregnancy for any reason. However, the principle of *double effect* does allow for an action to save the life of a pregnant woman, even if that action causes the loss of her pregnancy. In order for the conditions of double effect to be met, the primary intent of the action must not be the termination of the pregnancy but must be the saving of the life of the pregnant woman.

A recent abortion case in Phoenix tested the limits of the double-effect principle as well as public tolerance for such a principle in light of the corresponding value of saving a woman's life. In 2009, the ethics committee at a Catholic hospital encountered the case of a twenty-seven-year-old woman who was eleven weeks pregnant and experiencing acute pulmonary hypertension. Her attending physician estimated that the likelihood of her dying if the pregnancy continued was near 100 percent. The committee, including Margaret McBride, a Catholic nun in the order of the Sisters of Mercy and a hospital administrator, approved the decision to terminate her pregnancy through abortion. McBride was automatically excommunicated from the church for this decision, which was in violation of the Vatican's directive against direct abortion. Ironically, if the attending physician had performed a hysterectomy, a far more serious, dangerous, and irreversible surgical procedure, the action would have met the requirement of double effect. After the situation became public, outrage over how Bishop Thomas Olmstead handled the case was widespread. In addition to questioning the wisdom of excommunicating Sister McBride, prominent bioethicist Jacob Appel questioned whether pregnant women were safe when seeking medical care at Catholic hospitals; he warned women against taking their chances to find out.[22]

As someone who gave birth to my first child in a Catholic women's hospital because it was supposedly where the best obstetric care in town was available, this incident was particularly troubling. Although it was easy for me to remove the crucifix from the hospital wall when I arrived in the room (Protestants prefer the empty cross representing resurrection rather than the Roman Catholic crucifix, which emphasizes Jesus's death), it never occurred to me that if my labor and delivery had gone south and my life had been in danger, the doctors would have been required to sacrifice my life to try to save my child's. The ramifications of the Roman Catholic Church's prohibition even on emergency abortions to save the life of the mother are troubling, given that one in six people get their care from a Catholic institution, and ten of the largest twenty-five hospital systems in the country are Catholic. The church's extreme position that prenatal life and the life of the pregnant woman are equivalent lies in direct contrast to American law and public opinion.

When we look for the thread that holds together support for these seemingly disparate reasons to allow abortion, we find that compassion toward the pregnant woman transcends the assumed moral prohibition against abortion. This compassion is directly linked to patriarchal expectations about women's sexual behavior and their role as mothers. In the cases of rape or incest, because the pregnancy is a result of an unwanted violation of a woman's supposed sexual purity, she is not expected to honor her assumed moral obligation to continue any pregnancy that resulted from this sexual encounter.

In cases where the health of the prenate or the pregnant woman is in danger, compassion is extended to these woman *as mothers*. These health-related cases can be described as wanted pregnancies; the women have accepted their pregnancies and embraced their role as mothers. Only after they have accepted their expected role as mothers did a problem arise in their pregnancy. Under these conditions, the compassion that is extended is in line with what are considered reasonable expectations of pregnancy and parenting. While self-sacrifice continues to dominate expectations about motherhood, there is little cultural support for the notion that women must sacrifice their very lives for the sake of their prenates. The compassion that connects these exceptions, allowing for a breach in the supposed moral injunction against abortion, is only invoked for women who conform to traditional expectations about women's sexual behavior and motherhood.

The social control of women is clearly the foundation of the justification framework. Moreover, requiring women to have babies when they get pregnant is a blatant form of social control that has no cultural parallel for men.

The justification framework of abortion creates a culture of control that simultaneously silences and shames women for exercising their legal right to an abortion without ever deeply considering the real social problems that contribute to women's decisions to end their pregnancies. In a justification approach, people spend energy on arguing whether abortion is right or wrong and what circumstances create an acceptable moral situation for allowing women access to abortion services. The whole conversation is framed as one of judgment. Is it any wonder, then, that the cultural climate surrounding the topic of abortion is so judgmental?

The implications of the intrinsic logic of justification and its technique of shaming are rarely acknowledged: pregnancy is the result of sex; women who get pregnant must continue their pregnancies; therefore, women who do not want to have babies should not have sex. The stigmatizing rhetoric of the justification framework implies while PRIM abortions are allowed, forced pregnancy and childbirth are acceptable in all other cases. This argument is a continuation of nearly two thousand years of Christian attempts to control women's sexual behavior. While we regularly require women to justify their desire to end a pregnancy, there is no parallel requirement for women to justify keeping a pregnancy and subsequently becoming a mother. There are no competency tests that a person must pass, no age requirements, no health screenings or proof of employment or economic means. The state, quite rightly, does not interfere in women's pregnancies or reproduction *except in cases where women do not want to be pregnant or continue their pregnancy.* In fact, as we saw in the previous chapter, state interventions to limit women's fertility through forced sterilizations have since been judged immoral and abusive. Nevertheless, the fact that we do not require women to justify keeping a pregnancy or becoming a mother is further evidence of the extent to which women's capacity to mother is culturally accepted as a normative expectation for women, particularly those who are already pregnant.

The expectation that women are morally obliged to continue their pregnancies is supported in no small part by the theological belief that personhood begins at conception. This theological belief, though not shared by even the majority of Christians in this country, much less by many of the millions of women being denied access to quality reproductive healthcare worldwide, has helped shape public policy. For this reason, we must recognize the implicit theological foundations of abortion regulations that seek to restrict women's access to services.

As we have seen, the justification framework affects reproductive justice in several ways. The framework is biased against women and toward the prenate. It has generated extreme social consequences for women and for public dialogue. And it primarily aims to control women's social behavior. These reasons make clear why the justification framework needs to be rejected and replaced with a more justice-oriented approach to pregnancy, abortion, and parenting. This requires a new theory for thinking about pregnancy, the pregnant body, and prenatal life. We will take up this task in the next chapter.

Moving from Justification to Justice

CHAPTER 7

Reimagining Pregnancy

IN 1965, LENNART NILSSON introduced the prenate to the world in the pages of *Life* magazine with his groundbreaking photographs of life inside the womb.[1] With subtitles like "Weightless Ride in a Salty Sac" and images floating free in black backgrounds with starry skies, tethered to a life-support system through a visible umbilical cord, these images were crafted to evoke space travel and cast the prenate as the intrepid astronaut on an epic journey.[2]

For the first time in history, people could visualize what had always been hidden within women's bodies. Women's role as mediators between the prenate and the outside world was stripped away overnight as the whole world gazed inside women's bodies at the growing prenatal forms. Ironically, the very images that have come to symbolize prenatal life in the minds of people around the world were actually dead embryos and fetuses that had been surgically removed, rendering their amnion eerily more shroud than protective sac.[3] Nilsson collected the specimens from women's clinics in Stockholm, in Göteborg, and elsewhere across Sweden and then manipulated the fingers, hands, and tiny bodies to photograph them in visually stunning ways.[4]

Twenty-five years later, a follow-up *Life* story of Nilsson's new work exploited the public's fantastical identification of prenatal life with space exploration. The piece narrated a set of microscopic images of fertilization and implantation with rhetoric that moved beyond space travel to full-on colonization:

> Two hours. Like an eerie planet floating through space, a woman's egg or ovum has been ejected by one of her ovaries into a fallopian tube. . . . [A]bout twelve hours later the cell begins its incredible nine-month journey by taking the first step . . . down the fallopian tube toward the uterus.
>
> Two days . . . the blastocyst is attempting to pass through the narrowest opening of the fallopian tube just before entering the uterus. The space is so restricted the embryo can barely jostle and squeeze its way through.
>
> Four days . . . Gliding into the uterus . . . feeling its way for a comfortable home to spend the next 39 weeks. . . .
>
> Eight days. The blastocyst has landed! Like a lunar module, the embryo facilitates its landing on the uterus.[5]

Although both articles seek to establish similarities between the prenate and the space explorer, the 1990 version has not only erased the prenate's dependency on its mother, but has made the woman wholly alien, wholly other. The blastocyst is the intrepid explorer, its mission to conquer planet Uterus.

The radical cultural shift in how the public imagines the prenate in the twenty-five years between these two articles is evident in the differing understandings of the prenate's moral status in each article. The 1965 article claims, "In the Western world a person's life is reckoned from the day he comes out of the womb," whereas the German edition of the 1990 article now claims that a prenate is a human being at the moment of implantation: "Just a few moments ago there was nothing but a free-floating mass of cells. . . . Now communication has been established. The anti-bodies of the pregnant woman withdraw. 'We are accepted, we may stay!' It is a human being, one hundred percent."[6]

The blastocyst has managed to allay the threat of planet Uterus by forcing the hostile antibodies that are pervasive throughout the solar system known as Pregnant Woman to withdraw. The blastocyst has been cast as the hero who must struggle against all odds to tame and subdue the hostile forces of Pregnant Woman so that the colonization of planet Uterus might be successful.

The language in these *Life* magazine articles reflects an extreme version of how patriarchal perspectives and the male gaze have shaped our cultural understanding of pregnancy and prenatal life. Positioning the prenate as under potential attack at any moment from the hostile forces of its "host" constructs the pregnant woman and the prenate as antagonists. This viewpoint holds as much for the pro-life side (which sees the prenate as potentially under attack by its mother) as it does for the pro-choice side (when it frames the prenate as an unwanted aggressor that a woman has a right to repel). This kind of antagonism is rooted in an approach to pregnancy that seeks to understand the moral status of the prenate in light of a logic of individualism. Namely, when each entity—the pregnant woman and the prenate—is marked as separate individuals, they are positioned as potential antagonists. It is also this logic of individualism that undergirds claims of fetal personhood.

At the same time, the idea that an eight- or nine-month prenate is morally equivalent to that same fertilized egg doesn't feel right either. For many people, the moral status of the prenate is unclear. Part of the problem is the very limitation of our language and our moral theories. The moral boundaries between the pregnant woman and the prenate are more fluid than contemporary debate allows, and the liminal moral status of prenates simply does not fit into our extant moral lexicon, no matter how much we have tried to force it.

When we imagine pregnancy outside the male gaze and from the perspective of the pregnant woman and her body, we recognize how the pregnant body is ontologically different from both the male body and the not-pregnant female body. Similarly, the prenatal body is also ontologically different from the bodies of newborns, infants, or children. Both the pregnant body and the prenate defy the strict logic of individualism and exist instead within a liminal space defined by the potential for creation of new life. But potential is not actuality; many things can happen between conception and birth. In fact, 60 percent of fertilized eggs are spontaneously aborted before pregnancy is ever confirmed, and another 10 percent are lost in miscarriages.[7]

The problem that we face is a problem of moral imagination. For so long, we have been taught to think about women, sex, pregnancy, and abortion in particular ways. What we need is new moral language that expresses the complexity of pregnant bodies, liminal spaces, and the moral status of the prenate.

In this chapter, I reimagine pregnancy from the perspective of women and their reproductive bodies. The lives of most women today are not defined by their pregnancies; instead, pregnancies are chapters in a larger life story. Reimagining pregnancy from this perspective reframes it within the longer horizon of a woman's reproductive and sexual life. The category of liminality offers a theoretical framework for recognizing the moral status of the prenate as intrinsically valuable for its potential for life without reifying it as existing or actual life. The first task is to understand how the social construction of fetal personhood functions to erase the pregnant woman.

ERASURE OF PREGNANT WOMEN

Not only have the past fifty years revealed the hidden life of the prenate, but the prenate's visible and increasingly public status has become a major cause of shifting social attitudes about its moral status. Our cultural imagination about life inside the womb has only continued to accelerate as the technological development of fetal sonography, 3-D imaging, and fetal surgery have combined to create a hitherto unprecedented familiarity with prenatal life. Furthermore, these ubiquitous prenatal images have had an impact on women's experiences of pregnancy as well as their attitude and relationship with their developing prenate.

Prenatal images have erupted into our popular consciousness. As ultrasound technology has become more routinized in twenty-first-century prenatal care, most women in the US have numerous chances to see the prenate growing within them before they give birth. Pregnant women are also increasingly encouraged to talk to their prenate, read it stories, and play music for it. Women have always interacted with the moving entity inside their bodies and perhaps attributed characteristics to the prenate because of its activity. But today, the process of visualizing the prenate has encouraged a more fulsome construction of prenatal identity. The images allow parents to attribute personality and human characteristics in utero: "We saw the baby kicking his legs like he was riding a bicycle and we were like, 'Oh isn't that cute!'"[8] These images seek to tap into people's existing relationship with similar images—images of their own or their families' or friends' ultrasound pictures—and the affective response associated with wanted pregnancies.

This social construction of prenatal independence and fetal personhood is facilitated by the almost-complete erasure of the pregnant woman from these images—an erasure that began with those iconic images in 1965. As the pregnant woman's body is erased from our minds, the pregnant woman herself becomes disassociated from our psychological assessment of the images. In essence, technologies like ultrasonography and fetal surgery have produced a remarkable reversal, making the prenate visible while simultaneously making the pregnant woman invisible. That we think we see the truth or reality of pregnancy once we take the pregnant woman literally out of the picture is one of the most damning examples of misogyny I can imagine.[9]

PREGNANCY AS LIMINALITY

At least for now, prenates require the physical body of a woman in order to develop from a single cell into an increasingly more complex entity, an entity with the potential to become a human being. There is something remarkable about the way that the pregnant body responds to the presence of the prenate. The body acts without conscious thought or the permission of the pregnant woman herself. Our corporeality, or bodily nature, is often not under our conscious control. We do not ask our heart to beat or our blood to circulate. For the most part, we are not even aware of the millions of physiological events taking place within our body at any given moment. For most female bodies, pregnancy is a biological process that the body performs.

Since a woman does not willingly control the biological reaction of her body to a pregnancy, her body becomes pregnant before her mind or heart has any knowledge of the pregnancy or any ability to accept or deny the presence of the prenate. Remarkably, this corporeal response is entirely unbidden. A pregnant woman does not will the placenta to form or her body to increase the volume of blood by 50 percent; these physiological processes are triggered by the presence of the prenate. If the prenate were not there, the body would not respond, and if the body does not respond, the prenate cannot remain. The two exist together—woman and prenate, united and separate, two in one, a concept that troubles the Western metaphysical obsession with individual identity.

At the same time, most pregnant women also actively participate in the gestation of their prenates. Their participation is one characteristic that separates human reproduction from animal reproduction. Most women engage in purposeful activities related to their pregnancy, including changing their diet and otherwise altering their behavior.[10] Certainly, women who are not pregnant but trying to get pregnant can engage in many of the same activities that a pregnant woman does to contribute to the health of a pregnancy. These women might take vitamins, refrain from alcohol consumption, or eat a healthy diet. Generally speaking, such activities simply contribute to living a healthy lifestyle. But when a pregnant woman engages in these activities, the impact of these actions can exceed the individual impact they might have on the health of the woman—they can also contribute to the healthy development of the prenate.

Identifying the distinction between the body's response to pregnancy and the woman's knowledge of her pregnancy helps us recognize that there are two related but distinct moments that mark the beginning of a pregnancy—body-knowledge and self-knowledge. The first is physical; the second is social. The physiological response of the female body that initiates gestation is triggered by a chemical signal from the fertilized egg; the response represents the physical transformation of the female body from a nonpregnant state to a pregnant state. The social response occurs when a woman first discovers that she is pregnant. She can find out quite early with a home pregnancy test or, in the most extreme cases, quite late when she goes into labor and gives birth. The physical transformation of her body from not pregnant to pregnant, however, happens with or without her self-knowledge. Although the bodily experience of being pregnant represents a changed ontological status, only through the woman's knowledge of the pregnancy is any meaning made of the pregnancy. Meaning-making, which is the process of how people make sense of their life experiences, is primarily a social experience.

Philosopher Ann Cahill argues that the ontological experience of pregnancy transforms not only a woman's body but also her identity. Cahill argues that a pregnant woman's embodied subjectivity—her knowledge of her identity—is shaped by the very fact of the prenate's existence.[11] The very presence of the prenate reshapes the woman's identity when she responds to her knowledge of its presence; any action she takes is in response to its existence. Although the prenate depends on the pregnant woman for continued physical existence in a way that the pregnant woman is not physically dependent on the prenate, a pregnant woman's subjective knowledge of herself is constructed in response to the presence of the prenate. From an ontological perspective, in becoming pregnant, the woman will never again be a nulligravida, or someone who has never been pregnant. Whether or not she gives birth is beside the point at this stage; the pregnancy has transformed her. Cahill names this relationship *intersubjectivity* because the fact of pregnancy shapes the identity and existence of both the woman and the prenate. Even if the pregnant woman does not desire to continue the pregnancy, she must intervene in the physical relationship that exists between her and the prenate, to withdraw her bodily support for the development of the prenate. Whatever the woman's emotional response to the pregnancy might be—fear, sadness, anger, joy, resignation—the woman is responding to her transformed bodily identity.[12]

This transformation of identity by the pregnant woman and the process of gestation, of developing into a human being, are both examples of *liminality*. The concept of liminality refers to the experience of being between two worlds, on the threshold of becoming something new and different. The concept signals change and describes the transition from adolescence to adulthood, from being single to being married, or from life to death. Key places in human lives are clearly transitional; these places of transition, uncertainty, and in-betweenness are referred to as liminal.

People moving through liminal spaces in their lives occupy a special place in the social order. This place is often marked by special clothing (baptismal gowns, wedding dresses, shrouds); rituals and ceremonies (bar/bat mitzvahs, weddings); and celebrations (quinceañera, baby showers).

Pregnant women's liminal status and unique place in the social order is marked in many societies. There are various reactions to pregnant women, ranging from fear and discomfort to protection and familiarity, that often result in pregnant women being set apart and treated differently than other women in society. Most women change their style of dress (usually out of necessity), and the physical limitations of their burgeoning body often require adjustments to normal activities. Pregnancy can be dangerous; women still die in childbirth or from pregnancy-induced complications. Liminal events also usually last for a specified period, with a distinct beginning and end, also factors that apply to pregnancy. All these elements—being set apart, dressing and acting differently, standing on the threshold of life and death, and the nine-month duration—illustrate the liminal status of pregnancy.

Pregnancy, gestation, and birth are liminal spaces, but the transformations in each experience are distinct. In pregnancy, a woman's identity is transformed by her relationship to the prenate. Yet this transformation is not experienced in a universal and univocal way. The meaning of a pregnant woman's transformed identity depends on a variety of factors, including whether the pregnancy is wanted, whether it continues to birth, and what happens during and after birth. Experiences of miscarriage, abortion, stillbirth, live birth, as well as whether a woman places a child for adoption or chooses to raise it—all these factors will affect how she interprets her intersubjective relationship with the prenate and potential child.

Gestation, on the other hand, represents a very different sort of liminal experience. The liminal period of gestation is essential for the physical development of human life, as it takes roughly eight to nine months for the prenatal body to mature into a form that can function independently. During most of its gestation, the prenate cannot live outside the womb; it is utterly dependent on the body of the pregnant woman to continue to develop and grow into an independent life form. Even after the point of viability, which is itself variously defined and changes as medical technology improves, prenatal development within the pregnant woman's body—as opposed to in a hospital incubator—is safer and leads to better health outcomes.

Birth remains the final threshold that marks the transformation from prenate to newborn. While viability is a significant step in gestational development, a viable prenate is not equivalent to an infant. After all, one exists inside a woman's body, and the other outside. This difference is not merely incidental, but rather a fundamental factor in identifying the moral status of the prenate.

Building on Cahill's work on miscarriage, let's reimagine pregnancy. During the liminal period of pregnancy, the pregnant woman and her prenate have an intersubjective relationship: the woman and the prenate shape one another. In a wanted pregnancy, this intersubjectivity can be understood as a relationship of cocreation. When a woman chooses to keep a pregnancy, the prenate is becoming a human being during gestation even as the pregnant woman is becoming a mother (or its mother if she has other children). Perhaps it would help if we began to think about the prenate as a "human becoming" rather than a human being. The word *being* suggests the quality or state of conscious existence that does not yet exist for the prenate. The word *becoming* recognizes the "not-yet-ness" that is the defining feature of the liminal state of the prenate in the process of coming into being. The terms that we use to talk about pregnancy, developing life in the womb, and pregnant women matter enormously. These terms both shape and reflect our understanding of the moral experience of conception, pregnancy, abortion, and childbirth. Our existing language is profoundly inadequate in helping us think and talk about the unique reality of what happens during gestation.

Additionally, the US legal system is ill equipped to recognize the liminal status of the prenate as neither person nor not-person. The inability to deal with the nuances of prenatal ontology generates some of the most complicated divisions and confusion over the issue of abortion in American society. There is a danger in trying to invest the prenate with an established moral status and definition of personhood—a status that was created to define a different reality. Pregnancy, gestation, and prenates do not fit into our predetermined moral categories. We need new moral categories that acknowledge the unique position that prenates and pregnancy represent in our moral universe.

PRENATE AS NEW MORAL CATEGORY

The poet Adrienne Rich eloquently captures the fluid moral and physical boundaries of pregnancy when she describes her experience of her prenate "as something inside and of me, yet becoming hourly and daily more separate, on its way to becoming separate from me and of-itself. In early pregnancy the stirring of the fetus felt like ghostly tremors of my own body, later like the movements of a being imprisoned in me; but both sensations were *my* sensations, contributing to my own sense of physical and psychic space."[13] She goes on to say, "The child that I carry for nine months can be defined *neither* as me or as not-me."[14] Rich's words highlight the distinct dilemma that continues to confound us morally, legally, and theologically about gestation. Something remarkable happens as the prenate develops from a ball of cells into an independent living, breathing human being. Her naming of the prenate as neither me or as not-me hints at a new moral category that recognizes the prenate as neither person nor cells but something in between, as representing *nascent* life.

The current debate about abortion in the United States thus pushes people to take a conclusive stand on a question that has fluid rather than absolute boundaries. When does life begin? Given that there is no widely accepted definitive medical or theological answer to this question, many people remain ambivalent about what kind of legislation is warranted when it comes to abortion. The certainty, for some people, that life begins at conception has driven legislative attempts to definitively declare and codify when life begins through the implementation of fetal-personhood amendments. These amendments failed miserably across the country precisely because most people do not agree that life begins at conception. At the same time, many people intuitively believe that *something* happens along the way during a pregnancy as the prenate develops. Yet defining just what that something is, is more difficult. While the early prenate bears little resemblance to a baby, the external resemblance develops far faster than does the more intricate development of the internal organs, nervous system, and brain. Quite simply, the prenate looks like a baby far earlier externally than internally. Something happens during that nine months of gestation, but we have not yet articulated what that something is. Existing language fails us.

Throughout this book, I have used the term *prenate* to refer to the developing entity that exists inside the pregnant woman at any stage of development. I suggest that we not only adopt the term *prenate* to refer to the developing entity that exists before birth but also recognize *prenate* as a new moral category to be used instead of *person* when referring to developing life that occurs inside a woman's body. Adopting the term *prenate* provides a new way to describe and define the ontological and moral category of the nascent life that exists before a baby takes its first breath. Likewise, recognizing pregnancy as a state of liminality in which pregnant women and their prenates exist in intersubjectivity can allow us to develop a more nuanced awareness of the moral uniqueness of prenatal life. This new moral category makes important distinctions between prenatal life and newborn life. We can recognize that prenatal life represents the possibility of personhood while still recognizing an important ontological distinction between prenatal life inside the womb and newborn life outside it.

The prenate is fragile, contingent, potential, not-yet. Its very existence is fluid, in all the senses that that word encompasses—adaptable, unpredictable, changeable, unstable. It lives in a protective sac buoyed and secured by fluid, and its developing lungs are filled with fluid. It does not breathe until it enters the world. With this first intake of breath, the prenate crosses that threshold from nascent or potential life into the world of the living. The act of childbirth represents the threshold between worlds, between life and death, nothingness and being. Up until viability, this tiny developing prenate cannot exist outside the womb. It is growing and in process—not finished, not complete, and totally and hopelessly dependent on the woman within whose body it resides. Something happens when a child emerges into the world and takes its first breath and the umbilical cord is cut. Something shifts when the prenate moves from absolute biological dependency on a female body that transforms it from prenate to infant.

The emergence of the child from its mother's body is the pivotal moment of entrance into the human community and is an appropriate and meaningful marker that corresponds to its liminal character. Birth is an obvious biological transition: the profound physiological move from the absolute dependency of the prenate on the unconscious physical function of a pregnant woman's body for food and oxygen to the interdependency of a baby that is able to breathe independently but still relies on someone else for food and nurturance. Although many premature infants still hover in the liminal space between life and death and many may depend on machines to exist, their separation from their mother's body marks the transition from prenatal life and potentiality to newborn life and personhood. The physiological shift that is marked by birth corresponds to a changed moral status. A body that was two in one separates and becomes two apart, forever connected and marked by the experience—the newborn baby with a belly-button reminder of its connection to the birth mother, and the birth mother who will retain cells that crossed the placenta during each pregnancy and integrated themselves into her tissues.[15]

Interdependence is also a foundational aspect of our ontological essence, of what it means to be human. Although we rely on one another generally for survival as a species, there is no other period in our life when we require the specific conditions of a particular person or body for our survival. In pregnancy, the prenate and the pregnant woman are interdependent in an exclusive and absolute way. Before implantation, a fertilized egg can be implanted in any number of uteri. After implantation, however, the process is exclusive—only that pregnant woman can gestate that prenate. Each pregnancy represents an exclusive and absolute experience of interdependence. For a woman to remain pregnant in that circumstance requires the presence of that particular prenate; for that prenate to continue to gestate, it requires the cooperation and support of that individual pregnant woman. Pregnancy, a unique and exclusive experience of interdependency, corresponds to its unique status in our moral universe.

Another advantage of identifying the moral status of the prenate as a potential life rather than an existing life is that it reframes the question of abortion from a situation of conflict associated with competing rights to a situation of a developing moral obligation on the part of the pregnant woman. This position is consistent with women's experience of pregnancy, miscarriage, and abortion and with many pregnant women's increasing emotional attachment to the prenate and to a pregnancy as it progresses.[16] However, even if we accept the prenate as a new moral category to describe the ontological status of liminality during gestation, we still must define the moral status of the prenate.

MORAL STATUS OF THE PRENATE

In recognizing that the prenate exists as a separate moral category from personhood, we can also acknowledge that it possesses a different moral value. Many people, and most people of faith, hold that the potential for life represented in the prenate warrants some acknowledgment of moral value. This is particularly evident in how pregnant women, their partners, and their families interact with prenatal life in the context of wanted pregnancies. Many women remember celebrating the first barely perceptible butterfly movements that mark quickening and the surprisingly volatile distortions of the eight- and nine-month pregnant belly as limbs, butts, and heads push against the increasingly confining space of a mother's womb. Many women have known the joy (and pain and discomfort) of daily living with a growing prenate inside their bodies and the deepening bond that develops as the pregnancy progresses. Attachment or bonding, however, is a deeply personal and individual experience. For some women, it can happen in an instant, perhaps at the moment they confirm a pregnancy or when they first hear the heartbeat, see the sonogram, or feel prenatal movement. For other women, bonding develops over time.[17] For some women the bonding happens when they take their baby into their arms for the first time, whereas other women experience deep postpartum depression that makes bonding with their newborn extremely difficult.

This range of women's experience is normal, and one model of bonding is not good or right or perfect. In the language of cocreation, attachment is part of the process of calling the prenate into being and reflects the development of our social relationships with another, in this case, a prenate or a baby. For many people, this body-knowledge and personal experience of deep emotional attachment to prenatal life informs the belief that prenatal life has value.

Philosopher Hilde Lindemann offers a way to help us understand what is happening as women and families develop relationships with their prenates. Thinking about or describing the prenate as a baby is a form of anticipatory behavior that Lindemann describes as *proleptic*, or treating something that will happen as if it has already happened.[18] Speaking of one's prenate as one's baby is partly a linguistic deficit in the English language, which lacks a meaningful term that reflects women's understanding of the ontological significance of the developing life within them. Philosopher Kate Parsons acknowledges the inadequacy of our existing language to express the experience of her two miscarriages:

> For those, like me, who have staunchly defended the use of precise prenatal terms—*embryo* until eight weeks, *fetus* thereafter until birth—the recommendation to name the lost being as a *baby* can be simultaneously disquieting and compelling. I, for instance, had always maintained a firm distinction between prenatal fetuses and postnatal infants, to help defend my belief that abortion of prenatal beings is a decision best left to the women who sustain and carry them; yet, after my miscarriages, my confidence in the terms *embryo* and *fetus* began to slip away. Somehow these terms were starting to feel too cold, too detached, to name and reference beings about which I had been so excited and hopeful.[19]

The terms *embryo* and *fetus* are indeed cold and clinical and do not reflect pregnant women's expected relationship with their anticipated child. In this anticipatory act of treating their prenates *as if* they are babies, pregnant women begin initiating their prenates into the practice of personhood. The proleptic actions of pregnant women—arranging nurseries; buying clothes, diapers, and bottles; and creating social and physical spaces for their babies-to-be—are all part of identity formation, which Lindemann describes as "calling the prenate into personhood."[20] Personhood, she notes, is socially constructed by a host of narratives that tell and retell the stories of our lives, weaving together to shape identity. She defines it as "the bodily expression of the feelings, thoughts, desires and intentions that constitute a human personality, as recognized by others, who then respond in certain ways to what they see."[21] In this way, personhood is about relationship, it is embodied and social, and it reflects a certain recognition of our interdependence as a human species.

Lindemann says that the narrative work of constructing identity sometimes begins during pregnancy as parents engage in the earliest forms of identity construction for their prenates as a way of anticipating the future child's personhood.[22] One woman from my study explained how naming her prenate helped her in this process of identity formation: "As it approached the time for that ultrasound at eighteen weeks, we decided we were going to pick a name for the baby because I wanted to know who it was. Because it was in there and I was afraid, I was told you could lose the baby at any time depending on what's wrong. So I just wanted to give the baby an identity."[23]

Lindemann helps us see how pregnant women, their partners, their families, and communities work together to call the prenate into personhood during pregnancy in ways that are a meaningful part of becoming human. While none of these proleptic actions can matter to the prenate until it is born, these actions play an important role in the newly forming identities of the pregnant woman and her partner as their own identities shift in relation to the developing pregnancy and the child-to-be. Just as the prenate is not yet a baby, they are not yet parents, and these anticipatory actions are the actions of *expectant* parents.

A clear dividing line exists between the absolute physical or biological dependency of the prenate on the pregnant woman's body and the more social interdependence of human interactions after birth. Despite an existential continuity to human life that begins before birth and extends after death, the ontological difference between life and death is morally and legally significant. The moral status of personhood is bookmarked by the transitions of birth and death. So, what are we to make of the moral status of prenatal life?

Recognizing that the prenate has moral value does not mean that its value is equivalent to that of a newborn baby. We can value two things and not value them equally. After all, the relationships that we develop with animals, while deeply meaningful, are categorically different from our relationships with other people. Because we value different things in different ways, we can value prenates differently than we value persons. We ought to evaluate the moral value of prenates on their potential to become members of the human community; their moral value lies as potential persons. Because prenates represent the potential for human life and personhood, the decision to end a pregnancy is not trivial. At the same time, any value that might be afforded to prenatal life is not equivalent to the value of existing life; a prenate does not possess the *same* value that a person holds after he or she is born.

Even more important, the bulk of social-scientific research demonstrates that the vast majority of women who have abortions make the decision in the light of their capacity to be a good mother to a *potential* child.[24] Research examining both the complex reasons women cite for seeking an abortion and the complexity of women's lives at the time of their abortions also document the thoughtful nature of women's decision-making. The reasons that women offer for their decisions to end a pregnancy stand as affirmations that they recognize the significant moral and material obligations of having a child.[25] At the same time, because the prenate is not yet a child and does not hold equivalent moral status to a person, and because the decision to have a baby and to become a mother is a personal and private decision, the question of whether to continue a pregnancy can and should only be made by pregnant women with the support of their families and communities.

Since the prenate is not a person, there are no rights at stake. In an overpopulated world, the state has no reasonable vested interest promoting childbirth over abortion and therefore should not engage in any legislation related to limiting women's access to abortion. Like any other medical procedure, abortion should be performed under the direction of trained and licensed healthcare providers and subject to the normal regulatory processes of healthcare. The argument that third-trimester procedures need to be regulated or prevented because the state has a vested interest in protecting pregnant women or prenates is specious. As I've noted previously, third-trimester abortions are exceedingly rare, with only 0.08 percent of abortions occurring after twenty-four weeks.[26] They are only ever performed for reasons related to the health or welfare of the prenate or the pregnant woman. Not only is making laws to address nonexistent social conditions unwarranted, but such laws contribute to cultural attitudes that seek to portray pregnant women as threats to their prenates.

EVIDENCE OF UNIQUE MORAL STATUS OF PRENATE

That we already functionally recognize the unique moral status of the prenate is clear in the cultural and legal acceptance of abortion and the simultaneous rejection of infanticide. Most of us recognize a moral difference between the prenate and the newborn, even if we lack sufficient language to describe this difference. For women with unplanned and unwanted pregnancies, this distinction came up in their unprompted discussion of why they did not consider adoption a realistic option. One study found that women who already had children were even less likely to consider adoption for an unplanned or unwanted pregnancy. One woman who was living below the poverty line and already had two children indicated both a moral difference between a prenate and a child and a recognition that an emotional bond would certainly develop during her pregnancy: "If I go that far, I'm attached. I cannot just give my baby away to someone."[27] For this woman and for many others, at some point during the pregnancy a prenate shifts from a potential child to their baby. The fact that this shift happens in different ways for different women only contributes to the collective cultural confusion that exists as we try to think about the moral status of the prenate.

The fact that we have at least some practical acknowledgment of the unique moral status of the prenate in our laws and in public opinion is also evident in the thinking and behavior of women who have terminated wanted pregnancies after grave prenatal diagnoses. In my 2003 interviews, all thirteen women referred to their prenates as babies, not fetuses. Of these thirteen, five had undergone surgical abortions and eight had terminated through induced labor and delivery. Two of the five who had had surgical procedures named their children, and seven of the eight who had gone through labor and delivery did so. These women, by and large, had discovered their prenates' diagnoses between seventeen and twenty-four weeks. Yet, many of these women also acknowledged a certain ambiguity in identifying their prenates as their children. Because the pregnancies were wanted, the women had already entered into a social relationship with their prenates, including naming them, interacting with them, and imagining potential futures for their nascent children. These women clearly would not have advocated or even accepted the killing of their children *after* they were born. Indeed, one woman reflected on how she thought about her existing daughter when she received the news that the prenate she was carrying had Down syndrome and heart defects: "We thought about my older daughter. And we thought, gee, if she was in a car accident or something and was hooked up to life machines for years, we would be there. I mean, there's absolutely no question. We would knock ourselves out. We just learned these things about this baby, so shouldn't we dedicate our lives to this baby just like we would do to her? And we knew without a doubt, like I said, we're already madly in love with the baby. We knew we would love him no matter what."[28]

Nevertheless, this woman and her husband decided to terminate the pregnancy. They clearly drew a moral distinction between prenatal life and the life of their daughter. While often angry that they had to make the decision, all the women whom I interviewed recognized that there was a moral distinction between the potential life they carried inside them and a baby that they might give birth to and the children they already had. In these situations, women's discussions of their pregnancies offer evidence of the clear moral distinction that women make between their prenate and an existing child.

Reimagining pregnancy outside the logic of individualism is challenging for both sides of an abortion debate shaped by a logic of justification. Such a logic begins with the premise that the prenate and the pregnant woman are potential antagonists. And yet, most women do not experience pregnancy as a hostile experience; even women who have abortions do not commonly use such antagonistic language in describing their experiences.[29] Women's language of their pregnancies and abortions is, more than anything, pragmatic. For women who have unplanned and unwanted pregnancies, the prenate is not a threat, because they have the option of ending the pregnancy. Women with wanted pregnancies who terminate for prenatal or maternal health reasons see the prenates not as a threat but as their babies. When women can exercise their moral agency in shaping their decisions about their bodies, their families, and their futures within a framework of reproductive justice, the prenates are not a threat. When we reject the notion of personhood from conception, there is no person to be the subject of an attack.

The clarification of the moral status of the prenate that I offer here represents a more nuanced approach to thinking about pregnancy, prenatal life, and abortion than the dominant justification framework. It also is more in line with a contemporary understanding of the relationship between sexual activity and the desire to bear children. Reimagining pregnancy in the twenty-first century from the perspective of women's embodied experience also requires that we rethink motherhood and the task of mothering as well.

CHAPTER 8

Motherhood as Moral Choice

NOWADAYS, SEX IS NOT only for procreative purposes: the desire to have sex is not the same thing as the desire to have a child. And although most people do have sex when they want a child, the desire to have a child is hardly the primary reason that most people have sex. In fact, people *rarely* engage in sex for procreative purposes. As I mentioned, current estimates indicate that the average woman in the US spends less than three years pregnant, postpartum, or trying to become pregnant and three decades trying to avoid pregnancy.[1] If we assume an average of sixty-four years of sexual activity (beginning at age seventeen and presuming life expectancy of eighty-one for women), less than 5 percent of women's sexual activity during their lifetime reflects a desire to have a baby. Of course, these numbers don't mean that many people aren't willing to accept a pregnancy at other times, but it challenges the long-held Christian narrative that the purpose of sex is procreation.

The joining of an egg and a sperm is a potential consequence of having sex, but it need not be. Beyond contraception and abortion, the likelihood that the fertilization of an egg *will* lead to the birth of a child is very low. Less than 25 percent of fertilized eggs ever reach full-term delivery. In addition to the spontaneous abortion of the majority of fertilized eggs, there are hundreds of thousands of cryogenically frozen, fertilized eggs and embryos harvested during infertility treatments that will most likely be destroyed or held in endless stasis. (While minority groups of pro-life Christian activists promote "adoption" of these embryos, concern over their fate pales in comparison to the outsized public interest in preventing pregnant women from securing safe, legal abortions. This is further evidence that abortion politics are not about abortion, the status of prenatal life, or women's health, as much as they are about the social control of women.) Both our developing knowledge about reproduction and the changing medical landscape influence our moral assessment of the presumed obligation for women to carry pregnancies to term. Questions of overpopulation, children in the foster-care system, and cultural attitudes about women and children living in poverty also bear on any moral assessment of human reproduction and fertility.[2] Our changed historical circumstances challenge us to think differently, not only about pregnancy, but about childbearing as well.

When we think about the importance of families, raising children, and the sacred nature of parenting, it is even more puzzling that so many Christians continue to hold on to the belief that pregnancy is the "price women must pay" for sexual activity. Most Christians recognize that sexual activity between committed partners is one way they share their love and deepen the ties of their relationship. They also recognize that raising children requires love, commitment, time, and resources. Pregnancy is not something that should be undertaken lightly or without an express desire to become a parent. And becoming a parent is certainly not something that should either be forced on someone or viewed as punishment for having sex.

In the United States today, there are many women who do not associate their sexual activity with the desire or even the willingness to have a baby. For many of these women, taking responsibility for their sexual and reproductive lives includes the possibility of terminating an unwanted pregnancy. As we have seen throughout this book, many women who end their pregnancies do so because they recognize their inability to mother a child (or another child). For these women, abortion is a responsible moral decision. Recognizing women's decisions about abortion as a part of the long horizon of their reproductive lives and their hopes and desires for their own well-being as well as the well-being of their existing or potential family reframes how we think about the decisions that women make. Even more importantly, only the pregnant woman is in a position to know if she is ready, willing, and able to continue a pregnancy and to mother a(nother) child.

Forefronting childbearing and motherhood as the central issue in abortion decision-making requires that we think more deeply about mothering and motherhood. In this chapter, I will discuss childbearing as a deliberative moral act rather than an accident of nature. Childbearing thus requires society to respect pregnant women as uniquely able to make decisions about the health of their bodies, families, and futures.

CHILDBEARING AS A DELIBERATIVE MORAL ACT

The idea of motherhood as a moral choice is a positive Christian ethic of abortion rooted in a sexual ethic of responsibility that promotes sex within healthy and stable relationships, advocates the use of birth control, and recognizes that the primary purpose of sex is not procreation. In fact, many Christians already hold such a view. Within such an ethic, individual women and couples must recognize the possibility of pregnancy and be prepared to act responsibly if a pregnancy occurs. When we reframe the social problem as "how do we respond to an unplanned pregnancy?" we ask different moral questions. These questions don't presuppose a right and wrong answer but instead require us to think about how the whole context of a woman's life is part of the discernment process.

After all, the profoundly moral decision to have a baby will, at minimum, require significant alteration of a woman's daily life for the next nine months. The physical toll that pregnancy takes on a woman's body is remarkable. It includes fatigue, nausea, indigestion, cravings, back pain, sleeplessness, weight gain, not to mention labor and delivery or a C-section, or any of the pregnancy-induced conditions that can threaten a woman's life. And yet the decision to parent a child is an even more demanding and long-term moral decision than the decision to give birth. Given that less than 1 percent of women will choose adoption for their children, the majority of women who decide to accept and embrace an unplanned pregnancy are making the significant moral decision to welcome a child into their life.[3] While placing a child for adoption can be an admirable moral decision, qualitative research indicates that most women who do so are not choosing between adoption and abortion but are choosing between adoption and parenting.[4]

A recent study found that one-quarter of women who had abortions voluntarily voiced their rejection of adoption as a viable option.[5] In describing their unwillingness to bear a child and then place it for adoption, these women give voice to the reality that most women who do continue unplanned pregnancies do so with the understanding that they are deciding not just to have a baby but to mother a child. The intuitive recognition of the moral distinction between the prenate and the newborn baby makes it clear that, for these women, abortion is an acceptable moral choice for them in a way that adoption is not. One woman expressed her frustration with the unrealistic expectations of the pro-life movement this way: "I'm not . . . I don't want to give my child away to nobody, and I'm not . . . and that's the part they don't understand. I can't just be bearing a child for 9 months, going through the sickness and then giving my child [away]. I can't."[6]

The precipitous drop in the rate of women placing their babies for adoption after *Roe v. Wade* indicates two things. First, many women who placed their babies for adoption pre-*Roe* were forced into continuing their pregnancies, and many were coerced into placing them for adoption.[7] Second, when women are legally able to make their own decisions about what to do in the face of an unintended pregnancy, the vast majority are choosing between abortion and parenting. The data shows that when women are given an uncoerced choice about keeping their child or placing it for adoption, 99 percent keep their child.[8]

This reality is further confirmed by a recent study known as the Turnaway Study, which followed women who sought abortions but were turned away because they were past the gestational limit of the clinic. Researchers found that even though their study was composed exclusively of women who actively tried to terminate their pregnancies, only 9 percent of the women in that study placed their children for adoption.[9] The evidence indicates that when women decide to continue an unplanned pregnancy, the overwhelming majority are making a lifelong commitment to love, care for, and raise that child. Unwanted pregnancies can become wanted pregnancies, and most women who carry a pregnancy to term do develop an obligation toward their prenate—an obligation that translates into a desire to keep and raise their child. The Turnaway Study also found that although both women who received abortions and those who were turned away were in comparable economic positions when they were pregnant, one year later, 76 percent of the turnaways (86 percent of whom were living with their babies) were receiving federal assistance compared with 44 percent of the women who had received abortions.[10] In highlighting the economic struggles that some women seeking abortions face, the Turnaway Study shows that women's decisions are influenced by their very real concerns about their ability to financially care for potential children.

For many Christians, the question of whether to have a child is deeply theological. Theologian Kendra Hotz describes parenthood as a calling that not everyone is called to fulfill. She challenges us to think beyond the personal joy and gratification that raising children may bring and to think more deeply about whether the choice to have children is also "a faithful expression of what God is doing—through our lives—in the world." She argues that "the choice for parenthood is bigger than what pleases me; it is also about God's reconciliation of all things."[11]

In the Protestant tradition, individual well-being is intimately linked to vocational calling. The idea that there is deep and abiding value in the work of our lives and that we have a responsibility to discern our calling—vocationally and relationally—in communion with God reflects the importance Christians place on discernment. While discernment often includes consulting with one's community, discerning who God is calling you to be is ultimately a process between an individual and God. A willingness to accept one's calling is an expression of honoring God and respecting the holiness of life that is at the heart of living life as a Christian. Christians regard parenting as a sacred trust in which parents enter a covenant relationship to care for, nurture, and bring up a child to love and know God. It is not a responsibility to be taken lightly but one that requires full knowledge of the commitment and the sacrifices required. If a person is to honor God and the covenant, then any covenant commitment to parenting must be entered into willingly.

When we frame parenthood as a covenant relationship that parents establish with their children, we recognize the powerful social force that human relationships have in shaping personhood. Feminist social ethicist Beverly Harrison explains that personhood, as a reflection of the power of love in community, helps build up individuals by deepening relationships that bring forth genuine community. Her description of love as "the power to act-each-other-into-well-being" anticipates Lindemann and aptly depicts the loving act of a woman who embraces her pregnancy and assents to love her prenate into well-being with her very body and lifeblood.[12] We bring one another into being through our love, support, and care, and we cannot survive outside of community.

In recognizing the importance of relationships and love in shaping personhood and human community, and the unique role that birth mothers play in calling their prenates into personhood, we need to reconfigure our understanding of the moral relationship between the prenate and the woman. Only then can we develop a new moral understanding of both pregnancy and abortion. According to this new view, the woman must *assent to* the relationship after recognizing her pregnancy. A woman's acceptance of a pregnancy and her willingness to enter into a relationship with the prenate signals the beginning of her moral obligation to carry that particular pregnancy to term. Still, in a reproductive justice framework, this moral obligation is not absolute. Although childbearing is a calling and a covenant relationship to which a woman must assent, conditions in her life may change during the pregnancy such that she may feel the need to withdraw her assent and end the pregnancy. As a liminal category, pregnancy is inherently changing and often unstable. Because the process of becoming requires a pregnant woman's whole body and much more, her willing participation is a prerequisite for pregnancy to be understood as a moral act. Coerced pregnancy under any circumstances, for any reason, is a fundamentally immoral act that violates bodily integrity, respect for individual persons, and the human rights of individuals to choose to procreate or not to procreate.

To honor women's moral wisdom to discern God's calling, we must view a woman's moral obligation to a prenate as a covenant commitment that requires her assent. Actively embracing pregnancy as a covenant responsibility also reflects the moral conditions necessary for such a serious decision. With pregnancy, a woman is obligated to care for herself in particular ways and is later morally and materially obligated to the baby after it is born (either to raise the child or to entrust its care to an adoptive family).

Thinking about the moral status of the prenate as contingent on a woman's acceptance of her pregnancy is a more nuanced way of considering the question of the moral status of the prenate. It is also consistent with a Christian ethical approach to abortion, which focuses on a woman's assent to pregnancy as a necessary component. This approach reflects a Christian theological anthropology centered on relationship and interdependence. Christians believe that we were created to live together in communities of love and support. From this theological perspective, life is not simply about being born, but also about being named, claimed, and welcomed into community and nurtured into being. These characteristics of human dependence and interdependence are in stark contrast with a world that celebrates individuality and independence. They are also morally significant as we contemplate questions of pregnancy, reproduction, and parenting.

When women make decisions about their capacity to carry and bear children, they are also realistically assessing their own capacity to do what is necessary to nurture and care for a pregnant body and the developing prenate. Although the decision to accept a pregnancy and to protect and care for that prenate is an altruistic decision, the opposite decision—to terminate a pregnancy for which one is not ready or able to commit to—is also a responsible choice on the part of the pregnant woman. The decision to abort is often a reflection of self-care. The self-care may be motivated by a wide variety of circumstances. It might reflect a woman's desire to finish school so that she can get a decent job and care for herself and her family. It might reflect an attempt to protect herself in the midst of an abusive relationship. It might reflect her constrained economic reality and the difficulty she has in caring for existing children. It might reflect an acceptance of personal limitations in caring for a baby or another baby at that moment in her life. It might reflect the dissolution or fragility of her relationship with her partner. It might reflect a thousand and more different realities that represent the very real life circumstances out of which women daily make the decision to end a pregnancy so that they can tend to themselves and their current life circumstances. Self-care is not the same thing as selfishness. Until we recognize the difference, we will continue to misinterpret women's actions in misogynist and damning ways that shame women or that attempt to control their behavior.

The completely unfounded perception that women seek abortions casually or without completely understanding the ramifications of their decision can be traced back to those dominant cultural assumptions about woman's nature as the weaker sex, about women's social position as submissive to men, and about God creating women as helpers for men. The subtle (or not-so-subtle) message here is that women can't be trusted to make important life-altering decisions for themselves and that such decisions must be made by male authorities (doctors, the state, judges, priests) who are better able to assess what is in a woman's best interest. To develop our capacity to trust women to decide when and if they will bear and mother children, we must first examine why so many people find it difficult to trust women.

EVE AND THE MISTRUST OF WOMEN

Although the cultural distrust of women has been cultivated over millennia, our unwillingness to trust women to make decisions about their reproduction was intentionally initiated by the physicians' crusade in the nineteenth century. Up until 1867, the authority for deciding about a pregnancy resided with pregnant women. From 1867 until 1973, this authority was vested in physicians and hospital ethics committees (mostly made up of men). After *Roe v. Wade*, the authority shifted back again to pregnant women. Making abortion legal also addressed the public-health crisis of maternal mortality. While many celebrated the Supreme Court ruling as a moral victory for women's rights and women's equality, others were deeply disturbed by the *Roe* decision because of the power of self-determination that *Roe* gave to women. To understand these concerns, particularly among Christians, requires knowledge and understanding of how patriarchy and misogyny have shaped Christian attitudes about women, their sexuality, and their position in relation to men in our culture.

The traditional Christian narrative about women runs something like this—God created Eve from Adam's rib and gave her to Adam as a helper because he was lonely. Eve disobeyed God's direct instructions and gave in to the temptation to eat from the tree of the knowledge of good and evil. Eve then used her own seductive powers of persuasion to lure Adam into eating the apple. Their knowledge of good and evil made them aware of their nakedness, and they were ashamed; they covered themselves with leaves and branches and hid from God. But God knew what they had done, and God sought Adam and Eve and chastised them for their disobedience, cast them out of paradise, and punished them. Adam's punishment was that he was made subject to the back-breaking toil of tilling the earth, and Eve's punishment was great pain in childbirth and sexual desire for her husband, who God decreed would rule over her.[13]

To say that this is the traditional Christian narrative about women is not to validate or support such a perspective but to illustrate how deeply traditional interpretations of scripture are mired in misogyny. Certainly, Christians appeal to a lot more in the Bible when they want to argue for male leadership in the church, husbands' dominance in marriage relationships, and other patriarchal claims about male primacy. But the deepest cultural narratives about male superiority and female inferiority are found encapsulated in interpretations of the story of the Fall. For our purposes, the following cultural axioms can be directly attributed to the second creation story found in Genesis 2–3.

1. Men were created to rule over women; women were created to attend to men's needs.
2. Women are deceptive, seductive, and sexual creatures.
3. Nakedness is shameful.
4. Childbearing is women's punishment for disobeying God.

These axioms about gender, sex roles, sexuality, and childbearing have shaped cultural attitudes for centuries. But these stories haven't just molded Christian attitudes. Given Christianity's role in shaping culture and tradition in the Latin West, these axioms have been foundational in the development of public attitudes about abortion over the past forty years.

We see echoes of these cultural assumptions in the official statements that many Christian churches have made about abortion. Churches offer these statements for moral guidance to members of their church and to serve as the basis for political advocacy work related to abortion. This advocacy work takes many forms, including letters to Congress, testimonies on pending legislation, and amicus curiae briefs on cases before the Supreme Court. Since *Roe v. Wade*, the moral voice of Christian communities, particularly the Roman Catholic and evangelical Protestant churches, have had a profound influence on public opinion about abortion as well as on public policy. While many official statements of many Christian denominations support PRIM reasons for abortion, largely reflecting the dominant justification paradigm, many other statements identify and condemn particular reasons as *not* justifiable reasons for abortion. These include abortion as a primary means of birth control, for personal or social convenience, and for sex selection. These categories of abortion are singled out by Christian churches as immoral, and the implication is that abortions for these reasons ought to be prevented.

Since we discussed abortion for sex selection in chapter 3, I will focus here on the other two reasons singled out for censure by Christian churches—abortion as birth control and abortion for convenience. These two categories are quite prominent both in church attitudes about abortion and in the vast majority of political rhetoric. Not only are these categories deeply rooted in Christian theology, but they are also the primary rhetorical strategies used to promote regulations that limit women's access to abortion.

These two criticisms are certainly related to one another. Both betray a perception of irresponsibility on the part of the pregnant woman. The first charge, that abortion should not be used as birth control, is directed at women who get pregnant when they were not using birth control. The charge implies that if a woman didn't use birth control, then she was not being responsible, though any reference to her male partner's responsibility is virtually nonexistent in the conversation. So, now having denounced any abortion by a woman who didn't use birth control, they go on to denounce those who did use birth control by labeling them as motivated by convenience. This second charge, that women should not have abortions for convenience, is a catchall meant to cover any reason (other than PRIM) that a woman who used birth control might offer for why she does not want to have a baby. The criticism that women seek abortions out of convenience betrays both a profound lack of awareness or exposure to women who actually have abortions and a deep disregard for the serious moral agency and intellectual capacity of women to make informed and reasoned decisions about their bodies and their future. This charge reflects some people's fear that pregnant women who seek abortion have too casual an attitude toward what they perceive to be an entity with sacred worth. The idea of convenience is also simply a euphemism used by those who think that women who seek to pursue their education, need to care for the children they already have, or abort for any reasons associated with self-care are selfish. This charge echoes back to the accusations of the nineteenth-century physicians who judged women's actions similarly harshly and dismissively.

As shown throughout this book, in real life women approach the decision to have an abortion carefully and thoughtfully. The idea of women's irresponsible sexual behavior is rooted in images of Eve the seductress, the temptress, the woman who acts willfully out of her desire for knowledge (power) even to the point of disobeying God. Whenever the criticism of women's responsibility for "getting themselves in trouble" is invoked, it hearkens back to the mythical figure of Eve, who got all humanity in trouble and was punished by God with pain in childbearing. If Eve must bear this punishment as the consequences of her desire, then shouldn't all women bear the equivalent burden of bearing a child when they get pregnant?

RESPECTING WOMEN'S MORAL DECISION-MAKING

We have seen that the failure to trust women to make decisions about their reproduction is rooted in misogyny and sexism. But prejudice based on gender is complicated and intensified when it intersects with racial stereotypes about the sexuality and family values of black and brown women as well as class-based stereotypes about poor women. In her book *Killing the Black Body*, legal scholar Dorothy Roberts carefully outlines how "derogatory icons of Black women—Jezebel, Mammy, Tragic Mulatto, Aunt Jemima, Sapphire, Matriarch, and Welfare Queen" not only stereotype, demean, and oppress black women, but also undermine black women's access to reproductive justice.[14] These various mythologies weave an intersecting racist web that attacks black women from every possible angle—portraying them as paradoxically both domineering and lazy, wily and stupid, hypersexualized and asexual, as well as genetically deficient, hyperfertile and a host of other derogatory characteristics. This racist mythology laid the groundwork for legislation that incarcerates pregnant women for negligence, for sterilizing women of color without their informed consent, and for treating pregnant women who want abortions like children. Concerns that women make abortion decisions casually arise largely from middle-class, white ideas about what "proper" families should look like as well as moral assumptions about "proper" sexual behavior. Many white, middle-class Americans regard abortion regulations that reflect these middle-class, white assumptions as reasonable.

A Christian ethic of abortion rooted in reproductive justice begins with affirming that abortion is a decision with moral implications while also rejecting the narrow moralistic values that seek to police women's sexual behavior. A responsible ethical response to an unplanned pregnancy includes asking the very serious question of whether one is able to welcome a child into the world and to make a covenant with that child to be a loving and caring parent. When women ask themselves if they can accept an unplanned pregnancy, they are asking a serious moral question without exerting bias that there is a right and wrong moral response. A pregnant woman and her partner who are thinking carefully, morally, and responsibly about their situation, their existing moral obligations, and their capacity to embrace the joys and challenges of either parenting or placing a child for adoption are engaging in meaningful moral discernment. To say that abortion is a moral action is not a Christian argument but rather a moral one consistent with Christian teaching. Many of the actions related to our sexual behavior are moral actions: whether and when to have sex and with whom; whether to use birth control; whether to have children; and, of course, how to respond to a particular pregnancy. These actions have associated moral questions related to how we embody and express our sexuality. These are moral questions because they relate to two of the most fundamental and intimate aspects of our personhood and our identity—our sexuality and our bodies.

The ability to discern good from evil and to act for the good is what we call *moral agency*. It is this ability that Genesis 3 tells us makes humankind "like God." When we recognize that one of the most fundamental aspects of our humanity, our moral agency, is the result of Eve's actions, we can read this story in entirely new ways. Genesis is not a historical record; rather, it is full of stories known as *etiologies*, which are stories that people tell to explain or understand themselves and the world in which they live. As an etiology, the story of the Fall explained to our ancestors the physical dangers and realities of childbirth as well as why growing food was so toilsome. The millennia that separates our world from the world of our biblical ancestors means that people no longer read the Bible for scientific explanations. Instead, people of faith read it to seek its moral wisdom. Even as an etiology, the story of Eve seeks to explain why humanity can distinguish right from wrong; it marks our moral agency as part of what it means to be made "in God's image." Reinterpreting Eve's actions as the origin of one of humankind's deepest connections with the divine offers a new warrant for respecting the moral agency of women.

The assumption that just because you get pregnant means you should have a baby not only is outdated, but also reflects biased and demeaning assumptions about women, motherhood, pregnancy, and children. Whether it is an unplanned and unwanted pregnancy—or a wanted pregnancy in which the circumstances of the pregnant woman or the prenate have changed—women actively seek abortions as moral agents taking active steps to shape their future. In women's moral decisions about unplanned pregnancies, we see much of what psychologist Carol Gilligan found more than thirty years ago.[15] Gilligan notes that women base much of their moral reasoning on their existing moral relationships and obligations and that they evaluate the possibility of future moral obligations in light of their capacity to act responsibly in an imagined potential relationship. When women evaluate these possibilities, they consider many factors, including their financial ability to care for a child or an additional child, their ability to provide a safe and loving home for a child, and their ability to honor their own health and well-being, including their career and vocational plans.

Cultural expectations that women should welcome pregnancy and children are rooted in patriarchal expectations about what women should want and how women should respond to motherhood or potential motherhood. They are also rooted in middle-class, white assumptions about two-parent households where men make money to take care of their families. Romanticized expectations about how families ought to be ordered and what roles men and women play in these families continue to underlie cultural expectations about pregnancy and parenting. When women do not fit this mold, empathy and sympathy are often withheld from them and they are instead judged for their perceived moral laxity. This moral laxity is often associated with sexual activity: having sex outside marriage, having sex without the willingness to welcome a child, or having sex without contraception.

Women are not supposed to enjoy sex, desire it, or have sex unless they are willing to "suffer the consequences" or "accept their responsibility" or any other of the familiar cultural tropes that are used to portray expectations about how women should behave in light of an unplanned and unwanted pregnancy. Most women like sex as much as men do. Women's desire to have sex for pleasure and/or as part of their intimate relationships is normal and can be a healthy part of women's well being. For many women, having an abortion *is* "accepting their responsibility" in a situation where having a child or another child would be an irresponsible decision.

Men are lauded for being responsible when they think about their careers and prepare for them responsibly. When women express the same desire to follow their calling and find meaning in their work in the world, they are often reviled for being selfish. The underlying assumption in the different responses to the very same desire in men and women is that men should work so that they can support families and that women should privilege children over work. As we have seen, when women do not follow these cultural expectations, they are often called selfish and are accused of ending pregnancies for reasons of convenience. Arguably, many women who terminate pregnancies are making a more responsible decision about their future, their own health and well-being, and the welfare of their existing families than are some women who have babies simply because they get pregnant.

It is time to stop saying "Abortion shouldn't be used for birth control" and start saying "How can we ensure that all sexually active women have free and unimpeded access to effective forms of birth control?"

It is time to stop saying "Women shouldn't have abortions for convenience" and start asking what kind of support women need to raise the children they already have.

It is time to stop shaming women for being sexually active and start demanding that sex education materials include attention to how people can expect a healthy and safe relationship as a prerequisite for sexual relationships.

It is time to stop damning women for having repeat abortions and start ensuring that there is adequate affordable housing, drug treatment programs, public transportation, access to effective contraception, and affordable healthcare in their own communities so that women can raise the children they have and the children they hope to have.

When we shift from judgment to justice, we become the kind of community that helps women solve problems and live healthy and safe lives rather than blaming and shaming them for decisions they make in good faith about their future and their families. This reimagined vision of childbearing is the foundation of an ethic of reproductive justice.

CHAPTER 9

Celebrating the Moral Courage of Women

IN HER GROUNDBREAKING WORK, *Our Right to Choose: Toward a New Ethic of Abortion*, Christian ethicist Beverly Wildung Harrison reframes the moral debate over abortion as an issue of women having the right to the conditions of procreative choice that would allow them to exist as fully moral human beings.[1] This important moral argument in the early 1980s sought to recast the issue from one of individual morality to one of social justice and the common good. Harrison argues that society must recognize and provide procreative choice as an essential element of the social conditions necessary for women to thrive. While Harrison establishes a much broader social framework within which abortion is understood as a necessary legal option, her claim does not fundamentally challenge the prevailing assumption that the morality of abortion must be justified.

In this book, I have argued that the justification approach to abortion is a flawed moral framework that is inherently biased against women and that this framework is deeply rooted in the misogynistic history and traditions of Western Christianity. The modern conversation about abortion is deeply shaped by contemporary Christian arguments that misrepresent the Christian tradition's attitude and approach to pregnancy, contraception, and abortion. By exposing the misrepresentation in this argument, we can disrupt the claim that abortion has always been recognized as a moral evil. A framework obsessed with women's ability to justify their reproductive decisions pushes society to focus on controlling the decisions of individual women. When we are focused on influencing individual women's decisions, we are distracted from the larger moral question of how we shape our society so that women, who bear the brunt of responsibility in reproduction and child-rearing in our world, can embody and express their sexuality and their desire for childbearing and child-rearing in just ways. The justification approach diverts our attention from shaping public policy to create a just society that supports and protects women and their families.

The reproductive justice movement offers a more robust and demanding ethical theory for approaching women's reproductive health.[2] By starting with the concrete realities of women's lives, a reproductive justice ethic can rightly focus on healthy sexuality, empowered motherhood, self-care, and robust families. The movement was born in the United States out of the efforts of women of color seeking to broaden the traditional abortion-rights movement by responding to a fuller understanding of the issues associated with women's reproduction. Reproductive justice reflects the reality of the lives of women whose struggles have often been as much about the state's preventing them from having children as it has been about the state's preventing them from having abortions. The oppression of women has often taken the form of restricting, brutalizing, and controlling women's bodies, their sexuality, and their reproduction. Women of color and poor women have undeniably suffered the most at the hands of patriarchal and racist societies, and it is past time for things to change. The moral question we face is how to create a society where women's lives and well-being, and the well-being of their families and communities, are public-health priorities.

My methodological approach in this book has been informed by the work of the RJ movement. From storytelling to centering women's lives, to exposing the different ways women are hurt by the same forms of oppression that shape society, to emphasizing the necessity of addressing the concrete problems that different groups of women face daily in their struggle for wholeness, my argument is grounded in and embodies the spirit of reproductive justice. Other scholars have outlined the parameters of a theory of reproductive justice.[3] My work uses those insights to build a moral argument for trusting women to decide when and if they will become mothers. The work is informed by the prior work of women of color and others who have been theorizing and embodying reproductive justice in books, communities, and statehouses across the country for more than twenty years. This book does not seek to repeat that work but to build on it from the perspective of a social ethicist. I hope to dismantle the justification framework and offer a progressive Christian foundation for supporting and building the reproductive justice movement.

While the primary emphasis of this book has been to build a moral argument for trusting women as moral agents, a grounded ethic of reproductive justice rightly recognizes that justice is more than the ability to decide whether to bear children. Justice also requires that we recognize the right to parent children in safe and healthy environments. At a minimum, this right would include the following standards laid out in the United Nations Declaration of Human Rights: "the right to a standard of living adequate for the health and well-being of [themselves] and of [their] family, including food, clothing, housing and medical care and necessary social services, and the right to security in the event of unemployment, sickness, disability, widowhood, old age or other lack of livelihood in circumstances beyond [their] control."[4] Extending our public policy beyond the policing of women's sexuality and women's bodies is only one of the ways in which reproductive justice offers a more robust moral framework for public discussions about women's health and sexuality, pregnancy, abortion, and child-rearing. In this final chapter, after outlining the origins and commitments of the RJ movement, I will describe five concrete ways that the RJ framework can improve our public conversations.

THE BIRTH OF A MOVEMENT

In April 2004, my husband and I packed up our four-year-old daughter and headed to Washington, DC, to join with eight hundred thousand other people in the March for Women's Lives. While we are solidly pro-choice and felt it was important to include our daughter in this event, it was also difficult to try to explain to a four-year-old the complicated realities that lead women to seek abortion, much less the malignant politics that surround the debate. But young children can relate very well to the idea of choices. As a four-year-old, my daughter was all about having choices and learning how to make good ones. So, this was how we framed the issue for her—the March for Women's Lives was about helping to make sure that women could make good choices in their lives. As white middle-class parents, we felt it was important to help our daughter understand the basic concept that many women do not have access to the kinds of choices that our family might take for granted. But the march, the first national public initiative in support of access to abortion, pushed beyond the narrow liberal-feminist frame of choice that focuses almost entirely on the legal right to an abortion. The event was the result of an intentional move to an RJ frame to emphasize the importance of enabling real choices for all women by addressing the social and economic barriers that limit some women's options.

The march was originally slated to be called the March for Freedom of Choice, after the "big four" reproductive rights organizations—Planned Parenthood, NOW, the Feminist Majority Foundation, and NARAL—met in early 2003 to begin plans for the march.[5] Loretta Ross, a black feminist organizer and one of the founders of SisterSong Women of Color Reproductive Justice Collective, recalls that the narrow focus on choice did not resonate with women of color, many of whom felt that this framework did not reflect the complexity of the issues that women, particularly women of color, were facing: "We're dealing with the Bush administration, an immoral and illegal war in Iraq, the Patriot Act, poverty—I mean, all these things would not be challenged by just talking about freedom of choice. I mean, if we made abortion totally available, totally accessible, totally legal, totally affordable, women would still have other problems. And so reducing women's lives down to just whether or not choice is available, we felt that was inadequate."[6]

Many activists were also unhappy that the big four had set the agenda without consultation and representation from a broader group of feminist and women's health organizations. Eventually, three women of color organizations, SisterSong, the Black Women's Health Imperative, and the National Latina Institute for Reproductive Health, were added to the planning team. Their presence is credited with broadening the theme of the march from choice to women's lives.[7] This story of the March for Women's Lives represents a transformation of both the political movement associated with legal abortion in the United States and the moral framing of the question of abortion.

The term *reproductive justice* was coined by a group of twelve African American women who participated in a 1994 pro-choice conference advocating for healthcare reform. The conference occurred in the midst of the Clinton administration's healthcare reform efforts; Clinton's proposed plan had simply avoided the issue of reproductive healthcare as a way to build Republican support. The twelve women met at the end of the first day of the conference to discuss their concerns that women were being thrown under the bus to appease Republicans, a strategy that Ross notes ultimately failed.[8] It was in these conversations that this group of black leaders and activists began the work of theorizing the reproductive justice framework. These women felt that the emphasis on choice focused the moral conversation about abortion too narrowly on the termination of a pregnancy rather than on the broader social problems and structures affecting women's decisions about pregnancy, motherhood, and abortion.

Toni Bond Leonard, a colleague of mine and one of the twelve, describes the conversation:

> The RJ framework was born out of women of color wanting to broaden the reproductive health and rights discourse to go beyond access to abortion. We did this by centering ourselves—by putting ourselves at the center of the conversation, bringing in our lived experiences and the multiple oppression that impeded our access to the full range of reproductive health services, including abortion. We understood that an intersectional analysis was needed that highlighted how combined issues of race, class, and gender contributed to our reproductive oppression. Exclusive focus on rights-based language didn't work for us, because it ignores that for many women, that right oftentimes doesn't become a reality. So we centered ourselves and thought about our lives—we live in neighborhoods where safety is an issue, all forms of sexual and domestic violence, and for some black and brown communities, race-based violence is an issue.[9]

By starting from their own experiences and those of their communities, these women identified the need for a new approach to women's reproductive healthcare—an approach that brought black feminist theory together with the human rights framework and applied it to reproductive politics. In doing so, these RJ pioneers created a framework that was rooted in the lived experiences of women and that offered insight into the intimate ways that multiple socioeconomic factors preclude women of color from achieving optimum reproductive and sexual health.

The emergence of the reproductive justice movement reflected problems within the women's movement of the 1970s and 1980s: that the feminist agenda too often assumed that the concerns of middle-class, white women adequately represented the oppression and experience of *all* women.[10] As activist and scholar Jael Silliman described it, the narrow focus is "rooted in the neoliberal tradition that locates individual rights at its core, and treat the individual's control over her body as central to liberty and freedom," obscuring the social context in which women make choices.[11] In the work of reproductive justice, women of color activists and scholars pushed to shift the emphasis from a narrow focus on legal access to abortion and choice to a more comprehensive analysis that examined the structural constraints on women's agency.[12] The term *choice* masks the situation of women who end their pregnancies because they lacked the material support necessary to *choose* to have a baby (or another baby). A *choice* implies the ability to choose between options. The constraints of poverty and inequality in this country as well as the active oppressive forces of institutionalized racism mean that some women who end pregnancies do not necessarily experience that decision as a choice. Not only do the majority of women having abortions indicate that their so-called choices are affected by a variety of life crises, including domestic violence, poverty, and insecurity, but these same women's decisions are often dismissed as convenient, careless, and trivial.

RJ activists also emphasized that women's decisions about when and whether to have children and their ability to parent the children they already have are foundational aspects of human dignity and respect when reproduction is viewed within a human rights framework. Human rights are those afforded to all humans because of their membership in the human race; a great deal of international law is grounded in this premise.

Ross and Solinger describe the profound importance of grounding RJ work in a human rights framework because "interference with the safety and dignity of fertile and reproducing persons is a blow against their humanity—that is, against their rights as human beings."[13]

Thirteen years after the March for Women's Lives, my two daughters and I boarded a train and headed up to the nation's capital to participate in the 2017 Women's March on Washington. My seventeen-year-old had asked to go as her Christmas present. While this march was not focused on reproductive issues, it illustrates both how the RJ movement has shaped the national conversation and how far we still have to go as a country to build true movements of solidarity and justice. Concern for reproductive justice and the intersections of different forms of oppression dominated the signs that people carried and the messages that they chanted. Pussy hats dominated the scene as hundreds of women donned pink knitted caps that imitated cat's ears to defy the misogynist words and actions of the newly elected president. The double entendres on the signs and in the marchers' attire were so thick ("This pussy grabs back") that at one point, my youngest daughter turned to me and said, "Mom, what's a pussy?" At eleven years old, she is an avid human rights activist and a lover of cats, but it was clear to her that people weren't just talking about cats. While women of color and other people of color attended the March, many of my minority friends and colleagues expressed frustration and disappointment that again this major initiative was initially planned and organized by a group of white women. Even though the framework of reproductive justice offers a better way to approach issues of women's reproductive healthcare for all women, we must always remember that this framework arose from the voices, bodies, and activism of women of color and the work for justice must always include their wisdom and leadership.

HOW REPRODUCTIVE JUSTICE CREATES A BETTER PUBLIC CONVERSATION

An ethic of reproductive justice that places women's lives and reproductive needs at the center of our ethical inquiry lessens the inordinate emphasis on abortion in our culture and brings a different set of moral questions to the forefront of our collective attention. Starting with women's lives means that the RJ agenda begins with the reproductive health and needs of girls and youth and moves through the various reproductive needs that shape women's lives—including the need for healthy and safe communities to raise their families. This starting point allows for new ways of thinking about abortion and new approaches to public policy and legal opinions on the control and regulation of abortion services.

Identifying the right moral problem

We have seen how the justification framework focuses our attention on abortion as the problem by emphasizing the moral question of whether abortion is right or wrong. Identifying abortion as the problem is misleading. In framing the moral task as one of determining the morality of an individual woman's actions, this justification approach pushes us to focus on individual women's lives, situations, and morality. The approach plays well in a culture of individualism that emphasizes the importance of holding people accountable for their individual actions. The individualistic focus on behavior and accountability is also consonant with certain evangelical emphases on virtue ethics and personal morality as well as their emphasis on sin and salvation. Nevertheless, a progressive Christian approach to thinking about sin in the Bible focuses less on the sins of individuals and more on the sinful and disordering nature of power structures that oppress people. An emphasis on individual moral decisions prevents deeper recognition of the social structures that shape the moral world in which women are making decisions about continuing their pregnancies.

One of the primary strengths of the RJ frame is that it shifts our thinking away from the individual and the choices that individual women make in their personal lives to the larger social context within which individual women make choices. As Barbara Katz Rothman has argued, social policy should address social issues, not police the morality of individual citizens.[14] Unfortunately, the justification framework has focused public attention on the wrong social and moral problem. A more comprehensive critical analysis of the issue should begin (as all good social ethics should) with the question "What is the presenting moral problem?" Such a question emphasizes that abortion is not the presenting social problem—it is merely one solution to a prior problem.

The social problem that we need to address is a far larger one. The question of whether to terminate a pregnancy only ever arises within the context of an individual woman's life when she is faced with an unplanned or medically compromised pregnancy. Decisions about whether to bear a child are deeply influenced by the social world in which women live, by poverty, healthcare, safety, daycare, employment, and many other factors. Additionally, many women find that their life circumstances change during their pregnancies. Marriages or relationships break up; a situation of domestic violence may develop or intensify during a pregnancy; a woman may lose her job or have a child who develops a serious illness. Pregnancies happen in the middle of lives that are already in full swing. When women are faced with a crisis in their lives, they must manage many issues, responsibilities, and existing moral obligations. Under these circumstances, a pregnancy is one more thing to manage.

We must address as a society the social and cultural factors that might have an impact on women's decision-making. The fact that some women might make different decisions about unplanned pregnancies if the structures of our society ensured the care and well-being of all children is a moral issue. Structuring our society to care for the "least of these" is a moral issue. But right now, caring for the least of these is not our national social policy. This failure in our society hurts the ability of some women to turn unplanned pregnancies into wanted ones. Let me be clear: the state has no interest in ensuring that unplanned pregnancies become wanted. Rather, it should seek to create a social world where all women can make positive decisions about the size and shape of their families without being constrained by poverty, racial injustice, poor education, inadequate housing, low wages, or any other factors that prevent women from having real choices.

Public policy that promotes the health and well-being of women and families

When we acknowledge the fundamentally social nature of most abortion decisions, we can see that the legal approach to the issue of abortion has been misdirected from the earliest days of the *Roe* decision. *Roe v. Wade* emphasized the abortion decision as primarily medical and placed an inordinate amount of the decision-making authority with a pregnant woman's attending physician.[15] In an era of reproductive justice, abortion would remain decriminalized and would cease to be subject to governmental regulations. There is no medical reason to regulate abortion procedures separately from any other normal healthcare procedure. Current attempts by state legislatures to regulate away women's access to abortion services should be renounced as the discriminatory and abusive exercise of state power. The ethic of reproductive justice presented here supports the repeal of *all* abortion legislation and holds that abortion should be treated as no different from any other health decision with regards to governmental regulations, including provisions to cover the costs for the procedure by the government or by private healthcare providers.

When we shift our moral attention from the act of abortion to considering the health and well-being of women's lives and women's families we are able to ask better moral questions. Why are half of all pregnancies in the US unplanned? Why are women deciding to terminate their pregnancies? What kind of material and social support do women need to make good moral decisions about their pregnancies and the composition of their families? Appropriate public-policy responses begin with asking the right moral questions, paying attention to the realities of women's experiences, and including women who are affected by these issues as equal partners in the conversation.

Women who are juggling several jobs and struggling to care for one or more children know better than anyone what the care of a newborn requires and how far they can stretch their resources to care for another child. Today, it is not simply one more mouth to feed, though that in and of itself might push a budget beyond the breaking point. Mothers need much more than food for their children. They need high-quality daycare, clothes, formula, diapers, and money for doctor's visits and medicine. And these are just the material needs of a baby. Anyone who has cared for a newborn or raised a child is well aware of the time and energy also required for these responsibilities.

In 2014, some 44 percent of children under the age of eighteen lived in poor and low-income families.[16] White children make up the largest number of poor and low-income kids at 37 percent of the total, but nearly two-thirds of black, Hispanic, and American Indian children live at or near poverty. More than 1.5 million children live in families that are homeless, and 42 percent of these kids are under the age of six.[17] An additional 1.6 to 1.7 million young people per year become runaways, mostly living on the streets.[18] The mothers of these children are the experts on the support and public-policy changes they need to create safe and healthy families.

In the absence of social policy and the political will to ensure that children are adequately cared for from birth to age eighteen, poverty is a concrete moral factor that influences women's decisions about pregnancy. The future development of public policy should focus on creating equal opportunity for all women to have real choices about having or not having a child. For many poor women, young women, and women of color, this public policy should offer access to adequate resources to bear and raise children in safe and healthy communities. Among the resources these communities would offer are jobs that pay a living wage; access to affordable healthcare, childcare, and housing; and quality public schools where children could grow and learn in safe and supportive communities.

Promotion of public-health issues

By focusing on women's health and well-being more broadly, reproductive justice recognizes that issues related to women's fertility are primarily public-health concerns. A more comprehensive approach to women's health and well-being certainly attends to questions of unplanned pregnancies, but it does so in the context of broadly addressing women's healthcare needs. When we focus on the need to provide comprehensive reproductive healthcare to all women, regardless of their age or ability to pay as part of the task of shaping a healthy society and healthy families, we create a justice-oriented approach to our common good as a society. While such a comprehensive approach to women's reproductive health care would need to address a multitude of issues, I will focus here on the need for effective sex education as well as access to all forms of contraceptive services and equal and unbiased access to those services.

Beginning with girls and boys, reproductive justice argues that greater attention must be paid to sexuality education so that our young people are prepared to care for and maintain the health of their bodies throughout their lives. This education must include medically and scientifically accurate information about sexual activity, sexually transmitted diseases, contraception, and abortion. While abstinence should certainly be included as an important option, sex education programs should not rely exclusively on teaching abstinence. Abstinence-only programs that avoid teaching students how to think ethically about their sexuality and their intimate relationships are part of a public-health crisis in America. Because of this crisis, the country has a 50 percent unplanned pregnancy rate and one-quarter of sexually active girls contract sexually transmitted diseases such as chlamydia or human papillomavirus. Teaching children, teens, and young adults about the sacred value of our sexuality is a far more challenging and important ethical responsibility than simply telling them to wait until marriage. The data shows they aren't waiting. Teaching them respect for their bodies and their sexuality and how to make good decisions about when and with whom to share the most precious gift of sexual intimacy is a far more responsible and evidence-based approach to sexuality education.

Free access to safe and reliable forms of contraception is a central tenet of the RJ movement. Access to reliable contraception is especially important for young women between the ages of eighteen and twenty-nine, the group with the highest rates of unintended pregnancy.[19] Given the history of coercion and control of women's fertility, particularly of women of color, young women, and poor women, access to contraception and abortion in the United States is of paramount concern. Women need easy and free access to contraception to prevent unwanted pregnancies as well as to protect themselves from sexually transmitted diseases. The trick is ensuring access to contraception without coercing women and instituting state control of women's fertility. A recent experiment in Colorado sought to find out what would happen if teens and poor women were offered free IUDs and implants, or LARCs. The study, which was funded through a private grant from the Susan Thomas Buffet Foundation, had a tremendous response, with the teen birth rate plunging by 40 percent and the teen abortion rate by a similar 42 percent. Rates for unmarried women under twenty-five who had not finished high school were similar.[20] Not only do these programs allow girls and young women more control over their futures, but they also saved the state of Colorado approximately $5.85 in Medicaid spending for every $1 spent on the LARC initiative.

Public policy that supports the reproductive health and well-being of all women would include both free, universal access to all forms of contraceptive care (including the free insertion *and* removal of LARCs) and a repeal of the Hyde Amendment. The biggest contraceptive failure we face is the failure to provide contraceptives. Fully funded and accessible comprehensive reproductive health care for women at all stages of their reproductive lives is essential for the creation and maintenance of healthy and secure families.

Reframing of disability issues

Over the years, disability activists have raised deep reservations about the use of prenatal tests to diagnose the potential health and disabilities of prenates. These activists raise a serious concern about the impact that aborting prenates with disabilities might have on public attitudes, perceptions, and treatment of persons with disabilities. Reproductive justice helps us consider the moral challenges associated with scientific advancements that have resulted in the increased diagnosis of prenatal health issues. Instead of judging the personal decisions women make, reproductive justice looks at questions of social justice: how can we create a social world in which people with disabilities and their families are supported—socially, financially, educationally, and vocationally?

The ability to terminate a pregnancy for a known or suspected prenatal health issue is a relatively modern phenomenon. It is largely a result of scientific advancements in our knowledge of the existence of teratogens as well as increased understanding of human reproduction and the origins of conditions like Down syndrome and Tay-Sachs disease. By 1973, prenatal diagnosis was increasingly introduced into prenatal care as abortion became a legal option for pregnant women who discovered prenatal anomalies. Our capacity to screen and test for prenatal developmental and chromosomal anomalies has only increased since then. Prenatal tests now diagnose prenatal health earlier and earlier and with increasingly less invasive and less risky procedures. We know more about the health of our prenates than we did in any previous era of human history, and with that knowledge comes the burden of deciding what to do when you know. Several studies have shown that the diagnosis of a prenatal problem engenders an existential crisis as women and their partners are placed in a situation in which they must face the tremendously difficult decision about whether to continue a pregnancy.[21] While potential parents are faced with decisions about their pregnancy, some disability rights activists are deeply concerned about the high rates of abortion that accompany the discovery of serious prenatal anomalies.

These two groups, parents and disability rights activists, approach the issue of prenatal diagnosis and pregnancy termination from different perspectives. Parents approach the question on a micro level, attempting to discern whether they will be able to cope with their prenate's condition as parents in the societies in which they live. Studies indicate that the primary factors parents consider are the impact of the anomaly on the prenate or future child, on themselves, and on other family members, and their prior beliefs about abortion.[22] Disability rights activists approach the question on a macro level, voicing concerns that terminating disabled prenates with chromosomal abnormalities or other disabilities demeans the lives of people living with disabilities and threatens to undermine public support for people living with disabilities and their families.

This argument is known as the *expressivist argument*. The expressivist argument falls into the same fallacy as other antiabortion arguments do when it focuses on the moral value of the prenate as the singular factor for moral consideration. Interviews with women who terminate wanted pregnancies for prenatal health issues indicate a far broader moral equation than the individual value of the potential child. In fact, most women acknowledge that if they were to give birth or if an existing child were to become disabled, they would love their child unconditionally. The potential for a mother to love is not what is at stake here. Nor is the parent's regard for the value of people with disabilities. Rather, prospective parents consider a wide number of factors. Among them are their ability to care for a disabled child, the impact on existing or future children, the severity or potential severity of the diagnosis, the financial costs they might need to bear, and the impact on their marriage and their careers.

The individual decision of a woman and her partner about what to do with the information provided by prenatal diagnosis is primarily a social decision, not a medical one.[23] Even when prenates cannot survive birth or when they will only live for hours or days, there is often no medical need to terminate the pregnancy. The fact that different women with similar diagnoses will make different decisions reinforces the social dimensions of their actions. Some women will want to continue the pregnancy until its natural conclusion (stillbirth or infant death), whereas other women will elect to end the pregnancy. These decisions are always based on deeply personal faith commitments, self-knowledge of what the woman can manage emotionally, the impact on other children and family members, and many other social factors. The very personal nature of the circumstances and the difficulty involved in managing any decision in this situation underscores why it is only the pregnant woman who is ultimately capable of deciding what she can manage in this situation.

Parenting any child is a calling and a commitment. Parenting special needs children is rewarding and challenging in ways that are both similar to and different from parenting other children. Therefore, in the context of a prenatal diagnosis of disability, the covenant commitment of the parent or parents to nurture and raise the potential child must be reaffirmed. In the language of chapter 8, the pregnant woman must again assent to the continuation of the pregnancy and recommit to a covenant relationship with this potential child. In a world where extraordinary measures can and often are taken (and expected) in the care of disabled children and where this care falls heavily on the parents, this recommitment is a reasonable expectation. The decisions of parents to terminate after a prenatal diagnosis indicate only that couple's decision to parent or not parent under a particular set of circumstances. No one outside their situation is likely to know or understand these circumstances. As philosopher Eva Feder Kittay puts it, "To selectively abort because the fetus I carry is likely to develop into a child with profound disabilities does not send any clear and unambiguous message. And the morality of that choice must be weighed in the conscience of the woman who makes that choice. She alone can know just what her act meant and if it was carried out as a consequence of moral sloth and uncaring, or through a responsible choice."[24]

At the same time, we need to consider the concerns of disability rights activists in regard to cultural attitudes about disabilities and the impact of these attitudes on social policy. Cultural concern about parental obsession with the performance and success of their children, often referred to as the *perfect-child syndrome*, has led to the accusation that abortion can be used by parents as a form of social engineering that will guarantee healthy children. Christian ethicist Ted Peters raised this concern and speculated that it "may eventually lead couples to try repeated pregnancies, terminating the undesirables, and giving birth to only the best test passers."[25] Certainly, Peters has a valid concern for supporting the dignity of, and respect for, people with disabilities and ensuring that insurance companies, the state, or other outside agents do not pressure women directly or indirectly into having abortions. However, given the physical burden of pregnancy and the inconvenience and discomfort of abortion procedures, it is highly unlikely that women would routinely get pregnant and have abortions in pursuit of a "perfect" child. Even more importantly, the data over the past two decades has not borne out this fear. A comprehensive literature review in 2011 found that termination rates after a prenatal diagnosis of Down syndrome between 1995 and 2011 were between 67 and 85 percent, which is much lower than the 92 percent that an influential study from 1999 indicated.[26] Furthermore, ethicists were concerned that the search for "perfect children" might lead to callous decision-making in parents who might somehow fail to adequately value prenatal life. This concern is not only based on particular assumptions about how prenatal life should be valued but is also missing from the qualitative data about women and couples who choose to end their pregnancies. All the women I interviewed expressed hopes and dreams for their potential children, and the hopes were not expectations of perfection or excellence. One woman said, "I had thoughts that he was going to, you know, grow up and, I don't know, be an adult or work somewhere. I don't care where."[27] The desire for your child to simply *grow up* and become an adult is a fairly modest hope that any parent would desire for a child.

The parental desire to have children who will not suffer from painful and debilitating conditions is not morally equivalent to either the frivolous desire to choose a child's eye color or the more pernicious example of aborting a prenate because it might be gay. Accusing women of wanting perfect children discounts the serious prognosis that many women or couples face when confronted with the results of prenatal testing. They are often torn between the medical establishment's offer of more and more information about the potential child that they are carrying and an increasing social climate of hostility and judgment toward women who use this information to make moral decisions about the future health of their family.

Disability rights activists rightly believe that disability is socially constructed through the creation of impediments to the social inclusion of all people. One key impediment is the failure to provide adequate social support for people with disabilities and their families. We as a society need to address these concerns by responding to the needs of disabled persons and their families. Only when we actively address these needs will we begin to shape a social world in which potential parents would feel reassured that they could manage the increased responsibilities of parenting a disabled child. Likewise, the activists' concerns about our cultural preference for intelligence and how prejudice against all forms of difference affects people with disabilities are also very real.

An ethic of reproductive justice shares many of the concerns raised by disability rights activists and seeks to address them through working to shape social systems that support people with disabilities. State support for families who have children with disabilities is an essential aspect of a society. Women and families making decisions about their pregnancies with prenatal anomalies would know that they would have both the financial support and the social services to help in the education, care, and potential employment of their potential child. Furthermore, increased public support for and acceptance of people with all forms of disabilities can also help mitigate the social censure and ridicule that many families and children with disabilities face in society. Rather than blaming and shaming women who decide to terminate a pregnancy with prenatal anomalies, the emphasis of our public policy and social attitude should be on shaping a society in which it is easier to live with a disability and easier to raise children with disabilities.

Affirming women's sexuality and women's sexual activity

Our attitudes about abortion are intimately linked to our attitudes about women's sexuality. For women of faith, sexuality is also a profoundly theological issue. Given the pleasure and even ecstasy that can accompany the physical act of sexual intimacy and orgasm, it is hard to imagine that our sexual lives and our sexual desire are anything other than essential aspects of our very humanity and integral to our capacity for joy and deep intimacy with our sexual partners. A theology that affirms women's sexuality and women's bodies considers how our relationship with God relates to our sexuality, our sexual activity, and our capacity for reproduction, parenthood, and family. At issue here is our understanding of the nature of the divine being and humanity's relationship with God, both of which connect to how we think about God's role in conception, fertility, pregnancy, and childbirth. For Christians, our understanding of who God is and how God works in the world greatly influences how we assess the moral issues related to conception, pregnancy, and women's responsibility as sexual beings.

From a feminist theological perspective that affirms both the goodness and justice of God, I find it impossible to believe that conception and pregnancy, much less the fertilization of an egg by a sperm, are either the will of God or gifts or blessings from God. The theological ramifications of believing in a God who would give me a pregnancy while withholding one from another woman creates an image of God who is either capricious or who actively seeks to reward and punish individual people, often without those same people having any knowledge of why they are being rewarded or punished. Even more cruelly, believing that God creates prenates with hearts that cannot function or prenates that are missing vital organs is to imagine a most cruel and heartless God.

We need to let go of the belief that each pregnancy is a gift from God if we are to develop a theology of reproductive justice that centers women's sexuality and their moral agency as the most relevant theological issues. A theology of reproductive justice also undercuts the tendency to consider children as commodities, even if the gift supposedly comes from God. Children clearly bless us with their presence in our lives, but our capitalist-influenced understanding of blessing has distorted our theological understanding of this idea. In Genesis, when God first calls Abram away from his father's home and sends him to a new land, God tells Abram, "I will bless you, and make your name great, so that you will be a blessing" (Genesis 12:2). In this story, the sign of God's blessing is that Abram is to "be a blessing" to others. When we think about blessing in the context of pregnancy and children, we need to think of it as a verb, not a noun. Blessings are not possessions; the mere existence of our children is not a blessing, either. To be a blessing to another is to act in ways that bring joy, care, comfort, and honor to one another. Our children are blessings because they bring this joy and love into our lives, which is part of human flourishing. The fertilization of an egg with a sperm is a biological fact, not a blessing.

The Christian tradition has responded to women's sexuality in largely misogynistic ways that have sought to control women and their bodies. Perhaps the fear of women's ability to bleed without dying, to nurture life within their bodies, or to produce milk and suckle infants undergirds the misogyny that we often see in the Christian tradition. Not only have women suffered from the attitudes of a patriarchal Christian tradition, but the historic lack of women's leadership in the development of the theology and rituals of the church has also meant that we lack adequate theological resources for thinking about the sacred aspects of women's sexuality and reproductive lives. We lack rituals to celebrate and mourn their bleeding or lack of bleeding, their pregnancies or lack of pregnancies, and the milk that flows from their breasts or doesn't. We have inherited a tradition that has often demonized or labeled women as unclean for their connection to these bodily occurrences and a tradition so ambivalent and uncomfortable with women's bodies and women's sexuality that it has been unable to recognize and affirm the absolutely sacred aspects of women's sexuality and intimacy with their partners.

In a world where we recognize sexuality as an integral part of identity, the sexual activity of women must be affirmed as a good and healthy part of their lives. We know that half of sexually active women in the United States will have an unplanned pregnancy in their lifetime. Once we dislodge the assumption that women are obligated to carry every pregnancy to term and we establish that women must assent to a pregnancy before any moral obligation arises, the question that remains is how women discern what to do when they face an unplanned or problem pregnancy.

ABORTION AS A MORAL GOOD

The heart of an ethic of reproductive justice is the affirmation that women's capacity to control their fertility—whether that happens through contraception, abstinence, or abortion—is a moral good. *Moral good* refers to our human capacity to discern what is right and just and to act on it accordingly. For Christians, knowledge of what is morally good must be consistent with an understanding of God's justice and of God's desire for humanity and for the common good.

When we approach the question of what to do about an unplanned pregnancy from the perspective of a woman's life and reproductive story, we have shifted away from a justification frame. The moral questions are appropriately aimed at the moral actor—the pregnant woman. Now, the question of what that moral actor believes about the moral status of the prenate will invariably come into play as she discerns how to respond to her pregnancy. In this moral landscape, the appropriate place to consider the theological status of the prenate is not the public square (courtrooms, state houses, etc.) but the private sphere. Women of faith appropriately consider their theological beliefs about the prenate, pregnancy, and parenting as they make decisions about their pregnancies in the context of their families and communities. For some women, the moral status of the prenate will be of paramount importance in weighing their decision about whether to continue a pregnancy. It will also influence how they feel about their ultimate decision: either a morally good choice or a tragic one, for which they may feel the need for forgiveness from God. The important factor in reproductive justice is that women are recognized as the agents of their own lives with the capacity to engage in moral reasoning supported by their communities, including their communities of faith. When we shift the moral frame from justification to reproductive justice, the morality of abortion is no longer solely tied to beliefs about the personhood of the prenate.[28]

When an unplanned pregnancy is approached as a moral question, among issues like the health and well-being of a woman's life and her calling and responsibilities, the question of the moral status of the prenate is one question among many. The importance of this question will depend on the theological and moral sensibilities of the pregnant woman. For some women, the belief that a prenate already exists as a full moral being will be a significant aspect of their moral discernment. For other women, who hold that the moral status of the prenate progresses over time, the developmental stage of their pregnancy may play a considerable role in their decision. And for women who believe that a prenate is not a human being until after birth, the moral status of the prenate will not be a significant factor in their decision.

While there are many moral aspects to the question of whether to accept a pregnancy, the moral status of the prenate is what primarily shapes how people think about unplanned pregnancies and abortions. For those who believe that life begins at conception, unwanted pregnancies are experienced and understood as tragedy and are framed as moral dilemmas. Within this moral framework, a person must decide between two "bad" options—to carry an unwanted pregnancy to term or to have an abortion that will end a "life." For women who do not believe that life begins at conception, the question of abortion is still a moral *question*, but it may not be a moral *dilemma*. The fact that our public discourse frames the larger question of abortion as a moral dilemma illustrates how much one theological belief about when life begins has distorted the abortion debate in our country.

In light of the theological importance of supporting women's ability to discern their vocational and relational calling and live into this calling, women's capacity to control their fertility is a moral good. Abortion can be a good and responsible decision that women make faithfully, without regret, and without shame.

My argument that abortion *can* be a moral good does not necessarily mean that abortion is *always* a moral good. Women's experience of abortion is as varied as women's experience of pregnancy, miscarriage, childbirth, and motherhood. For some women, abortion is a moral good that is experienced as a positive moral action within the larger experience of their sexual and reproductive life. Even within this population of women who understand their abortion as a moral good, the emotional responses to the abortion itself range from happiness to relief to sorrow.

But sadness is the not the same thing as regret, and for the women who experience sorrow or grief in the face of a wanted abortion that they also believe is a morally good decision, their sorrow may very well be related to their recognition of the loss of a road not taken. Or they may feel frustration with the realities of life that have precluded the possibility of welcoming a child at this time. Women's sadness and grief in the face of an abortion can be mistaken—even by the women themselves—as guilt, regret, or shame about their decision to terminate a pregnancy.

In cases where abortion is not a moral good, the abortion may have been coerced or a woman may believe that what she is doing is morally wrong in light of her personal values and religious beliefs. An ethic of reproductive justice seeks to ensure that no woman is pressured or coerced into making any decisions, including abortion, against her will.

For many women, abortion is a morally good decision, a healing and life-giving experience. It allows some women to be responsible parents to the children they already have. For other women, abortion is a responsible decision that allows them to live life abundantly by finishing their education and becoming responsible adults. For still other women, not being pregnant helps maintain the thin thread of sanity that allows them to survive amid mental illness, poverty, divorce, domestic violence, or a host of other challenges.

In the midst of a culture that shames and blames women who have abortions, even calling them sinners, it takes a great deal of moral courage to terminate a pregnancy. It takes moral courage to ignore the bullies and hate-mongers who seek to shame you for your decision. To reject the Christians who want to make you feel guilty for making a potentially life-defining decision that you know is right with God. To navigate and survive the hundreds of state regulations that seek to pressure you to change your mind by showing you mandatory ultrasounds or making you wait for three days like a child in time-out to think about your decision—as if you haven't already given it deep thought. In the midst of a culture that blames and shames women who are seeking to act responsibly and faithfully in shaping the trajectories of their lives, I want to celebrate the moral courage of women who have terminated pregnancies as a morally good act in the larger story of a life well lived or at least as one small story on the journey to live the most faithful and moral life possible.

ACKNOWLEDGMENTS

IN WRITING A BOOK, authors encounter innumerable people who support and sustain them in obvious and not-so-obvious ways. I owe the deepest gratitude to so many people who have supported, guided, and otherwise made my life more livable in the days, weeks, months, and years that I have been working on this book.

Since I feel I have been preparing to write this book almost since I was born, I would like to acknowledge the incomparable influence that my family has had on my moral development and the particular ways that I think about and value the commitments of covenant relationship, parenting, and family. My father was a Presbyterian minister and an engaging and passionate person. One of my most vivid childhood memories is how he addressed me in his moments of deepest vexation with my behavior as "Rebecca Todd Peters, child of the covenant" before scolding me. When I was an adult and I asked him why he did this, he explained that invoking this baptismal language was an intentional spiritual practice meant to remind him that no matter how angry he was with my behavior, I had been named and claimed by God through my baptism and that as my father, he was responsible for shaping my moral attitudes and practices with grace and humility. My father lived long enough to baptize our oldest daughter, and I have found myself invoking this same baptismal formula in disciplining my own daughters.

As you have read in these pages, my mother was also a significant moral influence in shaping my attitudes about family, marriage, partnership, and mothering. She has taught me much over the years through her words and deeds about what it means to be a faithful Christian, a loving mother, a committed partner, and a loyal friend. She moved to Greensboro when our second daughter was born and has been an ever-present witness to the fact that working families need significant support with childcare to make ends meet. Without her willingness to pick kids up from school, care for them on weekends, and generally support us as a loving mother and grandmother, there would have been far fewer bike rides and conferences and much less ecumenical engagement and quality time with my husband.

My work on the topic of abortion began in my early twenties, when I served as a program assistant with the Justice for Women office of the Women's Ministry Unit of the Presbyterian Church (USA). In the two years that I held that position, I worked with two of the strongest advocates for women and justice that I have ever known. Mary Kuhns and Mary Ann Lundy taught me how to be a Christian feminist through their words and actions and, most importantly, through the way that they lived their lives. Their patience, care, and support of a young, eager, and naive colleague served as a witness to me of what it means to be a mentor. Our work together as advocates for women and reproductive justice laid the foundation for my own work on these issues as a scholar-activist.

After working at the Presbyterian national office, I went to Union Theological Seminary in New York to study liberation theology and specifically to study with Beverly Wildung Harrison. Bev's work in *Our Right to Choose* was groundbreaking in Christian ethics, and her support of me personally and professionally was unwavering. My coursework with her on reproductive rights and economic justice and endless hours of conversation about women, reproductive issues, and questions of justice helped prepare me for developing this ethic of reproductive justice. My debt of gratitude to Bev is beyond measure.

My formal research on abortion began in 2003, when I interviewed thirteen women who terminated wanted pregnancies in their second trimester. These women's willingness to share their stories with me was courageous, honest, and, for some of them, extraordinarily difficult. I was profoundly moved by their situations and the integrity with which they faced the challenges that their pregnancies posed for them. I am forever grateful for the gift of their stories. Like them, I hope that the telling of more abortion stories, in this book and in other places, helps to break the cultural silence about abortion that shapes our society.

Over the past fourteen years, I have had the opportunity to present pieces of this work in several places, including the Society of Christian Ethics (2015), the American Academy of Religion (2012), and the Association of Research on Mothering (2003). Thanks are due to colleagues who engaged my work and offered feedback at each of these venues. Thanks are also due to the *Journal of Feminist Studies in Religion*, where I published portions of chapter 3 in the spring 2014 issue in my paper "Considering Social Policy on Abortion: Respecting Women as Moral Agents."

Elon University has supported my research on this project through a sabbatical grant in 2014–2015, a summer fellowship in 2017, and several course releases for research over the past fourteen years. In particular, the support of Tim Peeples and Lynn Huber has been invaluable for my research. Thanks also to my department colleagues for their feedback when I presented material from this research in a faculty colloquium in 2015. The Wabash Center for Teaching and Learning in Religion and Theology supported my initial interviews with a summer research grant in 2003. In 2012, I was invited to participate in the Faith and Reproductive Justice Leadership Institute sponsored by the Center for American Progress. There I was introduced to several leading figures in the reproductive justice movement and a cohort of amazing scholars, activists, and all-around fabulous colleagues who have continued to support each other's RJ work over the years—my deepest thanks to all of you and to Sally Steenland and Eleni Townes, who organized and supported this initiative. In 2016, I was invited by the Religious Coalition of Reproductive Choice to participate in its Religious Leader Education and Theologies project; our group met several times with scholars and activists from across the religious studies landscape to educate ourselves about reproductive justice and to strategize about how to support one another in our work. It was through this work that I met Toni Bond Leonard and Rosetta Ross, both RJ leaders who have been generous in their support of my work. I also received rich and thoughtful feedback from colleagues in the Faculty Research Seminar at the Anna Julia Cooper Center at Wake Forest, where I presented in the spring of 2017. And special thanks to Melissa Harris-Perry, who invited me to participate.

As any scholar knows, there is often a multitude of friends and colleagues who offer material support to the research process in a host of ways—big and small. All of this support is most graciously appreciated and never forgotten. The librarians at Elon's Belk Library are all amazingly supportive, but Lynn Melchor's efficiency as our interlibrary loan coordinator has made the task of research infinitely smoother. Carol Robb and Marvin Ellison wrote letters of recommendation for grants, and Robby Jones of Public Religion Research Institute generously shared qualitative data from PRRI focus groups from their study on millennials' attitudes on abortion in my earliest stages of research.

A number of friends and colleagues have been generous interlocutors, and many have offered feedback on various aspects of the manuscript, including Toni Bond Leonard, Kate Ott, Grace Kao, Ellen Marshall, Jen Ayres, Caryn Riswold, Buffie Longmire-Avital, True Campbell, and Vanessa Haygood. Several friends were generous enough to offer feedback on the full manuscript; they include Mary Ann Lundy, Laura Stivers, Katey Zeh, Lee Hull Moses, and Marti Hazelrigg. Several work-study students helped with citations over the years; among these students are Rachel Zimmerman, Abbie Williams, and Joel Green. Several classes at Elon—including Approaches to the Study of Religion (2016), Sexual Ethics (2017), and Senior Seminar (2017)—read portions of the manuscript and offered valuable feedback. John Willse, master statistician and friend extraordinaire, graciously offered to create the graph that appears in the book when he heard me talking about how striking the data on contraceptive failure rates is. Special thanks are due to Marvin Ellison and Stephanie Egnotovich, who persistently encouraged me to write this book for many years. And special thanks to my friends Kris Thompson, Brooke Barnett, Ann Sargent, and Elizabeth Dick who were there for me when I needed them.

The editorial and production teams at Beacon have done an amazing job in working with me to produce this book. From my earliest conversations with my editor, Amy Caldwell, I was impressed with her interest in the project and her incisive questions about the material. I am extraordinarily grateful for her support of me and this book and for the many ways that her editorial hand has helped to strengthen and clarify the argument. Deepest thanks are also due to my copyeditor, Patricia E. Boyd. Her careful and meticulous attention to grammar and punctuation are remarkable, and her revisions and clarifications of my prose have certainly made the text read more clearly and easily. To the rest of the team at Beacon, especially Susan Lumenello, Beth Collins, Alyssa Hassan, and Molly Velázquez-Brown, thank you for your work on helping to launch this book.

My greatest professional debt is to my friend and colleague, feminist philosopher Ann Cahill, who not only read multiple drafts of the manuscripts but also has been extraordinarily generous with her time in talking through thorny issues and questions with me—often at a moment's notice.

To my husband and our daughters, it is impossible to convey the depth of my gratitude for your support of my work on this project over the past four years. From my husband's thoughtfulness in forwarding articles of interest from medical journals, to our oldest's feedback on chapters, to our youngest's eager questions about my research and progress—each of you has taken an active interest in my work and found meaningful ways to support me. The story of our family is woven into the fabric of this book, and part of my decision to finally write it is the fact that our daughters are coming of age in a world where there are serious threats to reproductive justice. It is my hope that this book, in some small way, will help to make the world a more just place for all families.

NOTES

INTRODUCTION

1. Christians are taught "Love your neighbor as yourself," a commandment that begins with the obligation to love and care for oneself.
2. Rachel K. Jones, Lori F. Frohwirth, and Ann M. Moore, "More Than Poverty: Disruptive Events Among Women Having Abortions in the USA," *Journal of Family Planning and Reproductive Health Care* 39 (2013): 36–43.
3. Rachel K. Jones and Megan L. Kavanaugh, "Changes in Abortion Rates Between 2000 and 2008 and Lifetime Incidence of Abortion," *Obstetrics and Gynecology* 177, no. 6 (June 2011): 1358–66.
4. Tracy A. Weitz, "Rethinking the Mantra That Abortion Should Be 'Safe, Legal, and Rare,'" *Journal of Women's History* 22, no. 3 (2010): 161–72.
5. Tom W. Smith and Jaesok Son, *Trends in Public Attitudes Towards Abortion: General Social Survey 2012 Final Report*, (Chicago: NORC, May 2013), 2. While the General Social Survey does not ask independently about incest, the nonconsensual nature of incest suggests that categorizing it with rape is a reasonable measure.
6. Lawrence B. Finer et al., "Reasons U.S. Women Have Abortions: Quantitative and Qualitative Perspectives," *Perspectives on Sexual and Reproductive Health* 37, no. 3 (September 2005): 113.
7. K. Daniels, W. D. Mosher, and J. Jones, *Contraceptive Methods Women Have Ever Used: United States, 1982–2010*, National Health Statistics Reports (Hyattsville, MD: National Center for Health Statistics, 2013); Elizabeth G. Raymond and David A. Grimes, "The Comparative Safety of Legal Induced Abortion and Childbirth in the United States," *Obstetrics and Gynecology* 119, no. 2, pt. 1 (February 2012): 215–19.
8. Loretta Ross and Rickie Solinger, *Reproductive Justice: An Introduction* (Oakland: University of California Press, 2017).
9. Myra J. Tucker, Cynthia J. Berg, William M. Callaghan, and Jason Hsia, "The Black–White Disparity in Pregnancy-Related Mortality from 5 Conditions: Differences in Prevalence and Case-Fatality Rates," *American Journal of Public Health* 97, no. 2 (February 2007): 247–51; Marian F. MacDorman, Eugene Declercq, Howard Cabral, and Christine Morton, "Is the United States Maternal Mortality Rate Increasing? Disentangling Trends from Measurement Issues," *Obstetrics and Gynecology* 128, no. 3 (September 2016): 447–55.

10. Loretta Ross, "Reproductive Justice Training," presented at the Religious Scholars Convening, Religious Coalition for Reproductive Choice, Washington, DC, March 3, 2016.
11. Jeffrey M. Jones, "U.S. Religious Groups Disagree on Five Key Moral Issues," *Gallup News*, May 26, 2016, http://news.gallup.com/poll/191903/religious-groups-disagree-five-key-moral-issues.aspx?g_source=position4&g_medium=related&g_campaign=tiles.
12. Michael Lipka and John Gramlich, "5 Facts About Abortion," Pew Research Center, January 26, 2017, http://www.pewresearch.org/fact-tank/2017/01/26/5-facts-about-abortion.

CHAPTER 1: YOU SHOULDN'T HAVE A BABY JUST BECAUSE YOU'RE PREGNANT

1. Finer et al., "Reasons U.S. Women Have Abortions," 110–18.
2. Presbyterian Church (USA), *Report of the Special Committee on Problem Pregnancies and Abortion* (Louisville: Office of the General Assembly, Presbyterian Church [USA], 1992).
3. Lawrence B. Finer, "Trends in Premarital Sex in the United States, 1954–2003," *Public Health Reports* 122 (January–February 2007): 76.
4. Ibid.
5. Ibid.; Guttmacher Institute, "American Teens' Sexual and Reproductive Health," Fact Sheet, Guttmacher Institute, New York, September 2016.
6. For a more detailed discussion of sex and the Bible, see Jennifer Wright Knust, *Unprotected Texts: The Bible's Surprising Contradictions About Sex and Desire* (New York: HarperCollins, 2011); Michael Coogan, *God & Sex: What the Bible Really Says* (New York: Twelve, 2010); David M. Carr, *The Erotic Word: Sexuality, Spirituality, and the Bible* (Oxford, UK: Oxford University Press, 2003).
7. Marvin Ellison, *Making Love Just: Sexual Ethics for Perplexing Times* (Minneapolis: Fortress, 2012); Margaret Farley, *Just Love: A Framework for Christian Sexual Ethics* (New York: Continuum, 2006); Marvin Ellison, *Erotic Justice: A Liberating Ethic of Sexuality* (Louisville, KY: Westminster John Knox, 1996); Carter Heyward, *Touching Our Strength: The Erotic as Power and the Love of God* (San Francisco: Harper & Row, 1989); Presbyterian Church (USA), *Keeping Body and Soul Together: Sexuality, Spirituality, and Social Justice* (Louisville, KY: Office of the General Assembly, Presbyterian Church [USA], 1991).
8. Pew Research Center, "Abortion Viewed in Moral Terms: Fewer See Stem Cell Research and IVF as Moral Issues," Pew Research Center, August 15, 2013, 2, http://assets.pewresearch.org/wp-content/uploads/sites/11/2013/08/Morality-of-abortion-8-15-for-pdf.pdf.
9. Hilde Lindemann calls this the "abortion intuition" and interprets this response as marking a set of "genuine moral considerations" about what pregnancy represents and "what we are stopping when we stop one." While I agree with her larger point about the moral responsibility that pregnant women have to "call the fetus into personhood," which I will discuss in more detail in chapter 7, I have a different interpretation of why so many women cannot imagine having an abortion. Hilde Lindemann, *Holding and Letting Go: The Social Practice of Personal Identities* (New York: Oxford University Press, 2014), ch. 2.

10. Jenna Jerman, Rachel K. Jones, and Tsuyoshi Onda, *Characteristics of U.S. Abortion Patients in 2014 and Changes Since 2008* (New York: Guttmacher Institute, 2016).
11. Carinne H. Rocca, Katrina Kimport, Heather Gould, and Diana G. Foster, "Women's Emotions One Week After Receiving or Being Denied an Abortion in the United States," *Perspectives on Sexual and Reproductive Health* 45, no. 3 (September 1, 2013): 127.
12. Brenda Major et al., "Abortion and Mental Health: Evaluating the Evidence," *American Psychologist* 64, no. 9 (December 2009): 885.

CHAPTER 2: ABORTION IN REAL LIFE

1. Madeleine Davies, "Amelia Bonow Explains How #ShoutYourAbortion 'Just Kicked the Patriarchy in the Dick,'" *Jezebel*, September 15, 2015.
2. Tamar Lewin, "#ShoutYourAbortion Gets Angry Shouts Back," *New York Times*, October 2, 2015.
3. Finer et al., "Reasons U.S. Women Have Abortions," 113.
4. Lawrence B. Finer and Mia R. Zolna, "Declines in Unintended Pregnancy in the United States, 2008–2011," *New England Journal of Medicine* 374, no. 9 (March 3, 2016): 843–52.
5. Adam Sonfield, Kinsey Hasstedt, and Rachel Benson Gold, *Moving Forward: Family Planning in the Era of Health Reform* (New York: Guttmacher Institute, 2014), 7.
6. Finer and Zolna, "Declines in Unintended Pregnancy," 843–52.
7. Jones, Frohwirth, and Moore, "More Than Poverty."
8. Data for one-year failure rates from James Trussell, "Contraceptive Failure in the United States," *Contraception* 83, no. 5 (May 1, 2011): 397–404. The three assumptions about change in failure rates over ten years (constant, decline by half, decline to zero) appear in the literature, for example, John A. Ross, "Contraception: Short-Term vs. Long-Term Failure Rates," *Family Planning Perspectives* 21, no. 6 (1989): 275–77. As in Ross, the monthly rate was calculated by taking the twelfth root of the one-year annual survival rate (i.e., no pregnancy; 1 minus the failure rate). Starting from the year-one survival rate, a cumulative monthly survival rate was then calculated using the previous month's cumulative survival rate multiplied by the current month's assumed survival rate under one of the three assumptions about change in risk of failure. These survival rates were then changed to failure rates (i.e., 1: survival rate) for plotting and discussion. Additional studies examining contraceptive failure rates include J. Trussell et al., "A Guide to Interpreting Contraceptive Efficacy Studies," *Obstetrics and Gynecology* 76, no. 3, pt. 2 (September 1990): 558–67; James Trussell and L. L. Wynn, "Reducing Unintended Pregnancy in the United States," *Contraception* 77, no. 1 (January 2008): 1–5; Kirsten I. Black, Sunanda Gupta, Angela Rassi, and Ali Kubba, "Why Do Women Experience Untimed Pregnancies? A Review of Contraceptive Failure Rates," *Best Practice & Research Clinical Obstetrics & Gynaecology* 24, no. 4 (August 1, 2010): 443–55.
9. Sonfield, Hasstedt, and Gold, *Moving Forward*, 41.
10. Eric J. Bieber, Joseph S. Sanfilippo, Ira R. Horowitz, and Mahmood I. Shafi, *Clinical Gynecology*, 2nd ed. (Cambridge, UK: Cambridge University Press, 2015), 968.

11. Sterilization has also frequently been used as a tool to control women's fertility without their consent. This will be discussed at more length in chapter 5.
12. Sonfield, Hasstedt, and Gold, *Moving Forward*, 41.
13. Rachel K. Jones and Jenna Jerman, "Abortion Incidence and Service Availability in the United States 2011," *Perspectives on Sexual and Reproductive Health* 46, no. 1 (March 2014): 3–14.
14. While this data is variable, Sonfield and his colleagues estimate that it was 54 percent in 2008 (Sonfield, Hasstedt, and Gold, *Moving Forward*, 8).
15. James Trussell and L. L. Wynn, "Reducing Unintended Pregnancy in the United States," *Contraception* 77, no. 1 (January 2008): 1, estimate the contraceptive nonuser rate at 10.7 percent. Sonfield, Hasstedt, and Gold, *Moving Forward*, 8, estimate the rate at 14 percent, and William Mosher, Jo Jones, and Joyce Abma, "Nonuse of Contraception Among Women at Risk of Unintended Pregnancy in the United States," *Contraception* 92, no. 2 (August 2015): 173, put the number at 16.5 percent.
16. All data in this paragraph is from Mosher, Jones, and Abma, "Nonuse of Contraception," 171.
17. Ibid., 174. Another study found the number to be even higher at 30 percent. See Mary D. Nettleman et al., "Reasons for Unprotected Intercourse: Analysis of the PRAMS Survey," *Contraception* 75, no. 5 (May 1, 2007): 361–66.
18. John Santelli et al., "The Measurement and Meaning of Unintended Pregnancy," *Perspectives on Sexual and Reproductive Health* 35, no. 2 (March 2003): 94; Mosher, Jones, and Abma, "Nonuse of Contraception," 173.
19. Mosher, Jones, and Abma, "Nonuse of Contraception," 173.
20. The numbers do not add up to 100 percent, as some women indicated more than one reason for nonuse of contraceptives.
21. Justine Wu et al., "Contraceptive Nonuse Among US Women at Risk for Unplanned Pregnancy," *Contraception* 78, no. 4 (October 2008): 284–89; Lori F. Frohwirth, Ann M. Moore, and Renata Maniaci, "Perceptions of Susceptibility to Pregnancy Among U.S. Women Obtaining Abortions," *Social Science & Medicine* 99 (December 2013): 18–26.
22. Kristen Upson, Susan D. Reed, Sarah W. Prager, and Melissa A. Schiff, "Factors Associated with Contraceptive Nonuse Among US Women Ages 35–44 Years at Risk of Unwanted Pregnancy," *Contraception* 81, no. 5 (May 2010): 427–34.
23. Kate Grindlay and Daniel Grossman, "Prescription Birth Control Access Among U.S. Women at Risk of Unintended Pregnancy," *Journal of Women's Health* 25, no. 3 (December 14, 2015): 249–54.
24. Ibid.
25. Jones and Kavanaugh, "Changes in Abortion Rates Between 2000 and 2008."
26. Jones, Frohwirth, and Moore, "More Than Poverty," 36–43.
27. Ibid.
28. Jerman, Jones, and Onda, *Characteristics of U.S. Abortion Patients*.
29. Ibid.
30. Jones, Frohwirth, and Moore, "More Than Poverty," 40.
31. Ibid., 39.
32. Ibid., 40.

33. Lawrence B. Finer and Mia R. Zolna, "Shifts in Intended and Unintended Pregnancies in the United States, 2001–2008," *American Journal of Public Health* 23, no. 3 (2014): e1–e9.
34. Rachel K. Jones, Lawrence B. Finer, and Susheela Singh, *Characteristics of U.S. Abortion Patients, 2008* (New York: Guttmacher Institute, May 2010), 12.
35. Sonfield, Hasstedt, and Gold, *Moving Forward*, 4.
36. Finer et al., "Reasons U.S. Women Have Abortions."
37. Ibid., 113.
38. Ibid.
39. Diana Greene Foster, "Socioeconomic Consequences of Abortion Compared to Unwanted Birth," paper presented at the American Public Health Association meeting, San Francisco, October 30, 2012.
40. Tara C. Jatlaoui et al., "Abortion Surveillance—United States, 2013," Centers for Disease Control and Prevention, *MMWR Surveillance Summaries* 65, no. 12 (November 25, 2016): 1–43.
41. The most comprehensive data on the incidence of abortion in the United States is published annually by the Centers for Disease Control and Prevention in its Abortion Surveillance report (ibid.). This report estimates that the number of abortions that occur after twenty-one weeks is 1.3 percent of the total number of abortions in the United States. See also Frances Kissling, "Is There Life After 'Roe'?," *Conscience* 25, no. 3 (Winter 2004–2005): 10–18.
42. The intact dilation and extraction procedure is known by many names, including intact D&E, intact dilation and evacuation, IDX, and D&X.
43. Rachel K. Jones, Lori F. Frohwirth, and Ann M. Moore, "'I Would Want to Give My Child, Like, Everything in the World': How Issues of Motherhood Influence Women Who Have Abortions," *Journal of Family Issues* 29, no. 1 (January 1, 2008): 79–99.
44. Diana Greene Foster and Katrina Kimport, "Who Seeks Abortions at or After 20 Weeks?," *Perspectives on Sexual and Reproductive Health* 45, no. 4 (December 2013): 213.
45. E. Janiak, I. Kawachi, A. Goldberg, and B. Gottlieb, "Delaying Factors Among Women Seeking Abortion Care in the Later Second Trimester," *Contraception* 86, no. 3 (September 2012): 302.
46. Foster and Kimport, "Who Seeks Abortions?," 210–18.
47. Ibid., 212.
48. Lawrence B. Finer et al., "Timing of Steps and Reasons for Delays in Obtaining Abortions in the United States," *Contraception* 74, no. 4 (October 2006): 334–44; Janiak et al., "Delaying Factors Among Women," 302.
49. Finer et al., "Timing of Steps and Reasons for Delays."
50. Foster and Kimport, "Who Seeks Abortions?," 215.
51. Janiak et al., Delaying Factors Among Women," 302.
52. Helen Statham, "Prenatal Diagnosis of Fetal Abnormality: The Decision to Terminate the Pregnancy and the Psychological Consequences," *Fetal and Maternal Medicine Review* 13, no. 4 (November 2002): 213–47; Anne Hawkins et al., "Variables Influencing Pregnancy Termination Following Prenatal Diagnosis of Fetal Chromosome Abnormalities," *Journal of Genetic Counseling* 22, no. 2 (April 2013): 238–48.

53. Aliza Kolker and B. Meredith Burke, "Grieving the Wanted Child: Ramifications of Abortion After Prenatal Diagnosis of Abnormality," *Health Care for Women International* 14, no. 6 (November 1, 1993): 520.
54. Anonymous, interview with author, Rebecca Todd Peters, "Examining Women's Moral Agency and Identity in the Tasks and Experiences of Mothering," unpublished interviews (hereafter cited as Peters, unpublished interviews), case 2, June 9, 2003.
55. Phoebe Day Danziger, "A Peaceful Death," *Slate*, February 5, 2014.
56. Anonymous, interview with author, Peters, unpublished interviews, case 10, June 20, 2003.
57. Anonymous, interview with author, Peters, unpublished interviews, case 4, June 17, 2003.
58. Rosamond Rhodes, "Abortion and Assent," *Cambridge Quarterly Healthcare Ethics* 8 (1999): 421.
59. Anonymous, interview with author, Peters, unpublished interviews, case 12, June 21, 2003.
60. Anonymous, interview with author, Peters, unpublished interviews, case 1, June 6, 2003.
61. Anonymous, interview with author, Peters, unpublished interviews, case 5, June 6, 2003.
62. Anonymous, interview with author, Peters, unpublished interviews, case 1, June 6, 2003.

CHAPTER 3: ABORTION POLICY AS THE PUBLIC ABUSE OF WOMEN

1. Guttmacher Institute, "The 334 Abortion Restrictions Enacted by States from 2011 to July 2016 Account for 30% of All Abortion Restrictions since Roe v. Wade," infographic, Guttmacher Institute, July 20, 2016, https://www.guttmacher.org/infographic/2016/334-abortion-restrictions-enacted-states-2011-july-2016-account-30-all-abortion.
2. Leslie Bentz, "The Top 10: Facebook 'Vomit' Button for Gays and Other Pat Robertson Quotes," July 9, 2013, http://www.cnn.com/2013/07/09/us/pat-robertson-facebook-remark/index.html.
3. Susan Ince, "Falwell's Baby Racket," *Mother Jones* 7, no. 5 (June 1982): 10.
4. Emily Bazelon, "Charmaine Yoest's Cheerful War on Abortion," *New York Times*, November 2, 2012.
5. Kate Sheppard, "Wham, Bam, Sonogram! Meet the Ladies Setting the New Pro-Life Agenda," *Mother Jones*, September–October 2012.
6. Guttmacher Institute, "States Enact Record Number of Abortion Restrictions in 2011," *News in Context*, January 5, 2011.
7. Ibid.
8. Provisions like mandatory ultrasounds, some clinic regulations, and required counseling may harass women without restricting their access to abortion. Ibid.
9. Guttmacher Institute, "States Enact Record Number of Abortion Restrictions in 2011."
10. Guttmacher Institute, "Counseling and Waiting Periods for Abortion," August 1, 2017, https://www.guttmacher.org/state-policy/explore/counseling-and-waiting-periods-abortion.

11. The states whose mandatory counseling asserts a link between abortion and breast cancer are Alaska, Kansas, Mississippi, Oklahoma, and Texas. The states offering inaccurate information about abortion and a woman's fertility are Arizona, Kansas, South Dakota, and Texas. See ibid.
12. Ibid.
13. Missouri, North Carolina, Oklahoma, South Dakota, and Utah. See ibid.
14. Americans United for Life, "Women's Ultrasound Right to Know Act: Model Legislation and Policy Guide for the 2012 Legislative Year," July 31, 2012, http://archive.org/details/405576-womens-ultrasound-right-to-know-act.
15. Kentucky, Louisiana, Texas, and Wisconsin. Guttmacher Institute, "Requirements for Ultrasound," Guttmacher Institute, New York, August 1, 2017.
16. Rick Ungar, "Virginia's Pre-abortion Ultrasound Law Medically Unsound—Violates Guidelines of American College of Obstetricians and Gynecologists," *Forbes*, March 8, 2012.
17. Ibid.
18. Jerman, Jones, and Onda, "Characteristics of U.S. Abortion Patients in 2014 and Changes Since 2008," 6, table 1.
19. Katherine M. Johnson, "Protecting Women, Saving the Fetus: Symbolic Politics and Mandated Abortion Counseling," *Women's Studies International Forum* 47, pt. A (November 2014): 36–45.
20. Alaska Department of Health and Social Services, Division of Public Health, "Informed Consent: Overview," in *Making a Decision About Your Pregnancy*, web page, updated September 2016, http://dhss.alaska.gov/dph/wcfh/Pages/informed consent/default.aspx.
21. Johnson, "Protecting Women."
22. Finer et al., "Reasons U.S. Women Have Abortions."
23. See the amicus curiae brief for Whole Woman's Health, et al., v. Kirk Cole, M.D., et al., at http://www.scotusblog.com/wp-content/uploads/2015/10/Medical-Associations-Amicus-Brief.pdf.
24. Maya Manian, "The Irrational Woman: Informed Consent and Abortion Decision-Making," *Duke Journal of Gender Law & Policy* 16 (2009): 233–34.
25. Planned Parenthood, "Planned Parenthood at a Glance," accessed September 25, 2017, https://www.plannedparenthood.org/about-us/who-we-are/planned-parenthood-at-a-glance.
26. Guttmacher Institute, "Induced Abortion in the United States," Fact Sheet Guttmacher Institute, New York, May 2016.
27. Rocca et al., "Women's Emotions," 122–31; Corinne H. Rocca et al., "Decision Rightness and Emotional Responses to Abortion in the United States: A Longitudinal Study," ed. Sharon Dekel, *PLOS ONE* 10, no. 7 (July 8, 2015).
28. M. Antonia Biggs, Heather Gould, and Diana Greene Foster, "Understanding Why Women Seek Abortions in the US," *BMC Women's Health* 13 (2013): 29; Finer et al., "Reasons U.S. Women Have Abortions."
29. South Dakota House Bill 1166, 2005.
30. Jackie Borchardt, "Bill Introduced to Regulate Men's Reproductive Health," *Dayton Daily News*, March 10, 2012.
31. Zack Ford, "Lawmaker Challenges Men to Accept Health Restrictions Like They Propose for Women," *Think Progress*, February 13, 2016.

32. Associated Press, "Georgia: No Murder Charge for Woman Who Bought Abortion Pills Online," *New York Times*, June 10, 2015.
33. Liam Stack, "Woman Accused of Coat-Hanger Abortion Pleads Guilty to Felony," *New York Times*, January 11, 2017.
34. Second-trimester abortions happen between fifteen and twenty-six weeks of pregnancy. Since pregnancy is dated from the woman's last menstrual period, prenates are developmentally between thirteen and twenty-four weeks.
35. Emily Bazelon, "Purvi Patel Could Be Just the Beginning," *New York Times Magazine*, April 1, 2015.
36. Charles Wilson, "Bei Bei Shuai Trial," *Huffington Post*, January 24, 2013.
37. Amie Newman, "Pregnant? Don't Fall Down the Stairs," *Rewire*, February 15, 2010, https://rewire.news/article/2010/02/15/pregnant-dont-fall-down-stairs/#story1.
38. Nina Liss-Schultz, "Tennessee's War on Women Is Sending New Mothers to Jail," *Mother Jones*, March 14, 2016.
39. However, sex selection is another abortion-related red herring used to stir up public emotions against abortion.

CHAPTER 4: MISOGYNY IS EXHAUSTING

1. John M. Riddle, *Eve's Herbs: A History of Contraception and Abortion in the West* (Cambridge, MA: Harvard University Press, 1997), 68.
2. Ibid., 35–36.
3. Ibid., 68.
4. John Riddle has carefully documented much of the history of these herbs and plants and their usage in the ancient world through the Middle Ages and into modern times (ibid.; John M. Riddle, *Contraception and Abortion from the Ancient World to the Renaissance* [Cambridge, MA: Harvard University Press, 1994]).
5. Riddle, *Eve's Herbs*, 14.
6. Ibid.
7. Aristotle, *Politics*, Book Seven, trans. Benjamin Jowett, Massachusetts Institute of Technology, Internet Classics Archive, accessed September 20, 2017, http://classics.mit.edu/Aristotle/politics.7.seven.html.
8. Hippocrates, "The Oath," trans. Francis Adams, Massachusetts Institute of Technology, Internet Classics Archive, http://classics.mit.edu/Hippocrates/hippooath.html, accessed September 20, 2017.
9. Riddle, *Eve's Herbs*, 44–46.
10. Hippocrates, "The Oath."
11. Riddle, *Eve's Herbs*, 39.
12. Ibid.
13. Michael J. Gorman, *Abortion and the Early Church: Christian Jewish and Pagan Attitudes in the Greco-Roman World* (Downers Grove, IL: Inter-Varsity Press), 30.
14. Ibid.
15. Ibid., 31.
16. Ibid.
17. Aristotle, *The History of Animals*, book 9, part 1, trans. D'Arcy Wentworth Thompson, Massachusetts Institute of Technology, Internet Classics Archive, September 20, 2017, http://classics.mit.edu/Aristotle/history_anim.9.ix.html.

18. Karen Jo Torjesen, *When Women Were Priests: Women's Leadership in the Early Church and the Scandal of Their Subordination in the Rise of Christianity* (San Francisco: Harper, 1993); Gary Macy, *The Hidden History of Women's Ordination: Female Clergy in the Medieval West* (New York: Oxford University Press, 2007).
19. April D. DeConick, *Holy Misogyny: Why the Sex and Gender Conflicts in the Early Church Still Matter* (New York: Continuum, 2011), 81.
20. Torjesen, *When Women Were Priests*, 142–43.
21. DeConick, *Holy Misogyny*, ch. 7; Torjesen, *When Women Were Priests*, ch. 4.
22. Torjesen, *When Women Were Priests*, ch. 4.
23. Tertullian, *De baptismo*, ch. 17, trans. S. Thewell, 1869, available at Christian Classics Electronic Library, Wheaton College, Grand Rapids, MI.
24. Tertullian, *De culta feminarum*, book I, ch. 1, trans. S. Thewell, 1869, available at Christian Classics Electronic Library, Wheaton College, Grand Rapids, MI.
25. DeConick, *Holy Misogyny*, 111.
26. Tertullian, *De virginibus velandis*, trans. S. Thewell, 1870, available at Christian Classics Electronic Library, Wheaton College, Grand Rapids, MI.
27. Augustine, *On the Trinity*, book 12, ch. 7, trans. Arthur West Haddan, in *Nicene and Post-Nicene Fathers, First Series*, vol. 3, ed. Philip Schaff (Buffalo, NY: Christian Literature Publishing Co., 1887), rev. and ed. for New Advent by Kevin Knight.
28. Martin Luther, *Table Talk or Familiar Discourse of Martin Luther*, trans. William Hazlitt (London: David Bogue, Fleet Street, 1848), 299, paragraph DCCXXV.
29. Karl Barth, *Church Dogmatics*, vol. 3, sec. 4 (Edinburgh: Clark, 1975), 158–72.
30. Southern Baptist Convention, "The 2000 Baptist Faith and Message," adopted by the convention on June 14, 2000.
31. L. K. Louise, "Mark Driscoll, Misogyny and Masculinity," *Feministing*, June 23, 2010, http://feministing.com/2010/06/23/mark-driscoll-misogyny-ad-masculinity.
32. Pew Research Center, "Global Views on Morality," *Global Attitudes Project*, April 15, 2014, http://www.pewglobal.org/2014/04/15/global-morality/table/premarital-sex.
33. Patricia Adair Gowaty, Yong-Kyu Kim, and Wyatt W. Anderson, "No Evidence of Sexual Selection in a Repetition of Bateman's Classic Study of *Drosophila melanogaster*," *Proceedings of the National Academy of Sciences* 109, no. 29 (July 17, 2012): 11740–45.
34. Beverly Wildung Harrison, *Making the Connections: Essays in Feminist Social Ethics* (Boston: Beacon Press, 1985), 138.
35. Kyle Harper, *From Shame to Sin: The Christian Transformation of Sexual Morality in Late Antiquity* (Cambridge, MA: Harvard University Press, 2013).
36. Ibid., introduction.
37. Ibid., 105.
38. Harper argues that Justin is the earliest example of a Christian co-optation of this belief for specifically Christian ends (ibid., 103).
39. While the following sources address the question of contraception and abortion in the Christian tradition, I am not aware of any feminist historiography of contraception and abortion within the Christian tradition. Beverly Wildung Harrison, *Our Right to Choose: Toward a New Ethic of Abortion* (Boston: Beacon

Press, 1983); John Noonan Jr., *Contraception: A History of Its Treatment by the Catholic Theologians and Canonists* (Cambridge, MA: Harvard University Press, 1986); Riddle, *Contraception and Abortion*; Susan E. Klepp, *Revolutionary Conceptions: Women, Fertility, and Family Limitation in America, 1760–1820* (Chapel Hill: University of North Carolina Press, 2009); Aline H. Kalbian, *Sex, Violence, and Justice: Contraception and the Catholic Church* (Washington, DC: Georgetown University Press, 2014).

40. For an early example of this pro-life perspective of history, see John T. Noonan Jr., "An Almost Absolute Value in History," in *The Morality of Abortion: Legal and Historical Perspectives*, ed. John T. Noonan Jr. (Cambridge, MA: Harvard University Press, 1970). For discussion of the history of Christian teaching and abortion, see Harrison, *Our Right to Choose*, esp. ch. 5; and Harrison, *Making the Connections*, 120.
41. Augustine, *Enchiridion: On Faith, Hope, and Love*, trans. Albert C. Outler (Grand Rapids, MI: Christian Classics Ethereal Library, 1955), ch. 23, p. 86.
42. Ibid., ch. 23, p. 91.
43. Noonan, "Almost Absolute Value," 15.
44. On May 31, 1889, the Holy See sent a letter to the Archbishop of Lyons declaring that craniotomies were not acceptable procedures to save the life of a pregnant woman even if it meant that both prenate and woman would perish (ibid., 41).
45. In *Casti connubii* in 1930, Pius XI condemned abortion in general and specifically in three instances: therapeutic abortion, which he called the killing of an innocent; in marriage to prevent offspring; and on social and eugenic grounds, as practiced by some governments. In 1965, the Second Vatican Council stated in *Gaudium et Spes*: "Life from its conception is to be guarded with the greatest care. Abortion and infanticide are horrible crimes" (ibid., 43–45; Melody Rose, *Abortion: A Documentary and Reference Guide* [Westport, CT: Greenwood Press, 2008], 33).

CHAPTER 5: PATRIARCHY AS SOCIAL CONTROL

1. James C. Mohr, *Abortion in America: The Origins and Evolution of National Policy, 1800–1900* (Oxford, UK: Oxford University Press, 1978), italics in the original.
2. Kristen Luker, *Abortion and the Politics of Motherhood* (Berkeley: University of California Press, 1984), 22.
3. These statistics are estimates made in Mohr, *Abortion in America*, 50. See ibid., 275n12, for Mohr's discussion of these estimates. Kristen Luker also summarizes the reported estimates of physicians at the time with the proviso that their estimates are likely inflated (Luker, *Abortion and the Politics of Motherhood*, 19–20).
4. Dorothy Roberts, *Killing the Black Body: Race, Reproduction, and the Meaning of Liberty* (First Vintage Books edition, 1997; repr., New York: Vintage, 1999), 10.
5. Ibid.
6. Ibid., 8.
7. Ibid., 8–19.
8. Rickie Solinger, *Pregnancy and Power: A Short History of Reproductive Politics in America* (New York: New York University Press, 2007), 21.
9. Ibid., 4.

10. For evidence that popular opinion traces family planning only to the late eighteenth century, see Riddle, *Contraception and Abortion*, viii; Angus McLaren, *History of Contraception: From Antiquity to the Present Day* (Oxford, UK: Wiley-Blackwell, 1992), 1. For recent scholarship on women's ability to control their fertility, see Mohr, *Abortion in America*; Riddle, *Contraception and Abortion from the Ancient World to the Renaissance*; Riddle, *Eve's Herbs*; Susan E. Klepp, *Revolutionary Conceptions: Women, Fertility, and Family Limitations in America* (Chapel Hill: University of North Carolina Press, 2009).
11. Klepp, *Revolutionary Conceptions*, 31, 76. See also Riddle, *Contraception and Abortion from the Ancient World to the Renaissance*; Riddle, *Eve's Herbs*; Mohr, *Abortion in America*, for detailed historical accounts of contraception and abortion in the United States; and Linda Gordon, *The Moral Property of Women: A History of Birth Control Politics in America* (Urbana: University of Illinois Press, 2007).
12. Klepp, *Revolutionary Conceptions*, 96–97.
13. Ibid., 97.
14. Klepp, *Revolutionary Conceptions*, ch. 1.
15. Historian John Riddle argues that the ancients had more knowledge of contraception than has been historically recognized. He documents his observation in Riddle, *Contraception and Abortion*.
16. Many physicians in the nineteenth century believed that women were most fertile during or just after menstruation and that the "safe" or least fertile period was between eight and sixteen days after the end of menstrual flow. Janet Farrell Brodie, *Contraception and Abortion in Nineteenth-Century America* (Ithaca, NY: Cornell University Press, 1994), 28, 79–86.
17. Klepp, *Revolutionary Conceptions*, 8, 43.
18. Ibid., 230.
19. Ibid., 231.
20. Mohr, *Abortion in America*, 4.
21. Ibid., 5.
22. Ibid., ch. 2.
23. Ibid.
24. Ibid.
25. Ibid., 41–43.
26. Mohr, *Abortion in America*, 73–74; Luker, *Abortion and the Politics of Motherhood*, 20; Klepp, *Revolutionary Conceptions*, 229–30.
27. Klepp, *Revolutionary Conceptions*, 182.
28. Mohr, *Abortion in America*, ch. 1.
29. Ibid.
30. Klepp, *Revolutionary Conceptions*, esp. chs. 1 and 5.
31. Ibid.
32. Ibid., ch. 5.
33. Ibid., 184.
34. Luker, *Abortion and the Politics of Motherhood*, 16.
35. Mohr, *Abortion in America*, 32–34.
36. Ibid., 32–33.
37. Ibid., 37.
38. Luker, *Abortion and the Politics of Motherhood*, 29–31.

39. Mohr, *Abortion in America*, 5–6.
40. Ibid., 156.
41. Horatio Robinson Storer, *Why Not? A Book for Every Woman* (Boston: Lee and Shephard, 1868), esp. 45–61.
42. Ibid., 47.
43. Luker, *Abortion and the Politics of Motherhood*, 22–23.
44. Storer, *Why Not?*, 74–75 (emphasis added).
45. Ibid., 76.
46. Ibid., 76.
47. Luker, *Abortion and the Politics of Motherhood*, 24–25.
48. Mohr, *Abortion in America*, 44, ch. 4.
49. Ibid., 35.
50. Luker, *Abortion and the Politics of Motherhood*, 23.
51. Ibid., 25–26. See also Mohr, *Abortion in America*, 164–66.
52. Luker, *Abortion and the Politics of Motherhood*, 25–26.
53. Laurel Thatcher Ulrich, *Good Wives: Image and Reality in the Lives of Women in Northern New England, 1650–1750* (New York: Vintage, 1991), 7.
54. Storer, *Why Not?*, 74.
55. Ibid., 63, 70.
56. Ibid., 63.
57. Jael Silliman, Marlene Gerber Fried, Loretta Ross, and Elena R. Gutiérrez, *Undivided Rights: Women of Color Organize for Reproductive Justice* (Chicago: Haymarket, 2016), 111.
58. Barbara Gurr, *Reproductive Justice: The Politics of Health Care for Native American Women* (New Brunswick, NJ: Rutgers University Press, 2014), 125.
59. Ibid.
60. Solinger, *Pregnancy and Power*, 5.
61. Philip R. Reilly, *The Surgical Solution: A History of Involuntary Sterilization in the United States* (Baltimore: Johns Hopkins University Press, 1991), 2–4.
62. Solinger, *Pregnancy and Power*, 6.
63. Ibid., 7.
64. Ibid.
65. Reilly, *Surgical Solution*, 2.
66. Peggy Cooper Davis, *Neglected Stores: The Constitution and Family Values* (New York: Hill & Wang, 1997), 170.
67. Ibid., 170–71.
68. Rickie Solinger, *Abortion Wars: A Half Century of Struggle, 1950–2000* (Berkeley: University of California Press, 1998), 24.
69. Rickie Solinger, "The Girl Nobody Loved: Psychological Explanations for White Single Pregnancy in the Pre-Roe v. Wade Era, 1945–1965," *Frontiers: A Journal of Women Studies* 11, nos. 2/3 (January 1, 1990): 45.
70. Ibid., 46.
71. Ibid., 49.
72. Rickie Solinger, *Wake Up Little Susie: Single Pregnancy and Race Before* Roe v. Wade (New York: Routledge, 2000), 17; Solinger, *Pregnancy and Power*, 149–53.
73. Carole Joffe, *Doctors of Conscience: The Struggle to Provide Abortion Before and After* Roe V. Wade (Boston: Beacon Press, 1995), 110.

74. Leslie J. Reagan, *When Abortion Was a Crime: Women, Medicine, and Law in the United States, 1867–1973* (Berkeley: University of California Press, 1997), ch. 5.
75. Ibid., 136–37.
76. Solinger, *Abortion Wars*, 17.
77. Reagan, *When Abortion Was a Crime*, 164.
78. Solinger, *Abortion Wars*, 18.
79. Reagan, *When Abortion Was a Crime*, 179.
80. Lawrence Lader, *Abortion* (Boston: Beacon Press, 1966), 24.
81. Joffe, *Doctors of Conscience*, 64.
82. Patricia Miller, *Good Catholics: The Battle over Abortion in the Catholic Church* (Berkeley: University of California Press, 2015), 41.
83. Ibid., 42.
84. James Voyles, "Changing Abortion Law in the United States," *Journal of Family Law* 7 (1967): 496–511.
85. Miller, *Good Catholics*, 280n62.
86. Ibid., 52.

CHAPTER 6: THE TRAGEDY OF FLAWED MORAL DISCOURSE

1. Storer, *Why Not?*, 75–76.
2. Luker, *Abortion and the Politics of Motherhood*, 193, italics in the original.
3. Lisa Sowle Cahill, "Abortion, Autonomy, and Community," in *Abortion: Understanding Difference*, Hastings Center Series in Ethics, ed. Sidney Callahan and Daniel Callahan (New York: Plenum Press, 1984), 265.
4. Although Cahill defines her position on the moral status of the prenate as "developmentalism," meaning that the moral value of the prenate increases over time, she describes her position as strongly biased in favor of the "fetus" and argues that there is a "heavy burden of proof" for women who seek to "justify" their abortions (ibid., 264).
5. Margaret Olivia Little, "Abortion, Intimacy, and the Duty to Gestate," *Ethical Theory and Moral Practice* 2, no. 3 (September 1, 1999): 301.
6. Ibid., 303.
7. Mary Anne Warren, "On the Moral and Legal Status of Abortion," *Monist* 57, no. 4 (1973).
8. Bioethicist Daniel Callahan addresses the "developmentalist" position in Daniel Callahan, *Abortion: Law, Choice and Morality*, new ed. (New York: Collier Macmillan, 1972), ch. 11.
9. Gene Burns, *The Moral Veto: Framing Contraception, Abortion, and Cultural Pluralism in the United States* (New York: Cambridge University Press, 2005).
10. Gallup, "Abortion" (collection of charts showing public opinions on abortion issues, 1975 to 2017), *Gallup News*, http://www.gallup.com/poll/1576/abortion.aspx, accessed September 21, 2017.
11. Gallup polls consistently show three-quarters or more of the population thinks abortion should remain legal, whereas Pew polls consistently indicate about half the public thinks abortion is morally wrong.
12. Pew Research Center, "Roe v. Wade at 40: Most Oppose Overturning Abortion Decision," Pew Research Center Religion & Public Life Project, January 16, 2013.

13. Joan Chittister, transcript of interview by Bill Moyers, *The Moyers Journal*, PBS, November 12, 2004, http://www.pbs.org/moyers/journal/archives/chittister_now_ts.html.
14. Frances Kissling, "Abortion Rights Are Under Attack, and Pro-Choice Advocates Are Caught in a Time Warp," *Washington Post*, February 18, 2011.
15. Robert P. Jones, Daniel Cox, and Rachel Laser, *Committed to Availability, Conflicted about Morality: What the Millennial Generation Tells Us About the Future of the Abortion Debate and the Culture Wars* (Washington, DC: Public Religion Research Institute, June 6, 2011), http://publicreligion.org/research/2011/06/committed-to-availability-conflicted-about-morality-what-the-millennial-generation-tells-us-about-the-future-of-the-abortion-debate-and-the-culture-wars.
16. Anna North, "Planned Parenthood Moving Away from 'Choice,'" *BuzzFeed*, January 9, 2013, http://www.buzzfeed.com/annanorth/planned-parenthood-moving-away-from-choice#.lbXvDkPw2.
17. Kristen M. Shellenberg, "Abortion Stigma in the United States: Quantitative and Qualitative Perspectives from Women Seeking an Abortion" PhD diss., John Hopkins University, Baltimore, 2010.
18. Katrina Kimport, "(Mis)Understanding Abortion Regret," *Symbolic Interaction* 35, no. 2 (May 1, 2012): 105–22.
19. Corinne H. Rocca, Katrina Kimport, Heather Gould, and Diana G. Foster, "Women's Emotions One Week After Receiving or Being Denied an Abortion in the United States," *Perspectives on Sexual and Reproductive Health* 45, no. 3 (September 1, 2013): 122–31.
20. Shellenberg, "Abortion Stigma," 178.
21. Peter Singer, *Practical Ethics* (New York: Cambridge University Press, 2011).
22. Jacob M. Appel, "After St. Joseph's: Are Women Still Safe in Catholic Hospitals?," *Huffington Post*, May 15, 2010. McBride's excommunication was lifted in 2011 (Kevin Clarke, "McBride Un-Excommunicated," *America, the Jesuit Review*, December 14, 2011, https://www.americamagazine.org/content/all-things/mcbride-un-excommunicated).

CHAPTER 7: REIMAGINING PREGNANCY

1. Lennart Nilsson, "Drama of Life Before Birth," *Life*, April 30, 1965. Barbara Duden notes that it is a misnomer to call Lennart Nilsson's work photography, which is an image made by the presence of light. She calls the work that he pioneered photo-*geny*, or the creation of an image through the use of light (Barbara Duden, *Disembodying Women: Perspectives on Pregnancy and the Unborn*, trans. Lee Hoinacki [Cambridge, MA: Harvard University Press, 1993], 18).
2. Nilsson, "Drama of Life"; Clare Hanson, *A Cultural History of Pregnancy: Pregnancy, Medicine and Culture 1750–2000* (Basingstoke, UK: Palgrave Macmillan, 2004), 156.
3. Nilsson, "Drama of Life," 54.
4. While the story contained seventeen embryonic and fetal images, only one is an image of a viable prenate still in the womb. Lennart Nilsson, "Behind the Lens: An Interview with Lennart Nilsson," *Nova*, PBS, 1996, http://www.pbs.org/wgbh/nova/odyssey/nilsson.html.
5. Lennart Nilsson, "First Days of Creation," *Life*, August 1, 1990.

6. Nilsson, "Drama of Life," 54; Duden, *Disembodying Women*, ch. 2.
7. N. S. Macklon et al., "Conception to Ongoing Pregnancy: The 'Black Box' of Early Pregnancy Loss," *Human Reproduction Update* 8, no. 4 (2002): 333–43. The most recent Centers for Disease Control and Prevention estimate of fetal loss (miscarriage) of 17 percent of pregnancies suggests an even lower estimate of the percentage of fertilized eggs that proceed to birth (S. J. Ventura et al., "Estimated Pregnancy Rates and Rates of Pregnancy Outcomes for the United States, 1990–2008," *National Vital Statistics Reports* 60, no. 7 [2012]: 4.
8. Anonymous, interview with author, Peters, unpublished interviews, case 4, June 17, 2003.
9. Thanks to Ann Cahill for this trenchant observation.
10. Lindemann, *Holding and Letting Go*, 38.
11. Ann J. Cahill, "Miscarriage and Intercorporeality," *Journal of Social Philosophy* 46, no. 1 (March 1, 2015): 53.
12. Ibid.
13. Adrienne Rich, *Of Woman Born: Motherhood as Experience and Institution* (New York: W. W. Norton, 1976), 63.
14. Ibid., 64.
15. Viviane Callier, "Baby's Cells Can Manipulate Mom's Body for Decades," Smithsonian.com, September 2, 2015, http://www.smithsonianmag.com/science-nature/babys-cells-can-manipulate-moms-body-decades-180956493.
16. A. Salisbury et al., "Maternal-Fetal Attachment," *Journal of the American Medical Association* 289, no. 13 (2003): 1701.
17. Kimport, "(Mis)Understanding Abortion Regret."
18. Lindemann, *Holding and Letting Go*, picks up on the idea of pregnancy as prolepsis from William Ruddick, "Ways to Limit Prenatal Testing," in *Prenatal Testing and Disability Rights*, ed. Erik Parens and Adrienne Asch (Washington, DC: Georgetown University Press, 2000), 95–107.
19. Kate Parsons, "Feminist Reflections on Miscarriage, in Light of Abortion," *International Journal of Feminist Approaches to Bioethics* 3, no. 1 (2010): 1–22.
20. Lindemann, *Holding and Letting Go*, ch. 2.
21. Ibid., 15.
22. Ibid., 18.
23. Anonymous, interview with author, Peters, unpublished interviews, case 5, June 17, 2003.
24. Jones, Frohwirth, and Moore, "'I Would Want to Give My Child.'"
25. Finer et al., "Reasons U.S. Women Have Abortions"; Biggs, Gould, and Foster, "Why Women Seek Abortions," 1–13; Jones, Frohwirth, and Moore, "More Than Poverty."
26. Frances Kissling, "Is There Life After 'Roe'? How to Think About the Fetus," *Conscience: The News Journal of Catholic Opinion* 25, no. 3 (Winter 2004–2005): 10–18.
27. Jones, Frohwirth, and Moore, "'I Would Want to Give My Child,'" 95; J. Jones, *Adoption Experiences of Women and Men and Demand for Children to Adopt by Women 18–44 Years of Age in the United States, 2002* Vital and Health Statistics series 23, no. 27 (Washington, DC: US Department of Health and Human Services, Centers for Disease Control and Prevention, 2008): 1–36.

28. Anonymous, interview with author, Peters, unpublished interviews, case 4, June 17, 2003.
29. In most narrative studies, women tell their stories of unplanned pregnancies from their discovery of the pregnancy to their decision to keep or terminate it, with an aim to explain or justify their actions. These stories demonstrate the thoughtful processes that women go through in making their decisions as well as the social pressure they feel to justify their decisions to external audiences (Jennifer B. Gray, "'It Has Been a Long Journey from First Knowing': Narratives of Unplanned Pregnancy," *Journal of Health Communication* 20, no. 6 [May 12, 2015]: 736–42).

CHAPTER 8: MOTHERHOOD AS MORAL CHOICE

1. Sonfield, Hasstedt, and Gold, *Moving Forward.*
2. Although the carrying capacity of the earth should bear heavily on discussions about family planning and fertility, population control movements in the 1970s and 1980s often targeted poor and minority communities and populations as "the problem" that needed to be addressed. While it is true that birth rates continue to be higher in countries in the global South than they are in the global North, the environmental footprint of babies in the global South is also far lower than babies in the global North. Any discussion about overpopulation needs to be sensitive to the very real history of racism and genocide that have accompanied these conversations in the past. See Betsy Hartmann, *Reproductive Rights and Wrongs: The Global Politics of Population Control* (Cambridge, MA: South End Press, 1999).
3. J. Jones, *Adoption Experiences*; Diana Greene Foster, Heather Gould, Jessica Taylor, and Tracy A. Weitz, "Attitudes and Decision Making Among Women Seeking Abortions at One U.S. Clinic," *Perspectives on Sexual and Reproductive Health* 44, no. 2 (June 1, 2012): 117–24.
4. Gretchen Sisson, "'Choosing Life': Birth Mothers on Abortion and Reproductive Choice," *Women's Health Issues* 25, no. 4 (July 2015): 349–54.
5. Jones, Frohwirth, and Moore, "'I Would Want to Give My Child.'"
6. Jones, *Adoption Experiences*, 95.
7. For more detailed social analysis of pregnancy and unmarried women before *Roe v. Wade*, see Regina G. Kunzel, *Fallen Women, Problem Girls: Unmarried Mothers and the Professionalization of Social Work, 1890–1945* (New Haven, CT: Yale University Press, 1995); Solinger, *Wake Up Little Susie.*
8. Foster et al., "Attitudes and Decision Making."
9. Gretchen Sisson, Lauren Ralph, Heather Gould, and Diana Greene Foster, "Adoption Decision Making Among Women Seeking Abortion," *Women's Health Issues* 27, no. 2 (March 2017): 136–44.
10. Foster, "Socioeconomic Consequences of Abortion Compared to Unwanted Birth."
11. Kendra G. Hotz, "Happily Ever After: Christians Without Children," in *Encountering the Sacred: Feminist Reflections on Women's Lives*, ed. Rebecca Todd Peters and Grace Yia-Hei Kao (London: T&T Clark, forthcoming).
12. Beverly Wildung Harrison, "The Power of Anger in the Work of Love," in *Making the Connections: Essays in Feminist Social Ethics* (Boston: Beacon Press, 1985), 12–13.

13. For a remarkable anthology on interpretations of the Eve and Adam story, see Kristen E. Kvam, Linda S. Schearing, and Valerie H. Ziegler, eds., *Eve & Adam: Jewish, Christian, and Muslim Readings on Genesis and Gender* (Bloomington: Indiana University Press, 1999).
14. Roberts, *Killing the Black Body*, introduction.
15. Carol Gilligan, *In a Different Voice: Psychological Theory and Women's Development* (Cambridge, MA: Harvard University Press, 1982).

CHAPTER 9: CELEBRATING THE MORAL COURAGE OF WOMEN

1. Harrison, *Our Right to Choose.*
2. Ross and Solinger, *Reproductive Justice: An Introduction*, 9.
3. Ibid.; Silliman et al., *Undivided Rights*; Gurr, *Reproductive Justice*; Joan C. Chrisler, ed. *Reproductive Justice: A Global Concern* (Santa Barbara, CA: Praeger, 2012).
4. Article 25 of the United Nations Universal Declaration of Human Rights. While the original language of the declaration in 1948 used masculine pronouns, it is widely accepted that the terms should be read as referring to all people, regardless of gender identity. The UN Convention on the Elimination of All Forms of Discrimination Against Women, adopted in 1978, extended definitions of human rights to delineate specific forms of discrimination against women.
5. Kimala Price, "What Is Reproductive Justice? How Women of Color Activists Are Redefining the Pro-Choice Paradigm," *Meridians: Feminism, Race, Transnationalism* 10, no. 2 (2010): 54.
6. Ibid.
7. Ibid., 55.
8. Ross and Solinger, *Reproductive Justice: An Introduction*, 63–67.
9. Toni Bond Leonard, conversation with author, January 18, 2017, and email with author, September 7, 2017. Ross and Solinger, *Reproductive Justice: An Introduction*, echoes the language of "placing ourselves in the center."
10. Zakiya Luna and Kristin Luker, "Reproductive Justice," *Annual Review of Law and Social Science* 9, no. 1 (2013): 335–37.
11. Anannya Bhattacharjee and Jael Silliman, eds., *Policing the National Body: Race, Gender and Criminalization in the United States* (Cambridge, MA: South End Press, 2002), xi.
12. Zakiya Luna, "From Rights to Justice: Women of Color Changing the Face of US Reproductive Rights Organizing," *Societies Without Borders* 4 (2009): 350.
13. Ross and Solinger, *Reproductive Justice: An Introduction*, 10.
14. Barbara Katz Rothman, *The Tentative Pregnancy: How Amniocentesis Changes the Experience of Motherhood* (New York: W. W. Norton, 1993), 9.
15. Paula Abrams, "The Scarlet Letter: The Supreme Court and the Language of Abortion Stigma," *Michigan Journal of Gender and Law* 19 (2012): 293–337.
16. These children lived in families that were up to 200 percent of the federal poverty threshold. People living in this category are widely referred to as poor, near poor, or low-income. Data on child poverty comes from Yang Jiang, Mercedes Ekono, and Curtis Skinner, "Basic Facts About Low-Income Children: Children Under 18 Years, 2014," National Center for Children in Poverty, Mailman

School of Public Health, Columbia University, February 2016, http://www.nccp.org/publications/pub_1145.html.

17. Yumiko Aratani, "Homeless Children and Youth: Causes and Consequences," National Center for Children in Poverty, Mailman School of Public Health, Columbia University, September 2009, 4, http://www.nccp.org/publications/pdf/text_888.pdf.
18. Ibid., 4.
19. Finer and Zolna, "Declines in Unintended Pregnancy," 847.
20. Sabrina Tavernise, "Colorado's Effort Against Teenage Pregnancies Is a Startling Success," *New York Times*, July 5, 2015.
21. Margarete Sandelowski and Julie Barroso, "The Travesty of Choosing After Positive Prenatal Diagnosis," *Journal of Obstetric, Gynecologic, & Neonatal Nursing* 34, no. 3 (May 1, 2005): 311.
22. Helen Statham, "Prenatal Diagnosis of Fetal Abnormality: The Decision to Terminate the Pregnancy and the Psychological Consequences," *Fetal and Maternal Medicine Review* 13, no. 4 (November 2002): 223.
23. Rothman, *Tentative Pregnancy*, xii.
24. Eva Feder Kittay with Leo Kittay, "On the Expressivity and Ethics of Selective Abortion for Disability: Conversations with My Son," in *Prenatal Testing and Disability Rights*, ed. Eric Parens and Adrienne Asch (Washington, DC: Georgetown University Press, 2000), 190.
25. Ted Peters, *For the Love of Children: Genetic Technology and the Future of the Family* (Louisville, KY: Westminster John Knox, 1996), 92.
26. Jamie L. Natoli, Deborah L. Ackerman, Suzanne McDemmott, and Janice G. Edwards, "Prenatal Diagnosis of Down Syndrome: A Systematic Review of Termination Rates (1995–2011)," *Prenatal Diagnosis* 32, no. 2 (2012): 142–53. A previous well-cited study from 1999 estimated that the termination rate for prenatal diagnosis of Down syndrome was 92 percent (Caroline Mansfield, Suellen Hopfer, and Theresa M. Marteau, "Termination Rates After Prenatal Diagnosis of Down Syndrome, Spina Bifida, Anencephaly, and Turner and Klinefelter Syndromes: A Systematic Literature Review," *Prenatal Diagnosis* 19, no. 9 [September 1, 1999]: 808–12).
27. Anonymous, interview with author, Peters, unpublished interviews, case 13, June 21, 2003.
28. Little, "Abortion, Intimacy," 295–312.

INDEX

Note: Page numbers in *italics* refer to illustrations.